The prints of WILHELMINA BARNS-GRAHAM

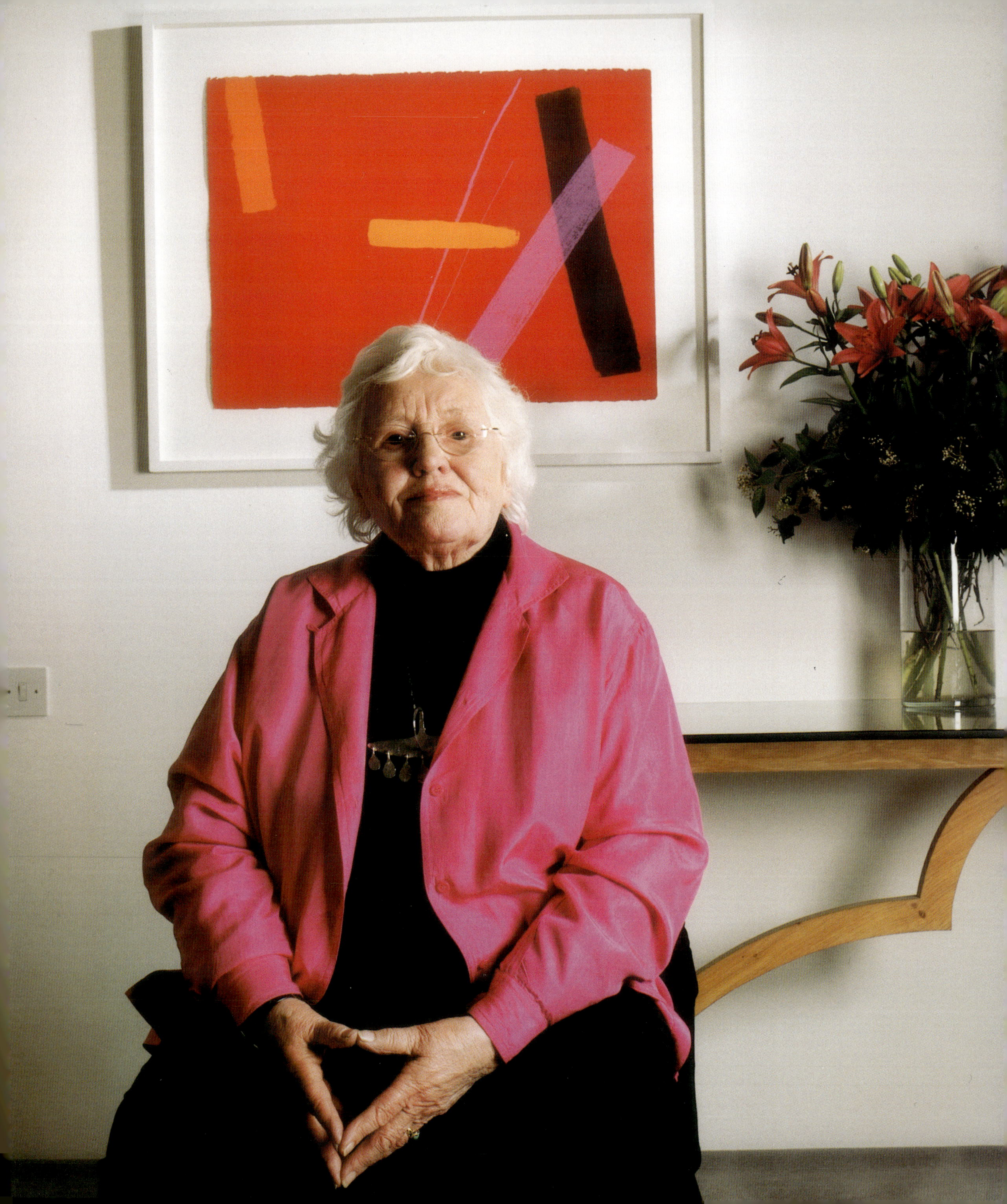

Ann V. Gunn

The prints of WILHELMINA BARNS-GRAHAM

a complete catalogue

LUND HUMPHRIES

In memory of Rowan James

First published in 2007 by

Lund Humphries
Gower House
Croft Road
Aldershot
Hampshire GU11 3HR

and

Lund Humphries
Suite 420
101 Cherry Street
Burlington
VT 05401-4405
USA

www.lundhumphries.com

Lund Humphries is part of Ashgate Publishing

British Library Cataloguing-in-Publication Data
Gunn, Ann
The prints of Wilhemina Barns-Graham: a complete catalogue
1. Barns-Graham, Wilhemina, 1912-2004 - Catalogues raisonnes
I. Title II. Barns-Graham, Wilhemina, 1912-2004
769.9'2

ISBN-13: 978-0-85331-969-6

Library of Congress Control Number: 2007929621

Edited by Maureen Street
Designed by Nigel Soper
Origination by MRM Graphics Ltd, Winslow, Bucks
Printed in Singapore, under the supervision of MRM Graphics

Frontispiece

Simon Norfolk, *Portrait of Wilhelmina Barns-Graham* (2000). Barns-Graham is shown sitting in front of her 1999 screenprint *Another Time*

CONTENTS

PREFACE

I FIRST HAD THE OPPORTUNITY TO STUDY THE SCREENPRINTS of Wilhelmina Barns-Graham when I ran a small gallery in St Andrews for a couple of years, specialising in contemporary Scottish Art. I enjoyed seeing the reaction of visitors when I revealed that these vibrant, joyful, abstract images had been produced by a white-haired lady of some 90 years who was still working, and still developing new ideas. Even on the greyest January afternoon, the glowing colours would light up the gallery – no doubt one reason why her prints sold so well. It was also a great pleasure to be able to study these works of art in detail when the gallery was empty, to look closely at the many-layered depths of, for instance, *Sunghrie II* (cat.76), to try to work out how it had been constructed and in how many strata, and to admire the thick, rich deposits and delicate, translucent washes of colour. It was frustrating to find that it was impossible to do full justice to these prints in reproduction, for instance on an invitation card for an exhibition opening. Not even the highest-quality commercial printing can properly reproduce the subtlety of the overlapping films of colour and the variety of finishes – matte, silky or glossy – that enliven the surface of the prints. These are not just flat images, but real objects with depth and they have to be encountered physically to be truly appreciated.

Barns-Graham's interest in printmaking was constant, if not dominant, throughout her working life. She began making prints in the 1940s, when she also started to collect prints by other artists. One of her earliest purchases was a drypoint by Ben Nicholson in 1949, and one of her last was from my gallery, a large aquatint by Craig Nugent, a recent graduate from Duncan of Jordanstone School of Art and Design in 2003. In between she acquired works by many other artists, including her contemporaries in St Ives, Barbara Hepworth, Denis Mitchell and John Wells. No doubt one reason for collecting their prints was to own a work by an artist she admired whose paintings or sculpture were beyond her reach financially. In 1949 the modestly priced Nicholson print still had to be paid for in instalments. And this is certainly one reason why she herself was interested in making prints, as her own paintings began to achieve prices beyond the reach of many collectors.

'Willie', as she was known to her friends, was an extraordinarily prolific artist and anyone trying to comprehend her progress and development over the sixty or so years of her professional life has to contend with a large body of work. However her prints provide, as it were, a readily graspable summation of the themes that preoccupied her for much of her career. She made just over a hundred prints between the early 1940s and her death in 2004, and in design and colour they consistently reflected the motifs she was working through in her paintings of the same time. Thus it is possible to encapsulate much of her career in the prints, and to give an overview of it in a rather more manageable manner.

I discussed the idea for this book with Willie in the summer of 2003. Subsequent meetings had to be cancelled due to her failing health, and sadly I never had the opportunity to talk to her about her printmaking. During the year following her death, in January 2004, I spent many hours with Rowan James, her friend and assistant, sorting through the collection, assembling the prints and making notes from our conversations.

At this point our discussions were unstructured, and I was planning a series of more organised sessions when Rowan herself became ill and then died, almost exactly one year after Willie. The two people who could have provided me with the most complete information about these prints were gone.

Instead I have relied on both the Barns-Graham archive – consisting of letters, diaries, notes, books and catalogues – and on the memories of people with whom she worked. Where possible I have used her own words from taped and published interviews, and the diaries she wrote almost every day. This book was written while the Trustees of the Barns-Graham Charitable Trust were still in the process of inventorying the extensive Barns-Graham collection, archive and library. It is therefore possible that I have overlooked some documentary evidence that might have filled the occasional gap. This also means that, at the time of writing, the archive had not yet been sufficiently organised for me to be able to give more than broad documentary references here for the use of future researchers.

I am very grateful to the many people who have allowed me to record interviews, to those who have answered letters and phone calls and especially to the printmakers with whom Willie worked. I would also like to thank the Trustees of the Barns-Graham Charitable Trust for their help and advice, and a number of friends and family who have read and commented on the text.

In particular I would like to express my gratitude to the following: Robert Adam, Geoffrey Bertram, Edward Bray, Brendan Cassidy, Norrie Colston, Iain Donald, Keith Fraser, Kip Gresham, Nicola Gunn, Stanley Jones, Rachael Kantaris, Fergus McLachlan, Breon O'Casey, Sheila Oliner, Ivan Polley, Nelson and Rose Rands, Carol Robertson, David Roche, Colin Ruscoe, Helen Scott, Diana Sykes, Kathy Watkin and Jim Whitlock.

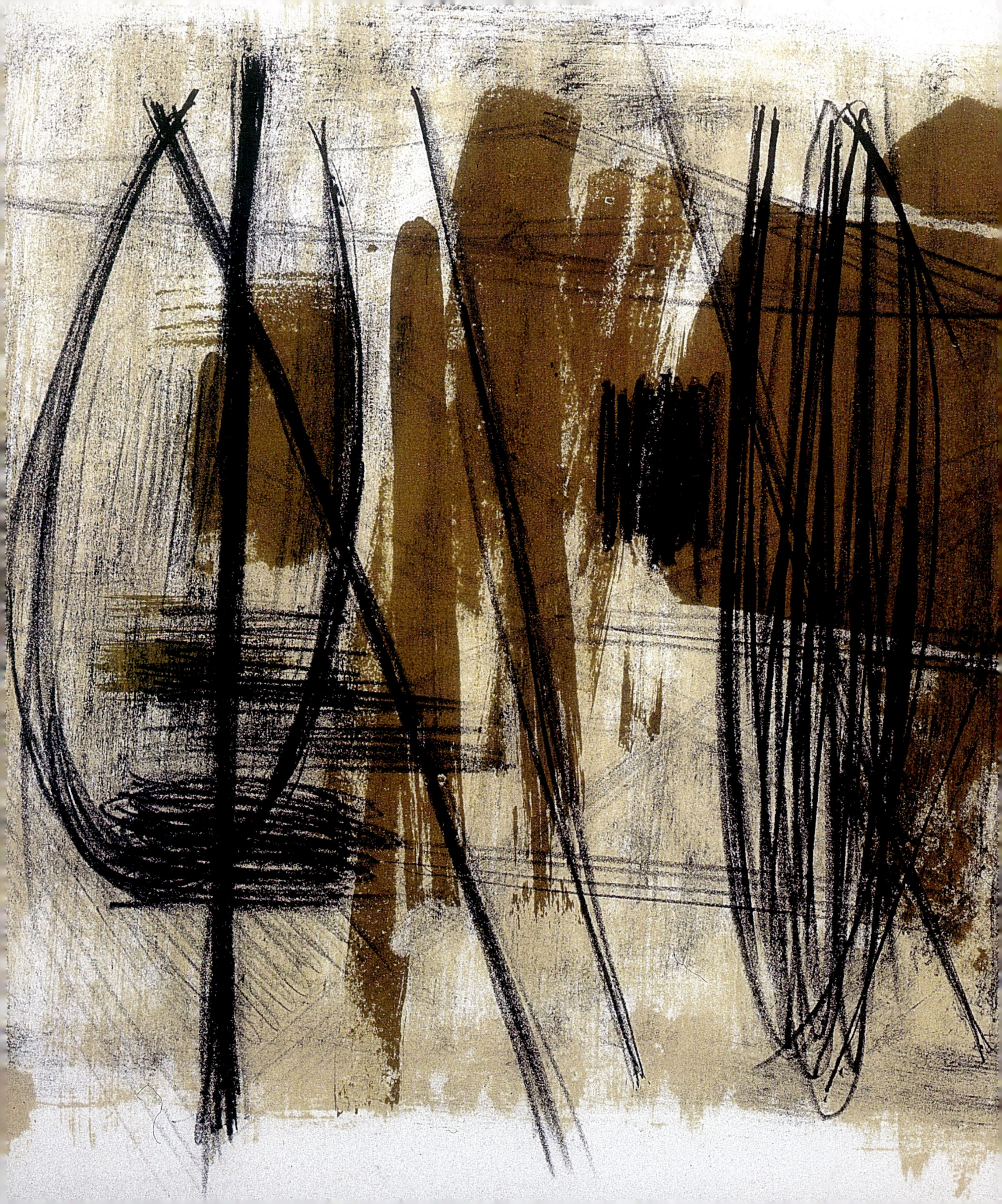

1

THE EARLY YEARS TO 1958

AT INTERVALS THROUGHOUT HER LONG ARTISTIC CAREER, Wilhelmina Barns-Graham engaged in printmaking. Although for much of her working life this activity was not consistent or sustained, there were some landmark years when she made significant strides in technique and understanding; and the images she produced always reflected her current artistic concerns and preoccupations. In the last decade of her life, the making of prints became an integral part of her artistic practice. A six-day visit to the Curwen Chilford Studio in Linton, near Cambridge, in November 1991, seems to have been something of a turning point, although not bearing immediate fruit – she published no further prints until 1995. But it is from about 1991 that writers of reviews and exhibition catalogues talk about the art of Barns-Graham undergoing a late flowering, an outpouring of work displaying extraordinary energy and a palpable sense of urgency. And although it was rarely, if ever, mentioned, that prolific activity included printmaking. In particular, from late 1998 until literally a few days before she died in 2004, she was working on screenprints.

In just over five years, in close collaboration with Carol Robertson, Barns-Graham produced a run of 44 editioned prints. A further 24 images were proofed but not yet editioned at the time of her death. This alliance with Robertson was the culmination of what can be seen as a search over the years for the perfect partner for her printmaking ventures. Only the prints she made in collaboration with a printmaker have ever been editioned and published. Other prints, mainly etchings, which relied on Barns-Graham doing her own editioning were fated to remain as experiments, trials and unpublished works.

Artists who have made prints, but for whom this is not their primary means of expression, have always relied on the

Detail of *Liner Abstract*, 1958 (cat. 22).

knowledge, expertise and craftsmanship of master printmakers. Often this relationship has been not just technical but creative and symbiotic, marrying together the knowledge and expertise of the printmaker with the ideas and skills of the artist to create work which neither could achieve alone. A number of partnerships produced the best of Barns-Graham's prints: with Stanley Jones in 1958, Kip Gresham in 1991, Rachael Kantaris in 1996–7, Alasdair Currie in 1998 and Carol Robertson from 1999 until Barns-Graham's death in 2004. In between she made other prints, but either the technique did not suit or the printmaker was at the other end of the country and the collaboration was unable to develop.

Many books have been published on the history of printmaking and the development of print techniques, and many others describe the processes for the student or practitioner. In this book I will therefore touch on the history and development of twentieth-century printmaking and publishing in Britain, only in so far as they impinge on the works of Barns-Graham. Although she benefited from a revival in printmaking and from technological developments as and when she made prints, she did not participate in major post-war developments such as, for instance, artists' lithographs at the Curwen Studio (apart from the St Ives project in 1958), or screenprinting at the Kelpra Studio or print publishing with Editions Alecto. These developments gathered pace in the 1960s, the one decade of her working life when she made no prints at all. But when she did turn to printmaking, the advances in working practices and techniques brought about by these enterprises influenced her work.

A brief outline of Barns-Graham's life will help to explain the progress and sporadic nature of her printmaking over the course of 60 years.[1] She was born in St Andrews in 1912, spending her early years there before moving to Carbeth in Stirlingshire. She studied at Edinburgh College of Art from 1931 to 1937, with gaps caused by ill health. A postgraduate award received in 1939 could not be used for travel abroad because of the outbreak of war, so at the suggestion of the College's principal, Herbert Wellington, she went to St Ives in Cornwall. Arriving in March 1940, she remained primarily based there until her death some 64 years later.

Wellington knew that St Ives and the surrounding area, already home to a colony of artists, were beginning to attract a new generation interested in modern movements in art, and would provide a congenial atmosphere in which she could work. Her contemporary at Edinburgh Margaret Mellis, and Margaret's husband Adrian Stokes, had moved there in 1939. When Barns-Graham arrived, Ben Nicholson and Barbara Hepworth, Naum Gabo, Bernard Leach, Denis Mitchell and Sven Berlin were already resident. Over the next few years other artists, who would also come to be identified as 'St Ives artists', came and went. Peter Lanyon was local but had joined the RAF just a few days before Barns-Graham arrived in Cornwall; he returned to live in St Ives in December 1945. John Wells and Bryan Wynter also arrived in 1945, and Terry Frost in 1946.

From the beginning Barns-Graham was a part of this group of modernist artists, though she also had friends amongst traditional painters such as John Park, Leonard Fuller and Borlase Smart. She was one of the modernist 'exhibitors round the font', at the shows of the St Ives Society of Artists in their gallery, the old Mariners' Church. In 1946 she became a founder member of the Crypt Group, a group of progressive young artists within the Society who showed their work separately in the basement of the church. She was also a founder member of the Penwith Society of Arts, formed in 1949 by a breakaway group from the Society. In that year she married David Lewis, a young South African writer who had arrived in St Ives in 1947. They lived in St Ives until 1956 when Lewis became a student at Leeds College of Art, studying architecture. Barns-Graham spent a year there teaching, but with the breakdown of the marriage (which was annulled in 1963) she returned to St Ives in 1958.

In 1960 she inherited Balmungo, a large house just outside St Andrews, from her aunt, Mary Neish. She had travelled regularly to Scotland to see her family, and was often not around when things were happening in St Ives. For example, although she was a founder member of the Crypt Group and its first meeting took place in her studio, she was in Scotland during its first exhibition in 1946 and had no work displayed or included in the catalogue. In the absence of this public sort of documentary evidence she has often been written out of the history of the early years of the St Ives group, although the facts of her involvement are contained in many, so far unpublished, sources. From 1960, her visits to Scotland became more frequent. Maintaining Balmungo took her there for extended periods of time. In the early 1960s she also lived in London for a couple of years, and then she bought a studio apartment in the newly constructed Barnaloft building, which became her St Ives home and workplace for the next forty years. In 1973–4 she spent 18 months in Scotland, getting the house and grounds at Balmungo sorted out, with the help of Rowan James. Rowan remained there and became the artist's permanent assistant, framer, promoter, exhibition organiser, archivist and friend. Thereafter Barns-Graham spent a part of every year in Scotland, re-forging her Scottish artistic links. It was in Scotland that she died in January 2004.

Her peripatetic career helps explain why her printmaking took place in a number of studios. In a continuing search for both tuition and partners for her printmaking endeavours, Barns-Graham worked with printmakers in St Ives, Cambridge, Edinburgh and Dundee. Over the years she worked in all the traditional print techniques: intaglio (etching and aquatint), relief (linocut), lithography, screenprinting and monotype (for brief descriptions of these techniques, see the Glossary at the end of this book).

Barns-Graham embarked on her career as an artist at a time when printmaking was at a very low ebb in Britain. The practice of printmaking had been severely disrupted first by the depression following the Wall Street crash of 1929, and subsequently by the outbreak of war. A vibrant market for etchings that had sustained artists, printers, publishers, print societies and publications collapsed almost completely in the 1930s, to be revived only in the mid-1950s. Artists who specialised in wood engraving were sustained mainly by providing illustrations for private presses such as the Golden Cockerel Press and the Gregynog Press. Only a few art schools were teaching printmaking in the 1930s, and there was no print training at Edinburgh College of Art when Barns-Graham was there.[2] Any prints made by artists in the 1940s and early 1950s were 'the result of individual initiatives, skills hastily acquired at evening classes, by observation of more experienced colleagues and by trial and error on the kitchen table'.[3]

By the late 1940s and 1950s, art-school teaching was expanding; intaglio and lithographic methods predominated, while silkscreen was still seen mainly as a method for printing signage and textiles, not artists' prints. Lithography was taught at the Central School of Arts and Crafts, at the Slade and at the Royal College of Art, all in London. Outside London, the Bath Academy of Art, established at Corsham Court, Wiltshire, in 1946, taught lithography and provided facilities for artists who were teaching there, some of whom came up from Cornwall. For those working in and around St Ives, it was possible to learn etching and engraving at the Penzance School of Art.

The year 1954 saw the opening by Robert Erskine of the St George's Gallery in Cork Street, London, which specialised in selling prints. This heralded the beginning of a print revival in Britain that gathered pace into the 1960s and 1970s. According to most sources, this resurgence was initiated almost single-handedly by Erskine as gallery owner and print publisher. While a student at Cambridge, he had seen exhibitions at Heffer's Art Gallery featuring prints made in Europe, where there was still a tradition of master printmakers. He could find nothing of this quality for his gallery from British printmakers. Works arrived from artists 'crooked [on] their paper, punched through with ugly registration slots, and seldom matching the colours of the accepted proof'.[4] So he set out to find printers to help artists produce prints of a more professional standard and quality.

Erskine worked with a number of printers, such as Harley Brothers Ltd of Edinburgh, but it was a collaboration with Timothy Simon of the Curwen Press that led to the establishment of a proper print studio, along the lines of continental operations. Curwen Press, based at Plaistow in East London, had long had a reputation for working with artists on commercial publishing ventures: advertisements, posters, calendars, leaflets and book illustrations, as well as artists' lithographs. In 1957, the Press took the decision to set up a separate lithographic studio, specifically to make editioned artists' prints.[5] In January 1958, Erskine went to Paris to persuade Stanley Jones, then working at the Atelier Patris, to return to England to run the studio. According to Jones, 'Erskine came across to Paris one day and said to me, "look I am so tired of sending my artists abroad to have their graphic work printed [and] we have this possibility of the Curwen Press rejuvenating their facilities for artists"'.[6] Jones agreed to return for a year or so to get the lithographic studio up and running, and Erskine could now commission and publish prints of professional quality.[7]

A parallel development was taking place with screen-printing. The Kelpra Studio was set up in London in 1957 by Christopher Prater, and the medium began to be used more widely by artists. The studio produced its first artist's print in 1961, and artists such as Richard Hamilton and Eduardo Paolozzi found there a way of working which perfectly matched their vision. The 1960s also saw the establishment of Editions Alecto, which began as a print publisher and later set up printing studios. The Marlborough Gallery joined the Redfern Gallery and St George's Gallery in showing contemporary prints in London. In Scotland, Edinburgh Printmakers was set up in 1967, the first open-access print studio in the country, followed over the next decade by print workshops in Glasgow, Dundee and Aberdeen. Then, in 1970 in Cornwall, a printmaking studio was established in St Ives with the help of the Arts Council. The Penwith Print Workshop was set up by Breon O'Casey, Roy Conn and others, in studio space above the Penwith Gallery. These years saw a growing awareness amongst British artists that printmaking was something they could undertake without necessarily having the requisite technical skills; the help of expert and professional printmakers could open up new creative possibilities and new markets for their work.

There was no printmaking culture, nor any facilities, in St Ives when Wilhelmina Barns-Graham arrived in 1940. Almost no prints were made during the war years. Nevertheless, from the mid-1940s, some artists were managing to produce a few prints of one sort or another in a casual way. Their aims were to explore new media and new forms of expression rather than to produce commercial editions. Bryan Wynter had his own table-top press, and he exhibited a lithograph at the Redfern Gallery in 1948.[8] He gave a print, *Crayfish*, to Barns-Graham as a wedding present in 1949.[9] In the same year, Ben Nicholson made some drypoints, though it is not clear where they were printed. Barns-Graham bought one then, paying in instalments: 'Dear Ben, I have chosen the Drypoint titled "Terendine" – from those we took away with us on Sunday. I enclose £2 & will send another £2 next month if that really is all right with you. How grateful I am.'[10]

Terry Frost also made some drypoint engravings in 1949, though as he lacked a press they were 'printed using manual pressure, and with inexperienced paper selection the results were disappointing'.[11] And the Crypt Group exhibitions included prints, although these were mainly monotypes, the principal method of St Ives printmaking in these early years. Barns-Graham, Sven Berlin, Bryan Wynter, Peter Lanyon, Patrick Heron and Terry Frost were all producing monotypes through the 1940s and 1950s.

Monotype has been variously defined, for example, as:

> A form of expression which defies easy classification as print, drawing or painting.[12]
>
> A single printing of an image incapable of being identically reprinted.[13]
>
> Essentially a single impression that has been pulled from any surface other than a fixed matrix such as an etching plate, lithographic stone, etc.[14]

One of its attractions was that it required no complicated equipment or special materials, both of which were in short supply during the war years. It also appealed because of the experimental and unexpected nature of the images – the accidental marks and the quality of the transferred paint or ink.

And each image was unique, not requiring time to be spent on the less creative activity of producing 20 or 50 identical prints.

Two methods of monotype were used by St Ives artists: printing from a sheet of inked glass, and what Barns-Graham called 'offset drawing'.[15] In the first method, paint or ink was applied to a piece of glass and then drawn into, using a brush or a sharp point. Paper was laid over the paint or ink and pressure was applied to the back. One impression could normally be taken (though sometimes fainter second or third impressions were possible). Often the monotype was then worked over with paint, being used as a background for a work. For instance, many of Bryan Wynter's early landscape paintings were worked over a substratum of monotype, the chance effects of which influenced the development of the composition.[16] Terry Frost learned this technique from Misomé Piele in St Ives, and it was also recommended by William Johnstone, the principal at Camberwell School of Art, where Frost studied from 1947 to 1950.[17] It was a way of freeing the imagination.

The earliest dated prints in the Barns-Graham archive are from 1948, although written notes indicate that she was making monotype prints as early as 1942, and in an interview with Sheila Oliner in 1993 Barns-Graham said that her first printmaking attempts were 'abstract monotypes [from] about 1943 continuing into the early 1950s'.[18] (She destroyed many of the early ones.)[19] The medium was attractive to her because she had always experimented with different mediums, and

> ... it was a cheap and easy way to develop ideas and encouraged freedom ... You could use printing oils – but I mainly used black oil paint, rolled on to glass. You could draw into this, use fingers, use added colour, press paper for image or use several papers as it dried, drawing on top of the placed sheet on the glass for different textures ... And one experimented with different states of the oil, thin, thick, loose or dryish.[20]

The most basic household utensils could be used, and Barns-Graham remembered discussing with Sven Berlin his use of the spoon to press the paper into the plate.[21] She preferred to use a roller to achieve a more even pressure. Examples of this kind of monotype include *Two Studies of a Horse's Skull* (fig.1), and *Fungi on Wood, Loch Long* (fig.2), both dated 1949.[22]

Another kind of monotype was the offset drawing, the origins of which can be traced to Paul Klee. In the early 1920s, Klee had developed a method of using a kind of 'hand-made "carbon" paper', which produced a scratched and grainy textured line.[23] The technique was brought to Britain by the Polish artist Jankel Adler, who had known Klee in the early 1930s in Düsseldorf, where they had occupied neighbouring studios. In the early years of the war, Adler served in the Polish army but he was demobbed due to ill health in 1941. He settled first in Glasgow, then moved to London in 1943 and lived in the same house in Kensington as Robert Colquhoun and Robert MacBryde, whom he had first met in Scotland. A number of artists picked up the technique from him, including Barns-Graham:

> I first heard of it from Adler, and then Colquhoun and MacBryde were doing it, and then Sven Berlin down here, he used a spoon if I remember right, and then I think other artists like Bryan Wynter started doing it ... But I pursued it for some time, because it was an attractive way of drawing.[24]

She had become friends with Colquhoun and MacBryde – 'the two Roberts', as they were known – when they were students in Scotland, and she had been introduced to Adler in Glasgow.[25] She visited the Roberts several times after they moved to London in 1942, and they also visited St Ives, staying with the poet W.S. Graham.[26]

The offset drawing method of making a monotype was one that Barns-Graham used and returned to over many years. Scrapbooks containing photographs of her works from the 1950s show dozens of landscape drawings, of glaciers, Cornish landscapes and the clay country of Chiusure in Italy (see figs 3–9). She later recalled:

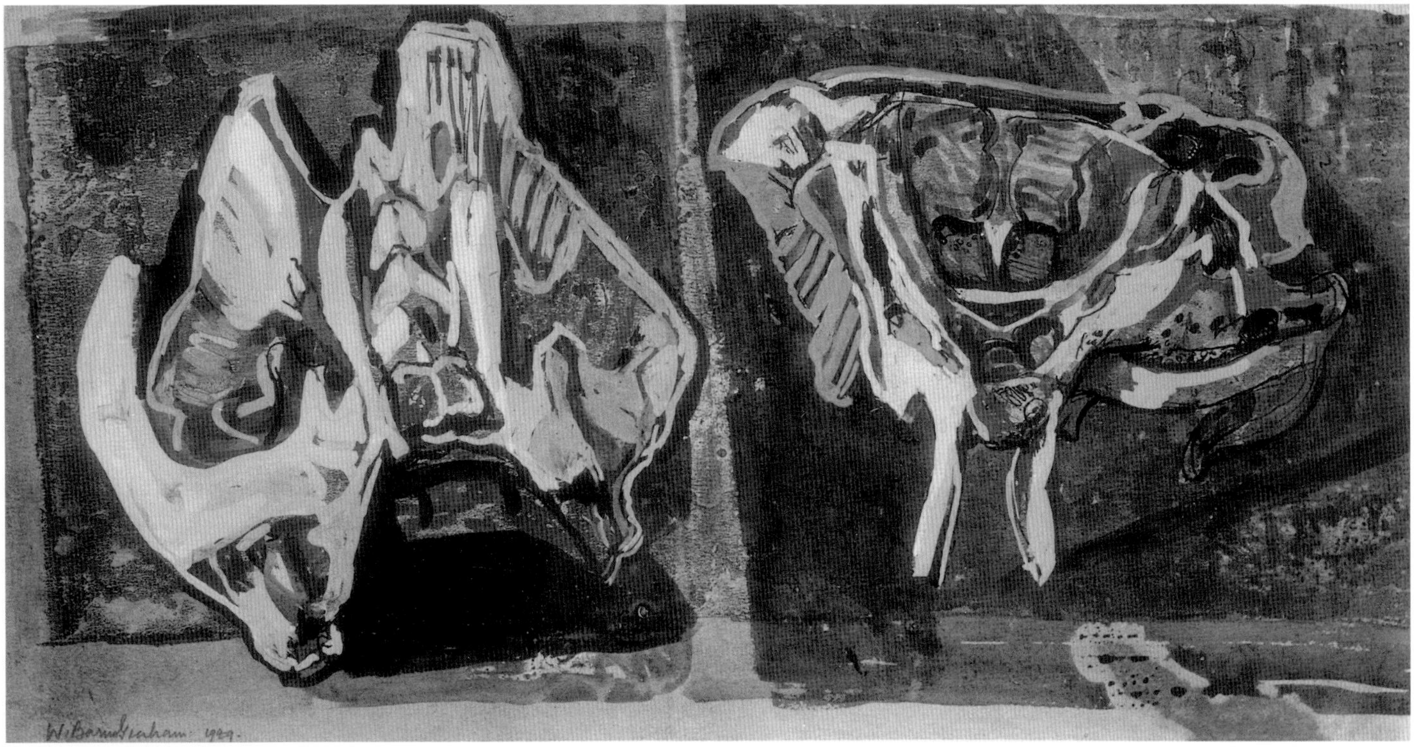

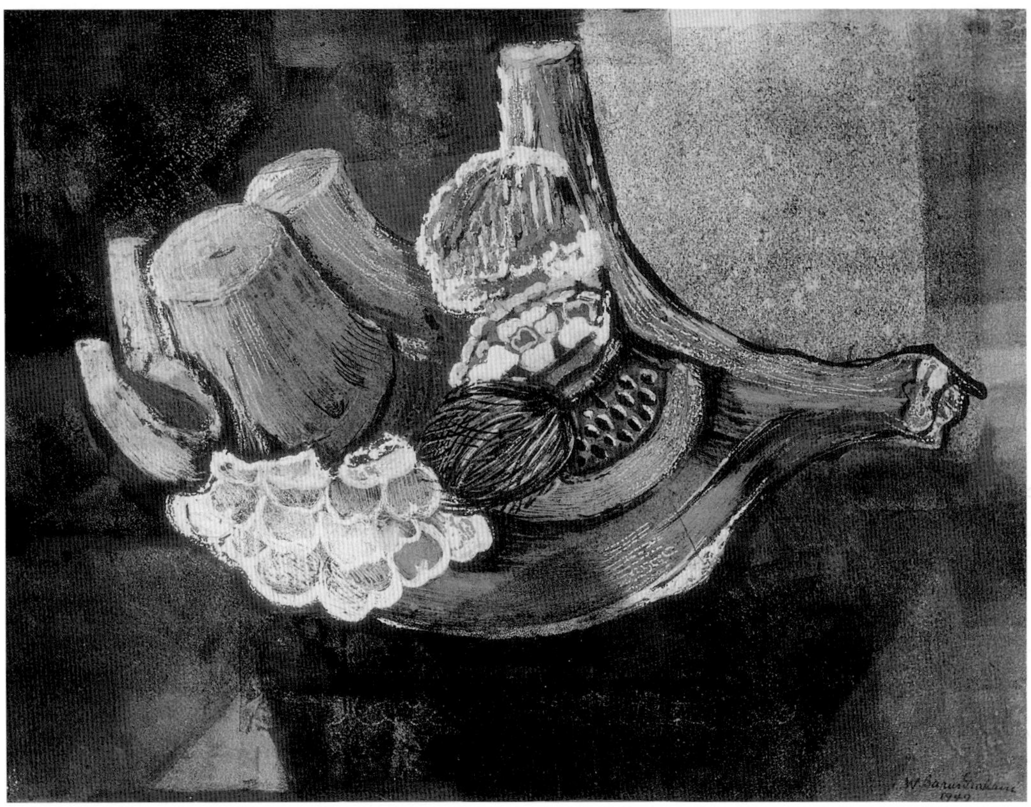

Fig.1.

Two Studies of a Horse's Skull, monotype and gouache, 1949.

Fig.2.

Fungi on Wood, Loch Long, monotype and gouache, 1949.

Fig.3.

Glacier Study with Guide Cutting Steps, offset drawing, 1949.

> You black a piece of tracing paper with printing ink, or I used oil paint, and when it's in a particular condition, sticky but dryish, you can draw through with a knitting needle or a nail or whatever sharp instrument you like. You take a tracing of your drawing on the other side of the tracing paper so that will give you the form that you want to draw through ... And sometimes the accidental smudge is useful. I did lots of drawings of St Ives at that time, and rock drawings ... Oh it was fascinating. A lot of us did it all round about the same time in the early fifties.[27]

Sometimes oil colour was rolled over parts of the monotype, and sometimes she pulled more than one impression of each image, though no two were ever the same. The main attraction was the texture of the line, fuzzy, scratched and broken, with unexpected, random areas of smudged ink, an accidental *frottage* which picked up the grain of the brush marks in the black paint as the hand drew with nail, knitting needle or stick. Barns-Graham 'used the accidents as surprise, freeing up one's work'.[28] Her archive contains a number of the original drawings, with black paint or ink on the back and scored or heavy pencil lines over the image on the front, as well as the resulting monotypes.

In the summer of 1948 Barns-Graham was invited to join her friends the Brothertons on a family holiday in Switzerland.[29] There she admired, climbed on and drew Alpine glaciers,

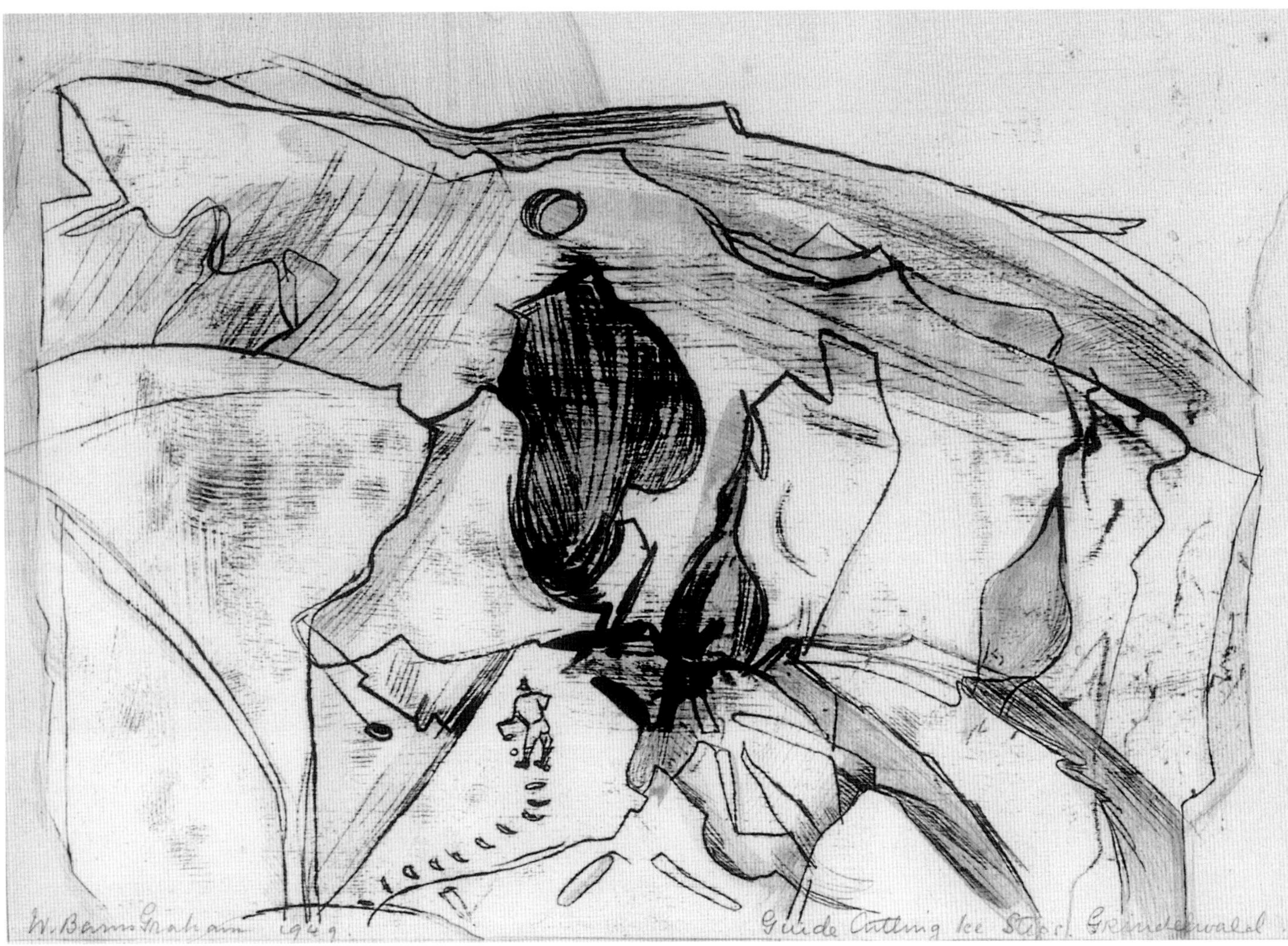

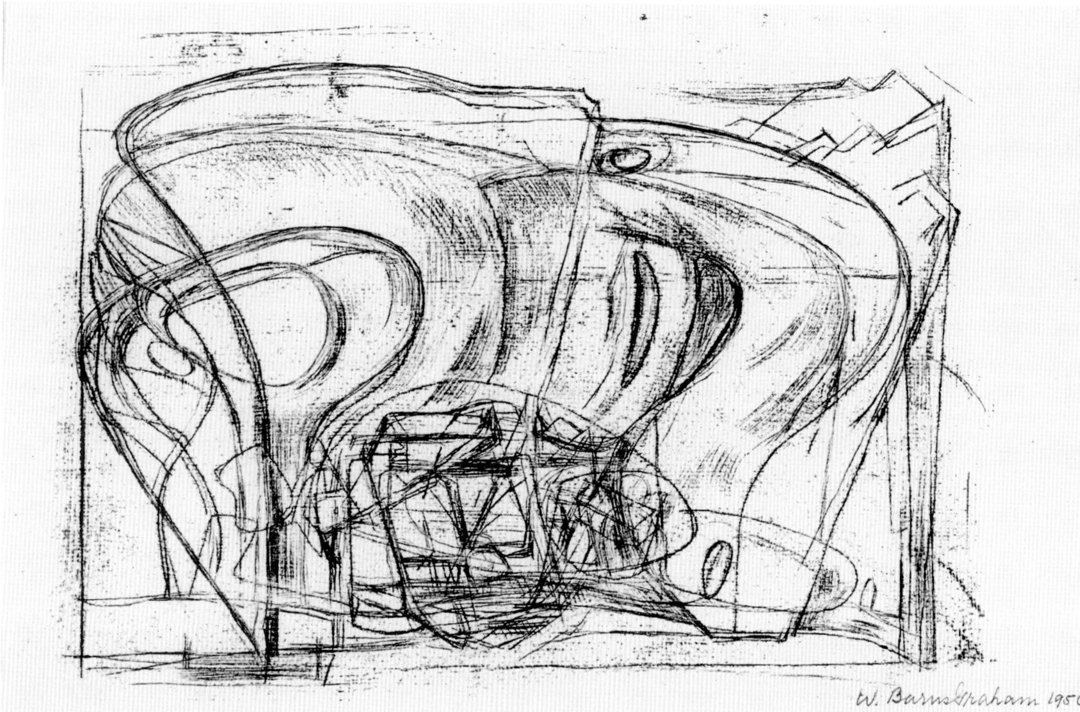

Fig.4.
Glacier Study, offset drawing, 1950.

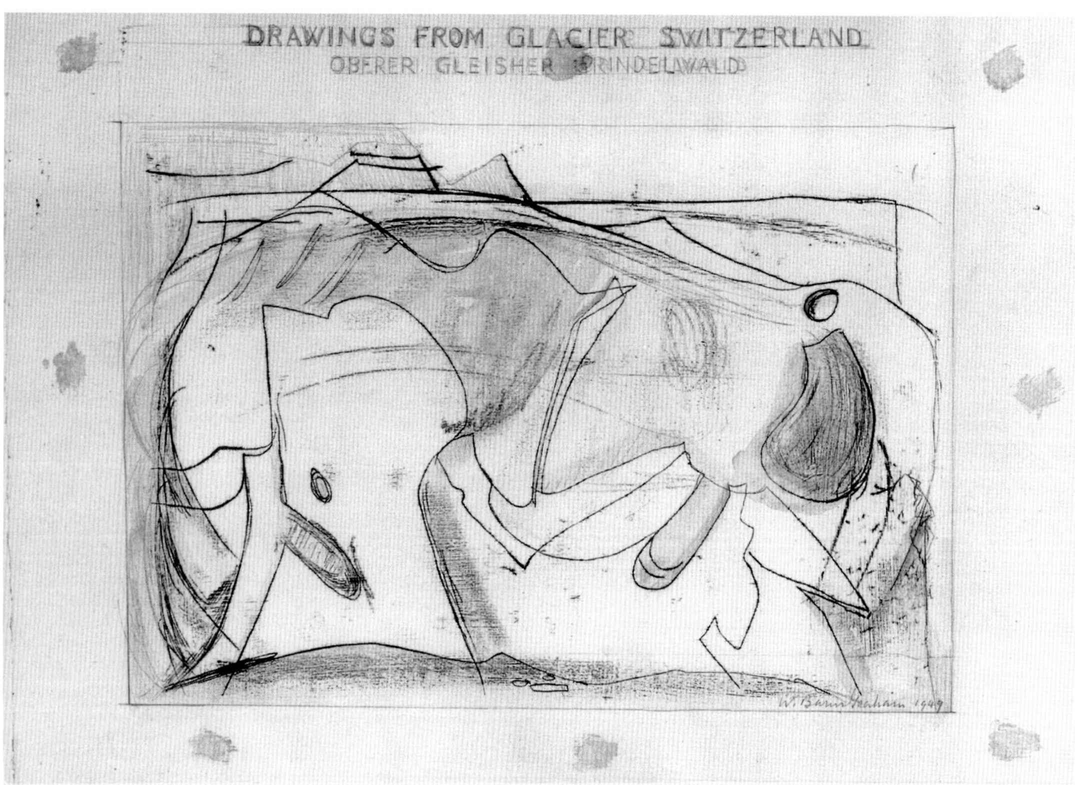

Fig.5.
Drawings from Glacier, Switzerland, offset drawing, 1949.

studying 'the effect of rain or heat and sunshine on the glaciers and the transparency and the colours and the forms and the big holes in them, and cavities… I did these drawings and watercolours and they gave me work for the next two or three years easily'.[30] Many of these works were shown in her exhibition *Recent Drawings, Monotypes and Paintings, Glacier Drawings* in July 1949 at George Downing's bookshop in St Ives. The exhibition was reviewed in the *St Ives Times* by fellow artist Misomé Piele: 'The public should enjoy this one-man show at Downing's bookshop, and admirers of Miss Barns-Graham's work may be startled at the changes in method and outlook in her present phase of painting.'[31]

The exhibition contained more monotypes and offset drawings than paintings. The reviewer appreciated the quality of the different media, picking out *Fungi* for comment:

> The green mottled oil base, washed with green and terracotta gouache, clinches the right character for an unusual subject.
>
> The Swiss towns and landscapes are graceful, but the glacier drawings more controversial. 'Grindelwald' with rococco [sic] spires and delightfully fussy buildings plumped into mountain valleys and 'Spietz' with an incurving glacier look effortless, and the environmental shock brings up a hint of Klee and the best of Emett … the glacier drawings … capture excitement and a wild sort of exploration.[32]

Later, in 1952, Barns-Graham also exhibited offset drawings at the Redfern Gallery in London, almost the only gallery giving space to modern prints at that time; she showed glacier paintings and offsets, which met with critical approval. J.P. Hodin had noted her monotypes in 1950, commenting that 'she has reached not only a material beauty – in a kind of off-set technique, developed by Paul Klee – but also a musical beauty through abstract forms'.[33] Two years later, reviewing the Redfern exhibition, he was able to record that 'amongst her drawings and pictures in offset technique we find probably the most mature expression of her work'.[34]

Offset drawing was particularly suitable for these glacier drawings, the fractured and scratchy nature of the lines suggesting both the fissures and cracks within the ice and the grit and gravel picked up as the glacier ground down the mountain. But Barns-Graham also used the technique for Cornish landscapes and views of St Ives, and combined the offset drawings with ink, watercolour and oil paint: 'You can't escape getting certain rhythms repeating in your work and I do a tremendous lot of drawing from landscape … I am interested in the effect of the weather on rocks, clay country … the curves of the bay here …'[35] She would go on expeditions with Ben Nicholson in the early 1950s, sketching, as David Lewis recalled, 'farms, villages, fields like patchwork with enclosing walls like seams, harbours and sea. Her's [sic] were oil offsets on textured paper …'[36] She also used the technique when travelling in Italy and Sicily in 1954 and 1955, finding it particularly appropriate for the 'extraordinary, deeply scoured landscape'[37] of Chiusure in the province of Siena:

> I went there more than once and did these drawings in offset, washes, sepia, and did a whole set of them after being there … I used oil paint on the Chiusure drawings, sometimes oil paint I rubbed in, slight brown colours, or terracotta red … mixed with turpentine, often using my finger.[38]

She returned briefly to the technique in 1991, when she responded to a request for information about the practice from Gordon Samuel, who was writing about monotype for a book edited by Robin Garton, *British Printmakers 1855–1955*. Her diary for that year records her working on small offset drawings again and reading about Degas's monotype methods.[39]

It was not until the early 1950s that Barns-Graham began to gain knowledge of, and to use, other more conventional printing techniques. At various points throughout her career she took etching lessons, first of all at Penzance School of Art,

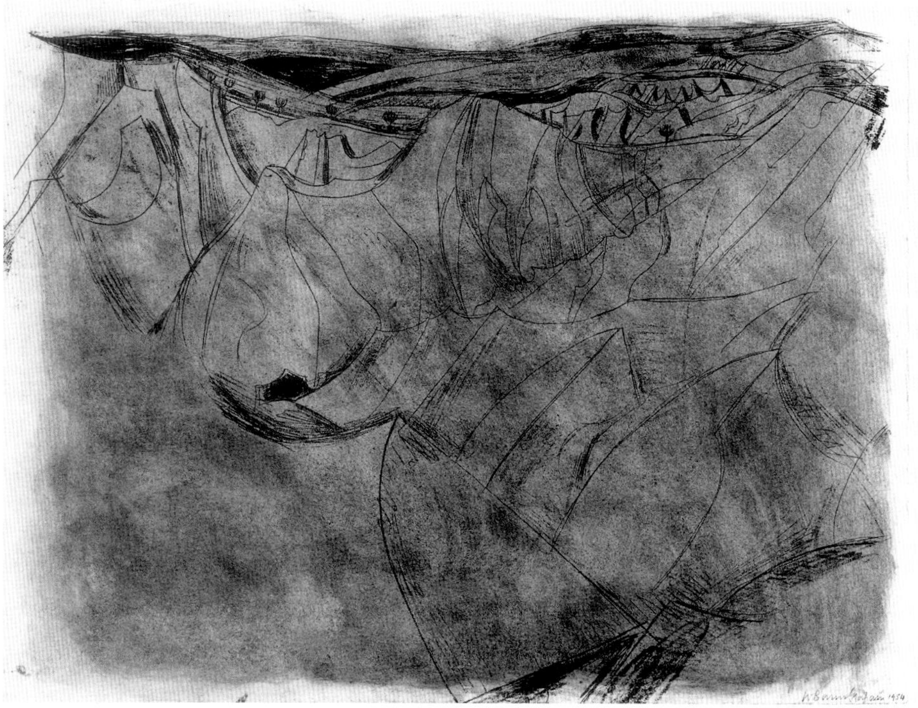

Fig.6.

Chiusure (Shadows), offset drawing on grey gouache, 1954.

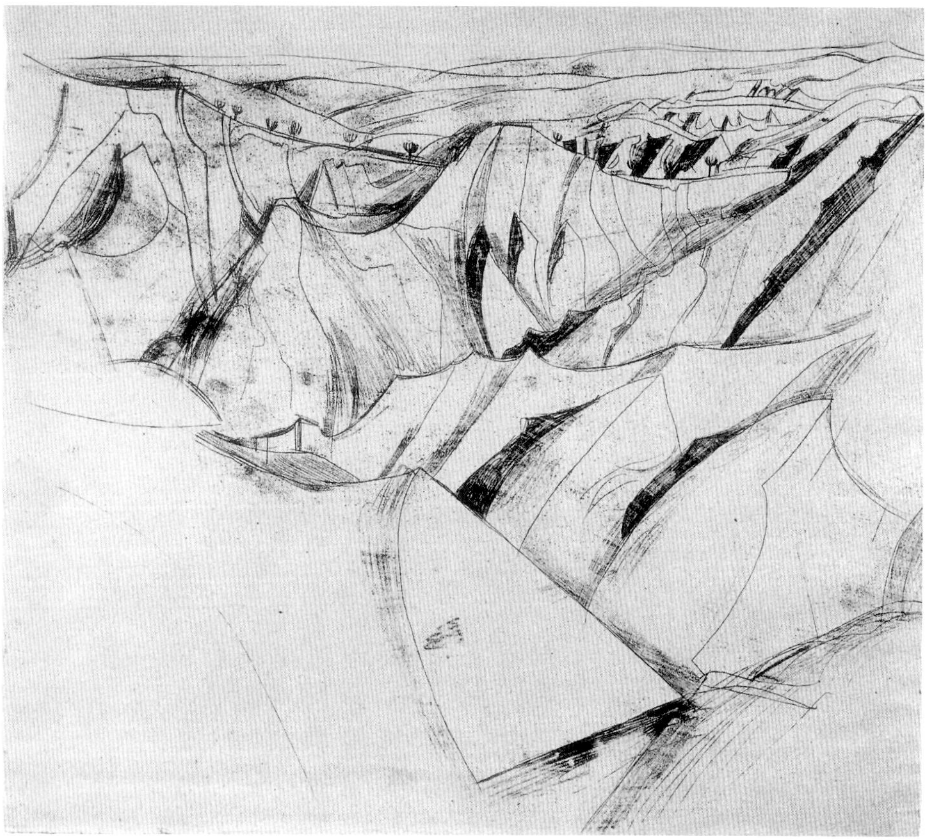

Fig.7.

Clay Country, Chiusure, offset drawing, 1954.

where the principal was the etcher and engraver Edward Bouverie Hoyton.[40] He had won the *Prix de Rome* for engraving in 1926, and had been Lecturer in Engraving at Leeds College of Art from 1934 before coming to Penzance in 1941. He encouraged artists to come and use the School's facilities; some also attended life-drawing classes there.

In 1952, Barns-Graham went to evening classes at the School with John Wells and Denis Mitchell, and they were taught etching by Bouverie Hoyton and John Tunnard. She made a print of a glacier which was not editioned but which exists in a number of states (cat.1). The linear quality of the glacier drawings and offsets translated easily into the etching medium. The first state is crisp and clean but the image becomes gradually more subtle through the states, as some lines are burnished out and new shapes and more crosshatching are introduced. The final state, number 6, exists in three versions, with inking by Barns-Graham and John Wells, and a mounted impression, inscribed 'Artist's Proof' inked by Bouverie Hoyton.[41] Examination of other prints by Wells reveals that he developed a distinctive way of inking up the plate, with soft shadows of ink remaining at the edges of the image and a framing line made from ink on the edges of the plate itself.[42] This is apparent in the glacier print made by Barns-Graham which Wells inked for her. An etching by Wells in the Barns-Graham collection dates from the same time.

The Penzance School of Art offered teaching but not a printing service. To print up an edition Barns-Graham would have had to do it herself. Perhaps this is why the glacier print was not editioned. On the other hand, she could make linocut prints in her own studio, without the need for a press. The colour linocut had its heyday in Britain in the 1920s and early 1930s with the work of Claude Flight and the Grosvenor School. From 1922 to 1928 Flight was a member of the Seven and Five Society which also numbered Ben Nicholson among its members. Nicholson had also made linocuts in the 1920s and early 1930s, and some of these were exhibited at the Castle Inn in St Ives in 1945.[43] This technique seems to have been taken up in St Ives from 1948 or 1949 by, among others, Peter Lanyon, Bryan Wynter and Terry Frost, as well as Barns-Graham. Linocut was an attractive technique because it did not require complicated equipment or materials. The lino blocks could be cut with simple tools, and printing required only the pressure of a roller on the back of the paper.

Barns-Graham made a small number of lino prints in 1953 and 1954, and they reflect a development in her art and motifs from ice to rock forms,[44] and in the use of geometry in the underlying structure of her compositions: 'I started using the Golden Section, and fitting the glacier experiments into that. So I worked on this scene for many years and it led me on to rock formations, again using the Golden Section and fitting shapes into this [making] single rock forms in very simple colours using black, grey and white.'[45] Her interest in the Golden Section was shared by other artists, notably Terry Frost, who in 1951 made a monotype entitled *Abstract Based on the Golden Section*.[46] His linocuts, and in particular one entitled *Double Quay* of 1952, must have had some influence on the rock-form prints Barns-Graham made in 1953. In Frost's print the lino block has been turned upside down and printed again so that the double images overlap.[47] Barns-Graham used this inversion when printing her linocuts the following year and a number of variants exist, including some with hand-colouring (cat.2). Some versions now in the archive have been mounted as cards so, while one cannot talk of a published edition, they clearly were distributed, probably as Christmas cards.

While rock forms appear in small and large paintings, there is an even clearer relationship between these two linocuts and the relief paintings Barns-Graham was making at the same time (fig.10). They share a similar small scale, most measuring no more than about 13 x 21 cm (5 x 8 inches). The flat planes are built up in layers on the relief paintings, and carved out on the lino block. The same triangular shapes, scooped-out half circles and diagonal lines dissecting the image, appear in both media. Another linocut, *Untitled Abstract* (cat.15), relates to a theme the artist was developing in her painting from 1954 onwards. This is the *Geoff and Scruffy Series*, the main components of which are a five-sided shape and a semicircle

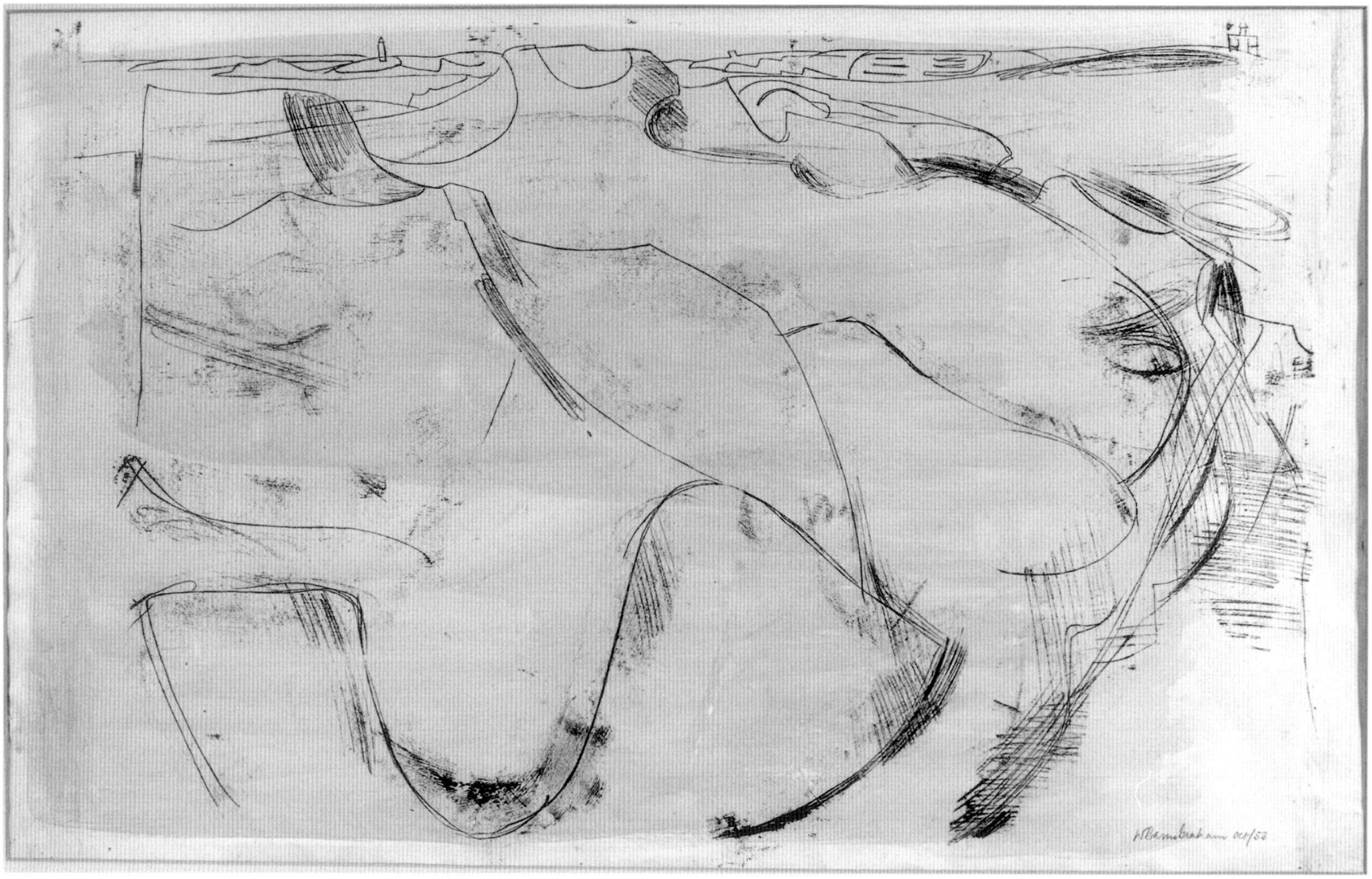

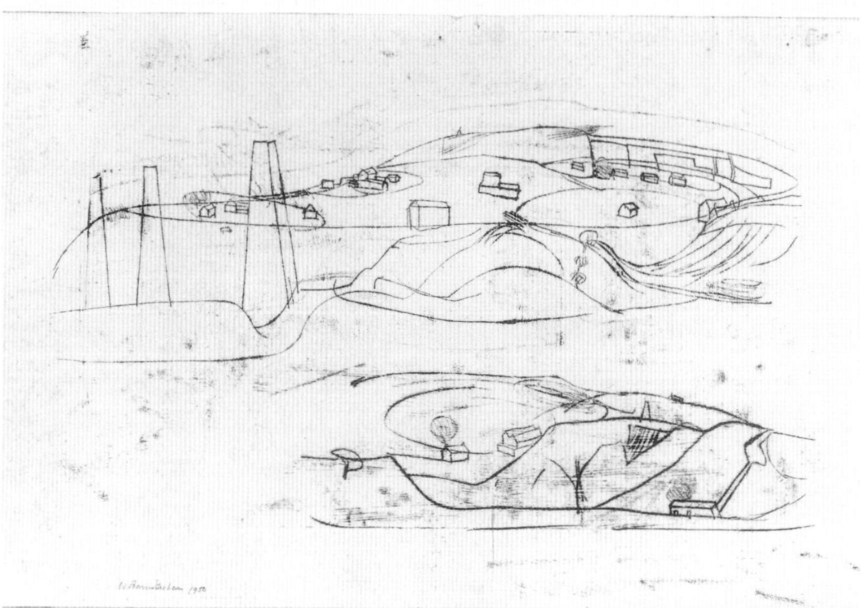

Fig.8.

White Rocks, St Mary's, Scilly Isles, offset drawing, 1953.

Fig.9.

Nancegollan, offset drawing, 1950.

Fig.10.

Rock Form, relief painting, 1952. This work is closely related to the linocut prints Barns Graham was working on at the same time.

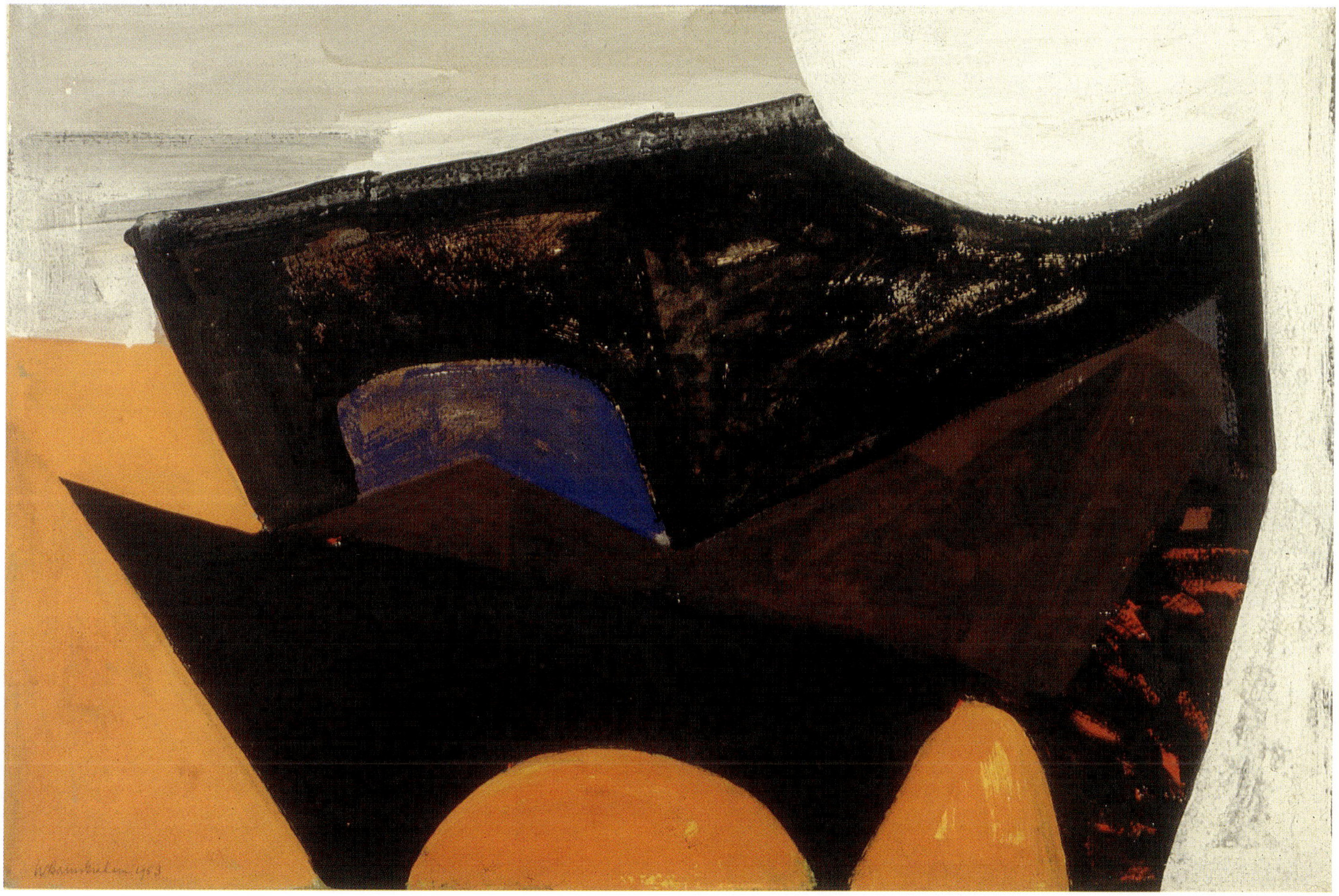

joined by two lines – shapes derived originally from 'drawings done in the war, of men painting buoys ... The shape got simplified, the half moon was the [Porthmeor] beach shape cut by the sea'.[48] A fourth linocut, *Night in Venice* (cat.14), was made following her visit to Italy in June 1954 with David Lewis to see Ben Nicholson's work at the Venice Biennale. Several states and variants exist with hand-colouring.

In 1955 Barns-Graham had her first encounter with screenprinting, the technique that would ultimately become her favourite means of printmaking. Once again, because it did not require a press, it attracted the interest of a number of artists who experimented with the technique. Peter Lanyon had made some silkscreens with Warren Mackenzie, an American who had come to St Ives in 1949 to learn pottery with Bernard Leach. They set up their studio above Leach's pottery. Denis Mitchell also had screenprinting facilities in his studio, and Terry Frost made his first screenprint here in 1953.[49] And it was also here that Barns-Graham's first screenprint was made.

This was her contribution to a set of linen table mats shown at Heal's department store in 1955. These were produced by Denis Mitchell and Stanley Dorfman under the name of Porthia Prints.[50] The exhibition, *Abstract Designs*, opened on 1 March 1955 at Heal's Picture Gallery and Craftsman's Market, and included paintings, sculpture and prints. Barns-Graham exhibited two paintings, *Orange, White and Red* (1955) and *Black and Pink* (1954). The screenprinted table linen was designed by Robert Adam, Barns-Graham, Stanley Dorfman, John Forrester, Terry Frost, William Gear, Barbara Hepworth, Patrick Heron, Roger Hilton, Peter Lanyon, Denis Mitchell, Michael Snow and John Wells. The table mats were available in sets of six, priced at £2 and 15 shillings per set.[51]

Barns-Graham's mat (cat.24) was printed in two colours,

black and yellow ochre, in an abstract design based on a painting that relates loosely to her rock-formation theme. There were clearly many of these mats left unsold after the exhibition, since there are a number of copies in the archive and some twenty years later Barns-Graham recorded in her diary spending time sewing the edges of some unfinished ones.[52]

By the mid-1950s, many of the St Ives artists were regularly engaged in printmaking and were beginning to find printing facilities in a variety of places. During these years many of them, though not Barns-Graham, were involved in teaching at the Bath Academy of Arts, housed at Corsham Court in Wiltshire, and some of them took the opportunity of learning lithography there with the principal teacher of lithography, Henry Cliffe. Lanyon, Frost and Wynter all taught at Corsham. They must have felt they were becoming sufficiently skilful in various printing techniques to instruct others, because Lanyon, Frost and Wells ran a summer school in St Peter's Loft in St Ives from 1955 to 1960 and the prospectus advertised etching, engraving, linocut and monotype.[53] Frost was also commissioned by the Miller's Press to make a print, and he and Bryan Wynter made lithographs for Robert Erskine and the St George's Gallery in 1956–8. Contact with them probably gave Erskine the idea of working with other St Ives artists as well.

In pursuit of his project with the Curwen Press, and while waiting for the new studio to be ready, Erskine decided that Stanley Jones should set up a temporary lithographic studio in St Ives. Erskine was keen to involve the St Ives artists and the pilot scheme would also help spread the word about the new Curwen venture.[54] Jones arrived in St Ives in January 1958 and over the next few months he worked with many of the resident artists, including Barns-Graham.[55] The St Ives artists were willing participants, said Jones:

> We began this small pilot studio complete with lithographic stones and press. People were keen to do this because they liked to ally themselves with movements on the continent ... like the School of Paris. Patrick Heron was very close in spirit to what was happening there – very conscious also of the New York people ... There was a great deal of activity going on at that time and making prints for them was something of a diversion but it was also a philosophy ... that they could [get] their work more publicly seen.[56]

The studio was set up at 36 Fore Street, Academy Steps, which was the studio of Bruce Taylor. He managed the printing project with his wife, Jennifer. One evening the artists all met in the Taylor's living room, as Stanley Jones recalled:

> Erskine gave a talk and he had visual illustrations that he projected on a screen to demonstrate various points ... [The] artists could ask questions and talk to him and talk to me and ... they then booked up the time they could come into this studio. It wasn't actually ready then; we had to spend a week or two preparing it.[57]

A local boat mechanic helped to get the press working.

On 10 January 1958 Erskine wrote to Barns-Graham, 'Enclosed is the promised document for you to study in connexion with our litho studio. I am sure that you will find lithography a great assett [sic] to your work. I do look forward to the prints which will transpire'.[58] The document gave details of the arrangements. Each artist was to have the use of the studio at 36 Fore Street under the supervision of Stanley Jones as printer for one week, having previously booked that week with Bruce Taylor. A booking fee of £3.00 included a contribution to 'stone-money'. There were no proofing or printing charges. The artist was to draw sets of stones for two colour lithographs, supervise the proofing and sign the final editions. The studio was to edition one print for the artist free of charge, and the artist would receive 30 copies of the print for nothing. Erskine would receive the set of stones for the second print in exchange, 'from which we would pull an edition for our own benefit of not more than 50 copies'. Artists would get artist's proofs of their edition, there would be two extra 'house copies' for publicity and Erskine would choose which of the two editions he wanted. Only the proofing of the prints would take place in St Ives, because the Fore Street premises were too small for the full-scale production of the editions. Jones was due to leave St Ives by the end of April, and so the artists were warned that there would be a delay in printing up the editions. These were to be produced in the order in which they had been made. Subsequently Barns-Graham received a letter from Jennifer Taylor about the 'Erskine Taylor' Plan, booking a week to work on a lithograph between 20 January and 27 April.

The resulting work (cat.22) relates closely in composition to other works by Barns-Graham from the period 1957–8.[59] The muted colour scheme and the calligraphic and scribbled bundles of lines appear also in paintings made that year, motifs which she subsequently developed in the *Spanish Island Series* and *Strung Form Series*.[60]

While the printmaking experiment, during the time it was based in St Ives, seems to have been successful, the subsequent outcome was less satisfactory. Jones moved all the equipment, presses, stones and proofs back to London. Barns-Graham's two prints were amongst them, and from that point on she had great difficulty in finding out what was happening to them. One image (which should have been hers to keep, according to the agreement) was printed in an edition of 30 and sent to her for signing, but the second was not:

> I had to go to Scotland, when I came back Stanley had vanished so I did the first lot which I took to a gallery in London and never heard another word to this day excepting that this year they are turning up in London and being bought by people and the Tate Gallery bought one of them. What has happened I don't know. I think they have been tucked away for – what is it about 30 years and suddenly have appeared ... one was exhibited in a collection at the Modern Art Gallery in Edinburgh.[61]

It was Erskine's practice not to invest in printing a whole edition at once, but to print on demand. Stanley Jones could not print the St Ives prints without Erskine's permission, since he was the publisher. Jones remembers that Erskine used to 'sit on

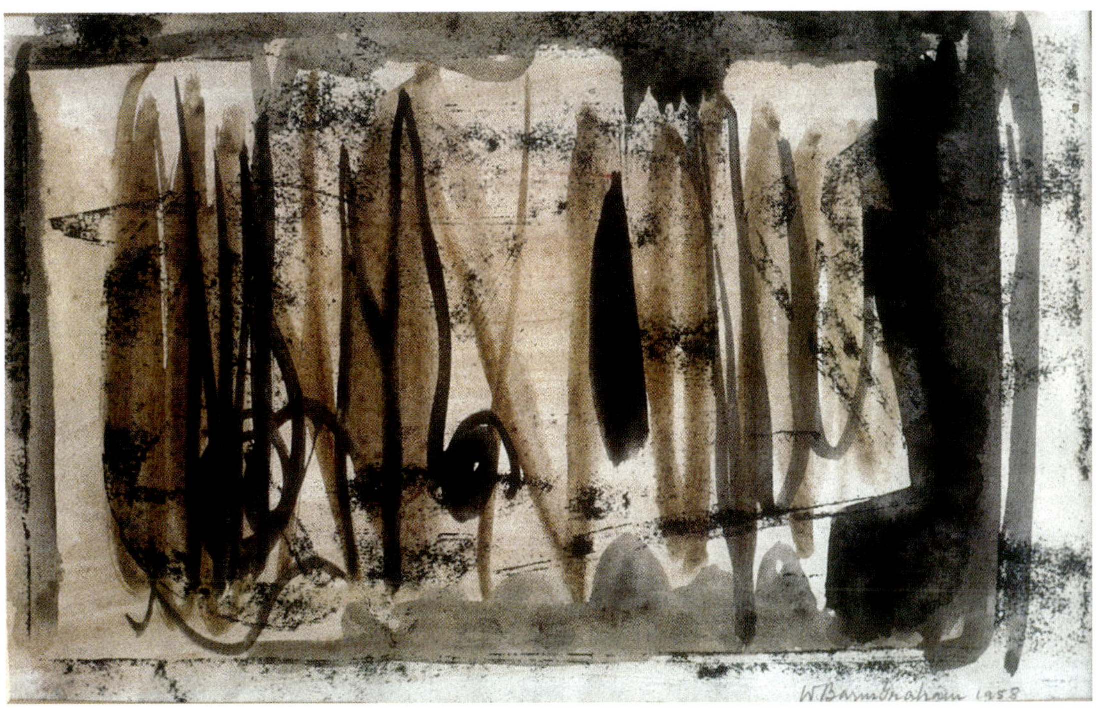

Fig.11.
October Painting, 1958, gouache.

proofs and show them to all kinds of potential buyers and if their reaction wasn't enthusiastic he would put them back in the drawer. I'm sure [Barns-Graham] herself would have published them if he hadn't because she was thrilled with the way of working which she'd never tried before'.[62] Barns-Graham tried to find out what had happened to her prints. She contacted Stanley Jones, by then working at the Curwen Studio in Plaistow, who replied to her on 8 July 1959:

> The situation regarding your print lies in the hands of Robert Erskine ... the position now being that he orders work from the press, and not from me personally. Although I have the stones and plates for your second print, I cannot myself go ahead and print it out – it has to be ordered from the Gallery.[63]

Barns-Graham was not the only artist to experience this problem. Few of the prints seem to have been fully editioned or sold by the St George's Gallery, though one print by Terry Frost was shown there in 1958.[64] Erskine became involved with Editions Alecto, established in 1962, and in 1963 the stock from the St George's Gallery was transferred to that organisation. It is unclear what became of the proofs and stones from the St Ives project, but one copy of Barns-Graham's print was purchased from Editions Alecto in 1965 by the UK Government Art Collection, and copies began to appear on the market in the 1990s.[65] A collection of twelve proofs appeared at a Phillips sale of *Old Master, Decorative and Modern Prints* on 9 April 1991 (lot 310), and were purchased by the William Weston Gallery.[66] Barns-Graham is not mentioned by name but the lot comprised twelve prints; ten other artists are named and the Gallery subsequently sold one Barns-Graham proof to the Tate Gallery and a second was sold to a dealer. Other copies turn up periodically.[67] The Barns-Graham archive holds a number of proofs, including one with instructions about signing and numbering.

Perhaps it was as a result of this experience, or of other circumstances in her life, that this was the last printmaking Barns-Graham undertook for over 12 years.

NOTES

1. For a fuller biography see Lynne Green, *W. Barns-Graham: A Studio Life*, Lund Humphries, 2001.
2. 'My Reflections or Notes written 1993–1996, Book I: the Blue Book', in the Wilhelmina Barns-Graham Archive (hereafter WB-G Archive): 'The College has been greatly extended since then and the war, we didn't have the printing or photographic & film departments.'
3. Frances Carey and Anthony Griffiths, *Avant-garde British Printmaking, 1914–1960*, London, 1990, p.21.
4. Robert Erskine, 'St. George's Gallery', in Charles Spencer (ed.), *A Decade of Printmaking*, London, 1973, p.20.
5. Pat Gilmour, *Artists at Curwen: A Celebration of the Gift of Artists' Prints from the Curwen Studio*, exh. cat., Tate Gallery, London, 1977, pp 95–6.
6. Author's interview with Stanley Jones, 9 November 2005.
7. Curwen Studio moved to Tottenham Court Road in 1965, and to Chilford Hall, Linton, near Cambridge, in 1989. Stanley Jones is still the studio's director.
8. Carey and Griffiths, *Avant-garde British Printmaking*, p.190.
9. Tamsyn Woollcombe, The British Library Sound Archive, National Life Story Collection (hereafter NLSC): 'Artists' Lives', *Wilhelmina Barns-Graham*, Tape Numbers F4747–4751, June 1994.
10. Tate Gallery Archive, 8717.1.2.292, letter to Ben Nicholson from Wilhelmina Barns-Graham, Tuesday, 29 November 1949.
11. David Archer, 'Terry Frost: printmaker', in Elizabeth Knowles (ed.), *Terry Frost*, Lund Humphries, 1994, p.208.
12. Carey and Griffiths, *Avant-garde British Printmaking*, p.148.
13. Riva Castleman, *Prints of the Twentieth Century: A History*, London, 1976, p. 209.
14. Gordon Samuel, 'The monotype 1900–1955', in Robin Garton (ed.), *British Printmakers 1855–1955*, Devizes, 1992, p.287.
15. This technique is described as a 'traced monotype' by Antony Griffiths in 'Monotypes', *Print Quarterly*, vol.5, no.1, 1988, pp 56–60, or as a 'carbon transfer process' by the same author in his book with Frances Carey, *Avantegarde British Printmaking*, p.21.
16. Chris Stevens, *Bryan Wynter*, London, 1999, p.28.
17. Samuel, 'The monotype 1900–1955', p.290. See also Archer, 'Terry Frost: printmaker'.
18. Quoted in Sheila Oliner, 'It's a beginning', *Printmaking Today*, vol.3, no.4, 1994, pp 8–9.
19. WB-G Archive, notes prepared by Barns-Graham in September 1991 for a letter to Gordon Samuel for his chapter in Garton, *British Printmakers*.
20. ibid.
21. ibid.
22. See Garton, *British Printmakers*, p.300, fig.559.
23. Carey and Griffiths, *Avant-garde British Printmaking*, p.148.
24. Woollcombe interview, NLSC, June 1994.
25. Green, *W. Barns-Graham*, p.80.
26. For instance Barns-Graham's diary for February 1951 records that, during a visit to London, 'I went to Colquhoun & McBride [sic]. Graham there & others. John Minton & Pat.' Her diary for 18 March 1951 records her working on offset drawings.
27. Woollcombe interview, NLSC, June 1994.
28. WB-G Archive, notes prepared in September 1991.

29. Green, *W. Barns-Graham*, pp 104–5.
30. Tate Gallery Archive, TV South West transcript, 8613, pp 297–319, p.304.
31. Review by Misomé Piele, *St Ives Times*, 8 July 1949.
32. ibid.
33. From J.P. Hodin, 'Cornish Renaissance', *Penguin New Writing*, no. 39, London, 1950, quoted in Green, *W. Barns-Graham*, p.117.
34. J.P. Hodin, 'W. Barns-Graham', *Art News & Review*, vol.4, no.2 (1952).
35. TV South West transcript, p.298.
36. David Lewis, *St Ives 1939–64: Twenty-five Years of Painting, Sculpture and Pottery* [1985], revised edition London, 1989, p.37.
37. Green, *W. Barns-Graham*, p.147.
38. Woollcombe interview, NLSC, June 1994.
39. WB-G Archive, diary entries for 1 July and 29 September 1991.
40. For a history of this art school see Peter Waverly, *Penzance School of Art 1853–2003*, Penzance, 2003.
41. WB-G Archive. The diary entry for 19 May 1983 records, 'Lunched with Sheila Lanyon ... Boots turned up with early engraving of Peter's I was able to verify the year done, Johnny, Peter & I having done a course at PZ art school under Bouverie Hoyton.' The diary entry for 3 May 1998 notes two errors in the exhibition catalogue by Matthew Rowe for the exhibition *John Wells: The Fragile Cell*, at Tate St Ives: 'one about the Crypt Group – for I was a founder member but didn't show first year, as had to go to Scotland – and it was me, not Denis Mitchell in 1950 went with Peter & Johnny to learn etching with John Tunnard at PZ Art School. A slip by Johnny I guess ... I don't remember Denis doing it at all & I have my etching & one of Johnny Wells.'
42. See, for example, works in the Tate Gallery Collection, P77131, *Abstraction*, etching 1950, and P77132, *Cliff Figure*, etching 1950.
43. David Archer, 'St Ives and Corsham', in Garton, *British Printmakers*, p.306.
44. The rocks were at Zennor, along the coast from St Ives. In a letter to Patrick Elliot dated 10 April 1990, discussing a painting of hers that had been bequeathed to the Scottish National Gallery of Modern Art, *Zennor Rock (Rose II)*, 1953, Barns-Graham recalled 'doing a series of Zennor Rock forms in different mediums ...'.
45. Woollcombe interview, NLSC, June 1994. The Golden Section is a particular proportion which artists throughout the history of Western art have thought possesses a special harmony, and it underlies the composition of countless works of art. It is used to divide lines or rectangles so that the proportion of the smaller part to the larger part is the same as that of the larger part to the whole.
46. Carey and Griffiths, *Avant-garde British Printmaking*, p.184.
47. David Archer, 'Terry Frost: printmaker', illus. p.210.
48. Green, *W. Barns-Graham*, p.142.
49. Carey and Griffiths, *Avant-garde British Printmaking*, p.185.
50. ibid.
51. Victoria and Albert Museum, London, Archive of Art and Design, Heal's Craftsman's Market scrapbook, AAD/1994/16/2693.
52. WB-G Archive, diary entry 23 October 1977: 'R & I worked on framing & I on mats hemming – silk screen D. Mitchell printed 1955'. A copy of the Barbara Hepworth design was included in an exhibition of Hepworth Prints at the Belgrave Gallery, St Ives, May–June 2003.
53. Carey and Griffiths, *Avant-garde British Printmaking*, pp 179–80.
54. Author's interview with Stanley Jones, 9 November 2005.
55. The other artists involved were Barbara Hepworth, Ben Nicholson, Terry Frost, Roger Hilton, Bryan Wynter, Peter Lanyon, Patrick Heron, Arnold Weschke, John Wells, Alexander Mackenzie and Trevor Bell; author's interview with Stanley Jones, 9 November 2005.
56. ibid.
57. ibid.
58. WB-G Archive, letter from Erskine to Barns-Graham, 10 January 1958.
59. The print has been variously named *Untitled, Brown and Tan*; *Brown and Yellow Composition*; and *Linear Abstract*. The last title has been used in this catalogue (see cat.22).
60. See Green, *W. Barns-Graham*, pp 172–3, figs 93 and 94.
61. Sheila Oliner, taped interview with Barns-Graham, 16 September 1993. The exhibition mentioned at the Scottish National Gallery of Modern Art was *New Beginnings: Postwar British Art from the Collection of Ken Powell*, 1992.
62. Author's interview with Stanley Jones, 9 November 2005.
63. WB-G Archive, letter from Stanley Jones to Wilhelmina Barns-Graham, 8 July 1959. Curiously, there is a diary entry for 12 July 1959, four days after Jones's letter, saying that Barns-Graham had sold a lithograph for £5, which must have been one of her artist's proofs of this print.
64. *Contemporary British Printmakers*, St George's Gallery, 1 July – 30 August 1958 (catalogue now in the Tate Gallery Archive, London), cat.16: *Brown Figure* by Terry Frost, lithograph in an edition of 30.
65. It is possible that copies were destroyed in a fire at Editions Alecto's premises in 1978.
66. Phillips sale Tuesday 9 April 1991, *Old Master, Decorative and Modern Prints*, lot 310, 'A Collection of St Ives Artists'. Lithographs, finished compositions and working proofs by various hands including Robert Brennan, John Wells, Bryan Wynter, Kenneth Armitage, Karl Weschke, Alexander Mackenzie, Peter Lanyon, Patrick Heron, Trevor Bell and Barbara Hepworth, the first six signed, some soft creasing and slight soiling, other minor defects, unframed, apart from the Armitage (12).
67. WB-G Archive, diary entry July 26 1994: 'Roll arrived [containing] my stone lithograph print I made with Stanley Jones 1958. Someone has bought and wanted signed – I've never got a penny for the set yet Tate has got one, one was on show in Modern Art Exh, Edinburgh, someone's collection ...'.

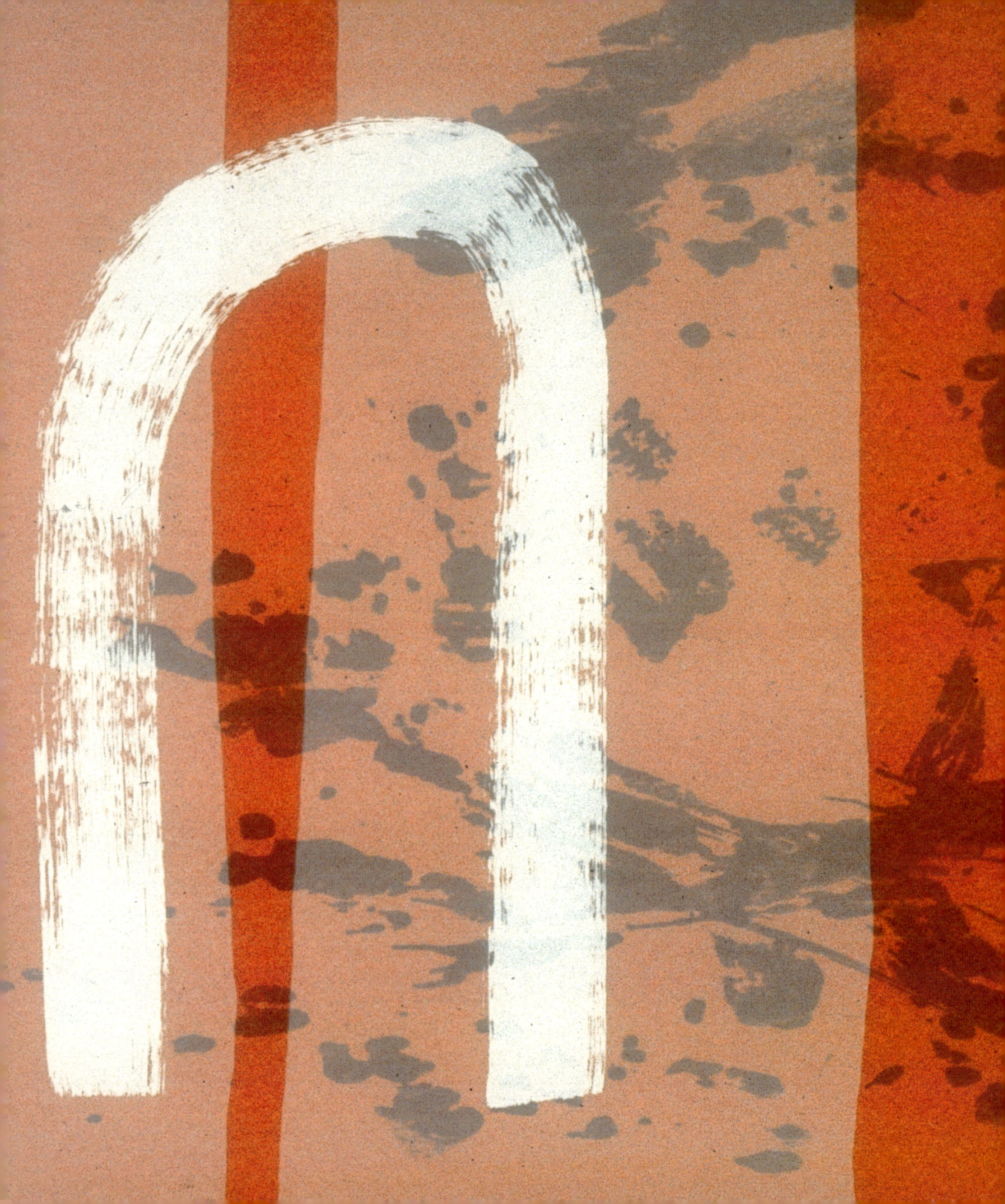

2

EXPERIMENTATION 1971-98

It was not until 1971 that Wilhelmina Barns-Graham once more turned to printmaking. Screenprinting, the medium she would finally make her own, had been increasing in use and popularity throughout the 1960s, and would have suited her hard-edged and geometric style of that decade.

Screenprinting is basically a stencil technique. A fine mesh (originally of silk, hence the terms 'silkscreen' and 'serigraphy', but now more commonly of a synthetic material) is stretched over a rectangular frame. Ink is then forced through the mesh with a squeegee onto paper. Each colour in a print requires a separate screen – a complex image can be made up from more than twenty screens. The image can be formed by the application of cut-out paper stencils to the screen, or by painting the screen with a screen-filler. Another method is to make painted marks with a screen-painting fluid and then to process this with a screen-filler stopping-out material, so that the ink prints only where the mesh is open.

A development from this process uses a light-sensitive emulsion for making stencils. The screen is coated with the light-sensitive emulsion, which hardens when exposed to ultraviolet light. The image is made by blocking the light with a positive (a transparent sheet holding opaque marks). The opaque marks form the area that will ultimately print. Artists

Detail of *November V*, 1991 (cat. 34).

may generate marks on their positive photographically, digitally or autographically (that is, with marks made by the artist's hand). As Barns-Graham always used the term 'separation' for these sheets, that term will be used here. She worked by hand with red, brown or black painting and drawing materials (tusches) which ultraviolet light cannot penetrate. The light-sensitive screen and the positive are held in contact and exposed to ultraviolet light. Where the light is blocked, the emulsion remains water-soluble and can be washed away, leaving the image as open mesh on the screen. When ink is passed through the open mesh of the screen, the mark originally on the positive is printed on the paper beneath the screen. It is important to remember that while the artist is imagining a coloured final image, or has a colour sketch or painting to refer to, the separation sheets that combine to make the final image each consist of a single monochrome layer. The final image can be built up from many printed layers and the effect of each layer of colour will only become apparent during the printing process.

This technique made it possible for artists to incorporate photographic images in their prints, which is why the method appealed to artists such as Andy Warhol and Richard Hamilton, who were experimenting in the 1960s with the inclusion of ready-made images in their work. A similar technique using separation sheets can also be applied to lithography and intaglio printing methods, using light-sensitive coatings to transfer images onto the lithographic or etching plate.

If Barns-Graham had had access to facilities and expertise close to home in St Ives, it is possible she might have returned to printmaking sooner. The opening of the Penwith Print Workshop in 1970, round the corner from her studio, seems to have rekindled her interest. She attended etching classes there in the winter of 1971–2, and again in 1976. Thereafter, sporadically throughout the 1970s and '80s, she made prints both in St Ives and in Scotland.

None of the etchings she made at the classes were ever published, and they can mostly only be dated by circumstantial evidence. One, for instance, can be dated by a newspaper from November 1971 in which the etching plate was wrapped (cat.2). In addition, these prints were always related to the subject matter she was exploring at the same time in her paintings. These early etchings reflect ideas which emerged from the work she was doing in the 1960s on 'the theme of "order and disorder of things of a kind", squares and circles, complimentary colours, hots and colds', as well as the studying of

> crowds, rush hours, fish swarms, bird flights, cell formations, backs of ferns, inside foxgloves plants, the dots ... the line drawings followed, they were things of a kind in a rythem [sic] that could be broken, hair, grass, etc, followed by my line drawings pen-and-ink of water rythems [sic] begun in the 1970s.[1]

Some of these preoccupations were also worked through in her printmaking in the 1970s. The *Untitled, 'Things of a Kind'* etching (cat.2) echoes her *Things of a Kind* paintings, in which squares or rectangles of different sizes, or in a formation, become disturbed and unbalanced. She was exploring 'the way they rely on each other and where they touch, [the] movement underneath as well as on top'.[2] As with the linocuts, this print also demonstrates her practice of reversing and doubling images, turning things around and looking at them upside down. *Untitled 'Things of a Kind'* exists in a number of states, some printed in brown ink and some printed reversed and overlapping in the centre. There is also one over which she had drawn with red and black ballpoint pen as she explored a different arrangement.

The same interest in shapes in order and disorder can be seen in a screenprint made in 1972, on which Barns-Graham worked with Jim Whitlock in the Penwith Print Workshop. *Vermilion Discs onto Turquoise Square* (cat.25) was based on her dot series of paintings and the theme of order and chaos. As she recounted in an interview, 'They were worked out and they were all calculated, the positions of these circles, and they were in fairly primitive colours, primary colours ... red and green and blue and yellow.'[3] This was screenprinting at its most basic. Barns-Graham was employing cut stencils and flat, opaque colour. Whitlock remembers that a lot of time was spent cutting circles and running proofs.[4] A large number of these proofs in a variety of colour combinations remains in the Barns-Graham archive. A small edition of 12 was published, and the print was exhibited at the Penwith spring show and at Newlyn. Several were sold at £25 each. The composition consists of a flat field of saturated turquoise with a swarm of vibrant vermilion circles and semicircles, in various sizes, pushing in from the left-hand side. Tonally the colours are very close, but are almost opposites on the colour circle, and the contrast gives the optical illusion that the colours are flashing where they meet. Technically, screenprinting was well suited to the image, but Barns-Graham found the limitations of the medium frustrating.[5]

For about 18 months in 1973–4 she produced no work at all, either print or painting, as she and Rowan James got the house and grounds at Balmungo organised. During this absence from St Ives, a portfolio of prints was proposed as a fundraising venture by the Penwith Society for the expansion of the Penwith Gallery. Barns-Graham was not invited to contribute. Her friend Bernard Leach wondered why and wrote saying:

> Dear Willi, I've never known you away for so long. We miss you, and I do hope that the slight of leaving you out of the first 12 of the Penwith Portfolio is not a contributory cause.[6]

He wrote again later in the year, saying:

> I have been making enquiries why several members were not included in the first list for the Penwith Portfolio, and find that the determination was made that financially the obvious thing to do which would yield most money, was to invite those artists most likely to contribute a litho who had an international reputation, leaving the second portfolio mainly to members of the Society in which you were included ... Their decision has resulted in sales approaching £50,000 which will be the bulk of our eventual debt on the six cottages etc. So it is clear that there was something to be said for the plan thus decided on.[7]

This portfolio was printed by the Curwen Studio, and of the twelve artists who contributed works only four had close St Ives connections.[8] In fact, Barns-Graham's printmaking activity mostly took place away from St Ives and was never a very visible aspect of her work there, and although over the years other St Ives portfolios were produced, she was never a contributor. The only portfolios in which her work appeared originated in Cambridge and in Scotland.

After a four-year interval Barns-Graham returned to printmaking in 1976, when she once again took etching classes at the Penwith Print Workshop with Roy Walker and Bob Crossley.[9] Two small prints, again not editioned or published, resulted from these classes (cats 3 and 4). In 1974 she had begun making small-scale pen-and-ink line drawings of sea movements, a subject she returned to many times over the next decades (see fig.12, for example). Composed of close parallel lines, occasionally broken or interrupted to make rhythmic patterns, these images translate naturally into etched lines. To one she added an aquatint ground as an equivalent to the washed or rubbed colour which she applied to her drawings.[10] But this was a learning exercise; these prints do not speak of a mastery of the technique, and are quite crude compared with the drawings.

But she now began to take advantage of print workshops that were being established in Scotland. Edinburgh Printmakers had been set up in 1967, and other print workshops followed over the next decade in Glasgow, Dundee and Aberdeen. In the autumn of 1977 she worked with Edinburgh Printmakers, making a screenprint with Ivan Polley, *Orange and Red on Blue* (cat.26). The process used here was rather more sophisticated than that used in St Ives in the work of 1972, though Polley recalls that the facilities were still rather basic.[11] The mesh for the screens was stretched over the frames by hand, rather than mechanically, and the screens were therefore sometimes unreliable, uneven or not taut enough. Changes in temperature and humidity in the building could also affect the paper. But they had moved on from hand-cut stencils.

Barns-Graham's arrangements with Ivan Polley were not

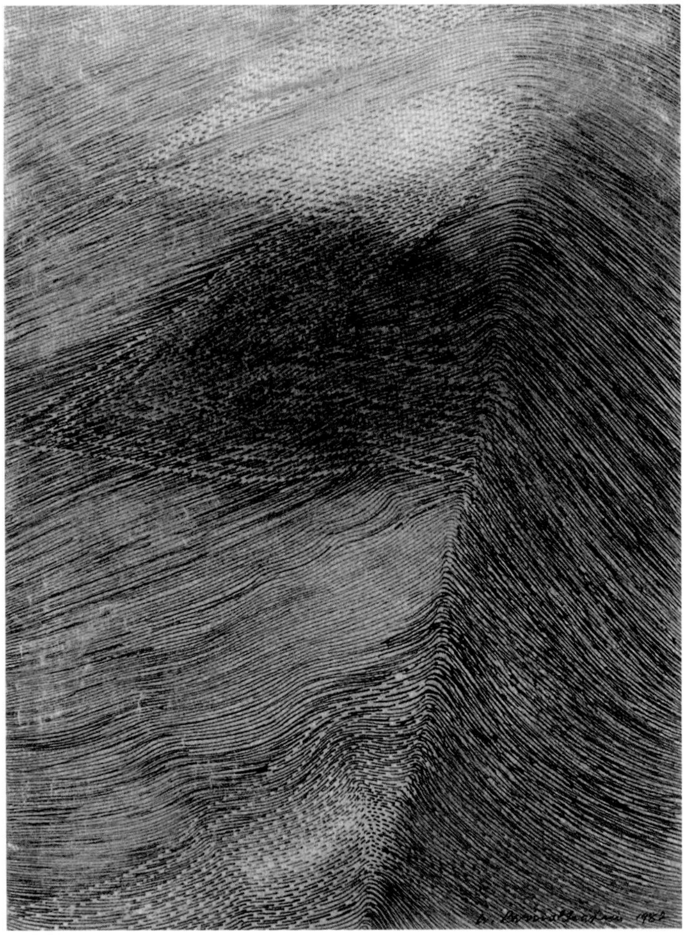

Fig. 12.
White, Red and Yellow Drifting, 1982, pen and ink drawing. This is typical of the images depicting wave and sand movements that also appear in the artist's early etchings.

a collaboration in the way that her later print projects were. She visited the print workshop and then made tracings for a silkscreen in the studio at Balmungo. This was an unfamiliar way of working for her and her diary records that she had to start again as she was using the wrong material.[12] Having handed the tracings over to Polley to be transferred to photographic stencil film, she returned a few days later to watch the printmaking, but played very little part in the technical side of the process. Polley remembers her watching from the window seat while Rowan James acted as a go-between. And Barns-Graham was not particularly excited by the process: 'He did the finishing of it. I can't say I learnt much there.'[13] The creative possibilities of screenprinting were not yet apparent to her.

Once again, the imagery of *Orange and Red on Blue* is closely related to paintings she was making at the time – a series of gouache paintings with similar colours and shapes, echoing balloons or kites, and variously entitled *Popinjoy*, *String Movement* and *Jubilee* (1977 being the year of the Queen's Silver Jubilee). The image, a geometrically constructed pattern of lines and circles and with crisply defined shapes and flat colours, demonstrates how well screenprinting was suited to hard-edged Op Art and abstraction. This print is a refined development of *Vermilion Discs onto Turquoise Square*, and shows the same interest in recurring shapes and in bright complementary colours. This was the first of Barns-Graham's prints to be made in a large edition, of 75. However, very few of the prints were numbered and signed, or framed up for exhibition. This was the only time she worked with Edinburgh Printmakers, and another five years were to pass before her next printmaking venture.[14]

At the opening of her exhibition *W. Barns-Graham: Paintings and Drawings*, in September 1982 at the Crawford Arts Centre in St Andrews, she was invited by Norrie Colston, then director of the Dundee Printmakers Workshop, to work there under a print bursary scheme, underwritten by the Scottish Arts Council.[15] She became a member of the Workshop and began attending etching classes at its Dudhope Arts Centre in St Mary's Place,

Dundee. She was taught by Andrew Hambleton and Keith Fraser, and between October 1982 and March 1983 she worked on two plates illustrating a tree root found near her family home in Stirlingshire, which she had first drawn in 1979 (cats 6 and 7; fig.13). She recalled:

> I enjoyed that very much ... They wouldn't allow me to do the designs I wanted to do – they wouldn't let me do my modern wave motives ... I got a stump of a tree which was part human, part animal and ... I was drawing on the plate from this drawing and they had one of these government young girl assistants and she came up to me, 'If you dinna mind me telling you I think you're awfully good for a beginner!'[16]

Fig. 13.
Tree Freak, pencil drawing, 1979. Barns-Graham found this tree stump on the Craigallan road near her family home at Carbeth in Stirlingshire.

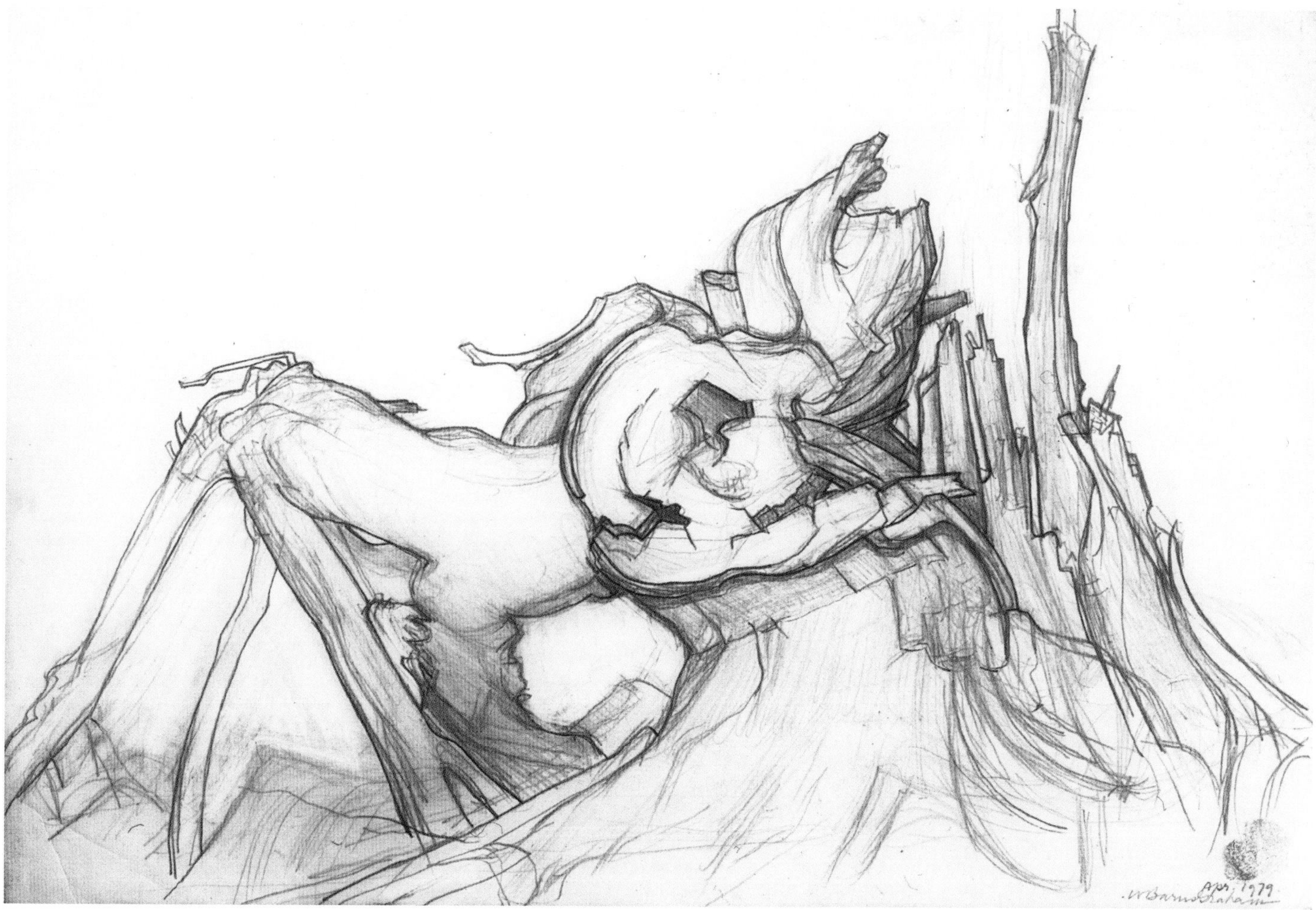

The 'modern wave motive' she mentioned was a development from her wave etchings done in St Ives in the 1970s. She made one tall, thin image of a wave that exists in two states (cats 3 and 4), and it is possible that the undated *Fish and Circles* etching (cat.8) also dates from this time.[17] Her diary for November 1982 details her progress, and a change of imagery, when she took along the drawing she had made in 1979 of the old oak tree root which, it was agreed, would make a good subject for an etching. A few days later when visiting her family at Carbeth she went out to find the tree stump to re-draw it from life:

> 2 hours work on tree stump 'Freak' along Craigallan Rd ... wet cold conditions – it has altered from 1st [drawing] on paper 1979 – this on card – but still fascinating and took some photographs. Would like to do more with the subject if get chance and I change to engrave... [18]

Over the next few days she went back several times to carry on with her drawing:

> 29 November. Manage to have 2 hours at 2nd go at tree stump 'freak' along Craigallan Rd, but very cold and wet and ice bound road.

> 6 December. Went to do a drawing direct on zinc prepared plate of the 'Freak' by Craigallan Loch – worked 1¾ hr and too cold.

Back in the warmth of the print workshop, she made two versions of the image, learning how to prepare a soft ground on the etching plate, and tracing the drawing reversed onto the plate. After taking a proof, she worked on the plate, scraping and burnishing. By Christmas she had reached the fourth state but still felt 'I've got a lot to learn in etching'.[19] To help achieve this, Rowan James gave her a book on etching and engraving as a Christmas present.[20]

These Dundee prints display a much firmer grasp of the etching medium than the wave line etchings, and they convey something of the energy and precision of her drawing style. She revisited Dundee and the 'Freak' subject in March 1983, learning sugar-lift and aquatint processes and taking more proofs up to State 13. At this point she was being taught by Keith Fraser, whose area of expertise was screenprinting. One day he showed her examples of his own work, which seems to have been something of a revelation:

> Keith showed me one of his [prints] drying out and one framed on wall of class room. Such a different approach here, free scribble over run of overlapping colours – like yellow pink to orange – his yellow-reds blues, building transparency yellow-green to the cobalt blue brush stroke. I've a lot to think about.[21]

She returned to St Ives at the end of March 1983 and the *Freak* etching was never editioned.[22] For the rest of that year she was preoccupied with collage or relief paintings, and her print-making was once more put aside. However, she did continue her relationship with Dundee Printmakers, exhibiting paintings in the galleries attached to the Workshop in 1983 and 1984.

A further collaboration took place with the Dundee Printmakers Workshop in 1988 when Barns-Graham was one of twelve artists commissioned by the Scottish Arts Council to produce works for a suite of miniature prints.[23] The prints, on the theme of Japan, were to complement an exhibition entitled *With an Eye to the East*, exploring connections between Scottish art and Japan. The exhibition was organised by the Arts Council's Travelling Gallery, and toured round Scotland throughout 1988. The prints were intended to be inexpensive, to encourage people who would not normally purchase contemporary art to acquire them.

Barns-Graham's contribution, *Peace Bird* (cat.27), of a stylised bird flying from left to right (to the East), seems strangely out of place in her *oeuvre* but it belongs to a period of experimentation in her work. In September of that year she wrote:

> There has been a change of direction ... in my larger

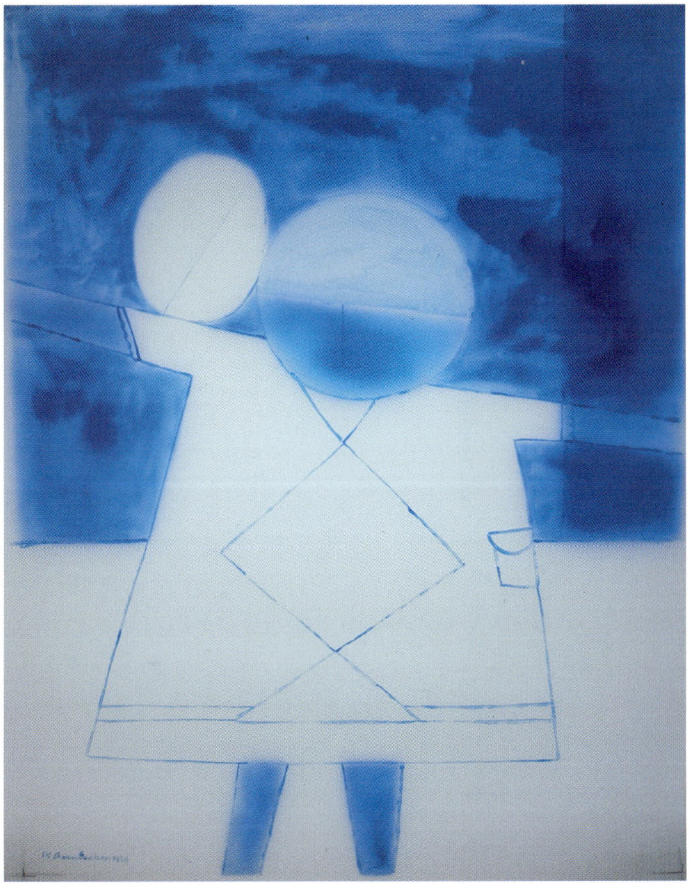

Fig. 14.
Rebecca, separations for an unrealised screenprint, 1989–1990.

gouaches and acrylics ... They are bolder, brighter, more free – simpler – 'a let go' with some daring or passion, abandoning – but not quite, the hard edge, the fastidious construction or perfectionist effort, allowing things to happen with a large brush – 'a so be it, to hell with it now attitude.' This is I believe an outcome of having been so ill January–February, the uphill struggle to regain strength.[24]

Alongside this loosening up of her abstract paintings, in the period from about 1987 to the early 1990s she also produced more non-abstract work than usual, some of it representational and some very stylid. This little print fits into this pattern. The paintings contain motifs of rocks and pebbles and mushrooms, whales and dolphins. A drawing, *Grey Whales*, was used for a Christmas card in 1988, using the same small format – a 4-inch square – as *Peace Bird*. Barns-Graham made several designs in March 1988 for the print, working with Fergus McLachlan at the print studio. She provided the hand-drawn and painted separations on tracing paper, which he photographed and applied to screens.[25] After seeing the first proofs she changed the colour scheme. The drawing of the bird, flying over undulating waves, is simplified to two curved black lines intersecting with a horizontal line and is set against bands of scarlet, yellow and orange.

This reduction of the motif to a few lines and simple shapes is seen again in an equally anomalous image of a child made at this time. Several drawings and paintings that Barns-Graham made in 1988 show a little girl playing variously with a skipping rope, a ball and a balloon. She also intended to make a print of this image, presumably at Dundee.[26] In May 1990 she was working on a series of separations begun in 1989, based on one of these paintings and entitled *Rebecca* (fig.14): 'Worked ... on Rebecca (Child with Skipping Rope 3) 1989 doing blue paint on tracing paper, the different sections for a print I'd begun months ago doing 2 parts – did 5 more sections. Not sure if using medium correctly.'[27]

The print was never made, but Barns-Graham had clearly remained intrigued by the possibilities of screenprinting that had been introduced to her at Dundee. Her real engagement with the method dates from a six-day visit to Cambridge in November of 1991. This visit was prompted by an introduction to the printmaker Kip Gresham by her friends Rose and Nelson Rands. The Rands lived in Cambridge but visited St Ives frequently, and Gresham visited them and met Barns-Graham there in the summer of 1991. He was working at the Curwen Studio, which in 1989 had relocated from London to Chilford Hall, Linton, just outside of Cambridge. The studio's director was still Stanley Jones, with whom Barns-Graham had worked over thirty years earlier in St Ives. The initial plan that came out of their first meeting was to reproduce three paintings in lithography and screenprinting. They considered several works, including the child with a ball, discussing which ones might be appropriate.[28]

The first project was *Orange and Red on Pink* (cat.28), based on a gouache painted in 1960.[29] The screenprint was made smaller than the painting, and Gresham wrote: 'We are very pleased with it and feel it has the colour balance between the Red-orange and Red-pink which is critical in the original. The change of scale seems to concentrate the image rather than reducing its power.'[30] Gresham visited St Ives again in September, bringing the finished screenprint and taking away the gouaches of *Two Circles on Purple,* to be used for a lithograph, and *Untitled 1991*, which would be screenprinted.

In October, proofs of *Untitled, April 1991* (cat.29) were sent to St Ives for comment. Gresham's letter accompanying the proofs drew attention to one aspect of the business of reworking a painted image as a print: 'There is a certain change of "touch" between gouache and printing ink; I'm afraid there is little we can do about this. We have printed this on a cotton/linnen [sic] paper called Moulin du Gué which helps the surface to move a little more.'[31] This is worth noting in reference to Barns-Graham's later work with Graal Press, where artists' paints rather than printing inks are used for screenprinting.

Proofs for the lithograph *Two Circles on Purple* (cat.23) were ready the following February, and the editioned prints were sent in March 1992. Barns-Graham wrote:

> I could hardly wait to open the litograph [sic] print when it arrived this afternoon ... I am really pleased with what you have achieved. The red circle really sings as does the emerald and the blue lines now go under both these forms, and there seems to be more contrast and life generally.[32]

These prints sold well, particularly *Untitled, April 1991*, but Barns-Graham had some worries about them as she was beginning to recognize that there was a difference between making prints as original works of art and as reproductions of her paintings. In January 1992, after her visit to Curwen Chilford, she wrote to Stanley Jones that she felt 'guilty having used your time in a reproduction of one of my gouaches when I realise I could have used the time in learning from you something about lithography'.[33] Later in the year she wrote to one of the printmakers there, saying, 'I met with a lot of controversy over "Reproductions" and I am so inexperienced and ignorant of the whole thing, I'm beginning to realise the different approaches'.[34]

This question of the originality of a print has been a perennial problem for artists, printmakers and collectors. In his 1962 book *About Prints*, S.W. Hayter tried to categorise degrees of originality. At the highest level the artist physically makes the image on the printing matrix, undertaking the inking and printing personally. A second level might be where the artist has physically made the marks on the printing plate or lithographic stone but a technician has made the prints. At a third level, the artist makes the image which is transferred by photomechanical means; having made a mark on a clear plastic sheet, that mark is transferred onto the screen, stone or plate, which is coated in a light-sensitive emulsion. At a further distance from the hand of the artist is the reproduction of a work of art originally made in another medium, such as Barns-Graham's three prints made at Curwen Chilford. These are made by photographically scanning the image and making colour separations, which are then transferred in the same way as in the third level. It is debatable as to whether these prints deserve the somewhat pejorative epithet of reproductions. To an extent, they are altered by the change in medium and can be seen rather as reinterpretations. The resulting lithograph or screenprint requires the same technical skills as more 'original' prints and cannot be compared to mass-produced reproductions made by commercial half-tone processes. Certainly, Barns-Graham's works presented challenges to the printers at Curwen, and required extra separations to get them just right.

The ongoing discussion about the hand of the artist in the process of printmaking was something that concerned Barns-Graham. Considering this issue in 1993 with Sheila Oliner, she stressed her interest in learning more about making her own prints:

> I'm a beginner and ... I'm very keen to do more printing and I'm very keen to do original prints not reproductions. There's been a lot of arguments about this and although my experimental ones were original ones, the reproduction ones ... I worked on ... but I think there is another stage which I want to look into of working direct on stones or plates or screens and there's a lot I want to learn, I don't understand the colour etching, these mixed mediums, I'd like to know more about it.[35]

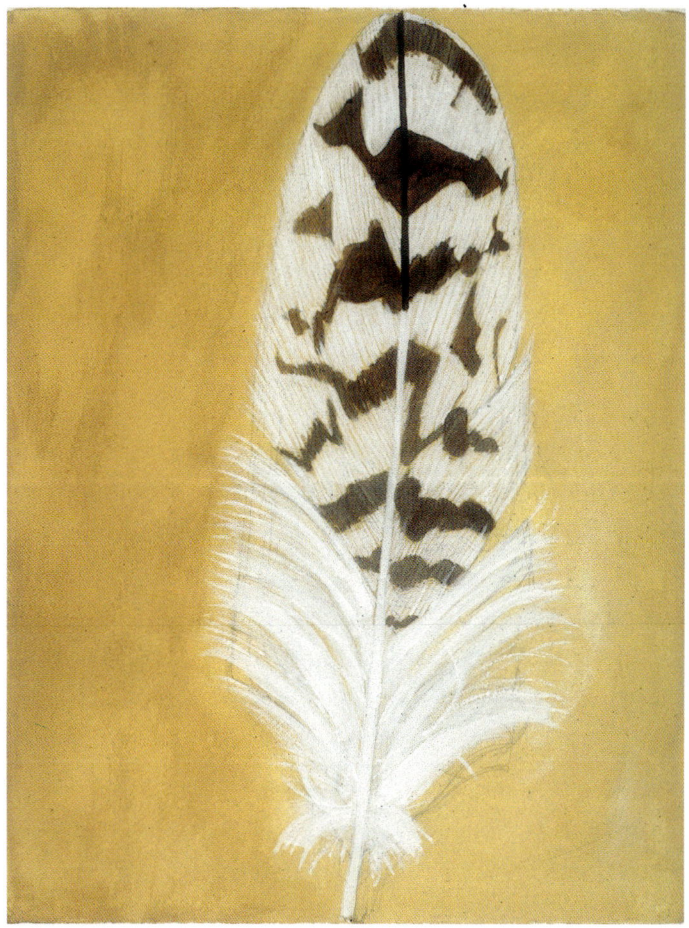

Fig. 15.
Gull Feather, gouache, 1991.

These experimental prints were made during the six-day visit to Cambridge in 1991. Prior to the visit Kip Gresham had left some materials, including tusches and translucent plastic sheets, for Barns-Graham to experiment with to make images directly for lithography and screenprinting. She began with a drawing of a feather (fig.15) from an immature seagull, which she found on her doorstep. The feather contained 'some marvellous brown semi-human shapes on it – and links to each form like a thread! Amazing'.[36] She first painted it in gouache on paper, and followed this with versions using the lithographic inks and crayons on separation sheets. Later on at Curwen some trial proofs were taken of *Gull Feather* (cat.10) in one or two colours, but this was never editioned.

During October she continued working with the printing

materials, making two further designs, one of which she called *Sacrifice* in her diary.[37] One design incorporated the head of a goat, possibly based on a sketch from 1989 of the three goats that were kept at Balmungo.[38] These designs were sent to Cambridge and were printed up. These works were not only experimental in technique but also in imagery. The strangeness of the imagery can partly be explained by a mistake in the printing, when the separations for the two designs were intermingled and printed as one (see cat.11). A small number of lithographs were pulled at Curwen by printmaker Serena Castle with a variety of different colours and, on arrival at the studio in November, Barns-Graham noted that they 'showed me the lithograph studies done with notes I'd sent up but Serena had put one on another and it totally confused me – and not inspiring design anyway but interesting possibilities'.[39] She later wrote to Serena, 'What a pity you never seemed to have got the letter I sent along with these designs ... 1 and 2, though unfortunately a bit similar, were different and separate'.[40] Never one to waste work, Barns-Graham used some of these proofs as the basis for mixed-media works, painting over with crayon and gouache, and calling them *Goat Series*. Even taking this mistake into account, though, these designs are quite unlike anything else she produced and, like the little girl with a ball, they represent an experimental path not taken.

She must have been in an experimental frame of mind during this period. In October 1991 she took a six-day visit to Barcelona, to visit the Tàpies and Miró Foundations and the Picasso Museum. Her diary records the Tàpies museum as being 'all marble effect in cement, pale ochre colours – very harmonious with his work. Great deal of matt black and white impasto – and sometimes hanging unframed on loose fabric – used corrugated brown paper – I'm very impressed and stimulated'.[41] She returned to the museum and bought a catalogue of Antoni Tàpies lithographs: 'I ... find his work strong, simple (though not really) sort of protests – very Catalan – very painterly and the colours are sombre.'[42] She returned to Cornwall 're-fuelled and my mind widened'.[43] This was just a few weeks before her trip to Cambridge in November. Passing through London en route to Cambridge, she went to see a Tàpies exhibition of sculpture at the Waddington Gallery in London, and bought a book on his work in Cambridge the next day.

It is tempting to see the influence of Tàpies and of her experiences in Barcelona in the first print Barns-Graham made at Curwen Chilford (cat.30). One day in Barcelona she had seen

> a yellowish wall with great big red brushstrokes on it and squiggles and writing in grey ... and for a mile or two walls, parts of buildings had this red paint – and there is a work by Tàpies I've seen in a catalogue of a yellow wall with white graffiti and 5 broad perpendicular red brush strokes. Catalan protests.[44]

The original plan for the six days at Curwen had been to work on lithographs with Stanley Jones and Serena Castle, and they did work on *Untitled, April 1991*, but due to changed circumstances they decided she should work with printmakers Kip Gresham and Andrea Bowden making experimental screenprints. She looked through a box full of other artists' prints to explore the range of possibilities. She was fascinated by colour separations and the way images were assembled, and she needed to understand the process and be part of it to see the possibilities for her own work.

The excitement she experienced during this visit is palpable in her diary entries of the period. They detail both the creative and the technical progress she made (cats 30–6):

> 28 November. 1st proper day and it was decided to work with Kip on my 1st print I was to call the 'November Series' 1, 2, 3, 4, 5, 6!! etc. I was highly nervous and asked to make marks on [a] type of tracing paper. To unwind I asked if I could make 'a splash' with black gouache ... [which was] done on the ground; the splash marked the floor over the paper a good 36"! Which I did – then a large brush mark L.H. side. We printed this on cream coloured paper with black splash and the big brush mark, red, a yellow form R.H.S. This was No 1 and I thought possibly a

bit aggressive? too close to it to acess [sic]. We made a similar one running over a purple stain ... which turned the yellow into a brownish mustard and lowered the red and black, a lovely harmonious purple. We later cut the first one by removing the yellow shape and letting the final spots and splash [illegible] up into corner. All very exciting and Andrea mixing the colours and I kept seeing forms in the different processes like washing down the image after photography, seeing the blue coming off and exposing the brush work – and my adrenalin started pulsing – so began No 2.

29 November. We began No 3 – another black splash which became ... a cross form something like a St. Andrews Cross; this was realised much later. Again on cream paper with a texture ground of yellow and then grey onto yellow ... and a lilac blue band on left hand side top to base and a hook U form under it, top LHS to the side going out and not filled in, done with finger. Just happened. I didn't know what to think of this one. Bold, courageous, but was it too big for the sheet? was it nonsense? But I was seeing things, shadows, shapes, everywhere a heightened state of awareness and was moved to excitement. Kip wonderful at helping to pull out ideas. So enjoyed today. ... I was very tired and happy and learning new processes ... Such a good atmosphere – John Allcock in the office bringing us cups of tea or coffee – eating our sandwiches at the lunch hour together.

The time at the studio was broken by a weekend during which Barns-Graham worked on further ideas.

1 December. Spent the morning working on ideas for the next print in sketch book ... I didn't want to flounder or waste time but in actual fact I had to tame my ideas there! Anyway I worked on a few including the 'Green Field to Margaret series' – using colour ... I am thinking nearly all the time about work in the print shop – shapes, ideas, colours, and I go upstairs to rest and think and think and I find it difficult to sleep! I wish I'd done this years ago, on the other hand I'm at a stage in life and work that I can be adventurous and bold!!!

2 December. We began No 4 print, a great struggle after playing around with bits of paper and chalk and thinking – It was the 'Green Field to Margaret Series' started with a brilliant phlorescent [sic] yellow ground. Then a green, varying tones from base to lighter. Colours mixed by Andrea and then I put the large black brush shape around 3 sides starting from R.H.S. across and round to L.H.S. RHS open, and white 1" strip at base. This is a smaller print. But it wasn't working and none of us liked it – and I felt despair, yet reminded myself I was not here to make pictures but to learn ... when a deep blue was run over it, and to all our joy the white strip unexpectedly became a surprising lilac which made it, the green darkened at base, and the textured yellow (same textured ground as No 3) was showing a curious movement and the yellow spread over the edge, not approved of by Kip or Andrea but delighted me, approved of by Stanley ... Printed in 6 colours (incl. green) on Fabriano Tiepolo paper.[45]

3 December. We began No 5 print and here the fun became intense! I was supposed to do a small one, when Kip produced a beautiful large sheet, French paper specially made for them. We made a rich bracken-orange-tan shape at R.H.S. by throwing water on a blocked screen, got a movement, design ½ way or less across in blobs by circular movement with grey over, it became a greyish brown.
2 pieces of thin paper laid down by Kip gave me the idea to retain them and painted a double ∩ shape [which was] really [a] prepared trial 2 size brushes for 'Green Field,' and then a wettish, thin, not quite white alongside and because [of] the RHS design abandonned [sic] the idea of a third in grey. The black was good on the orange particularly LHS and the white on the tissue sheets, effective and we looked

at one another in surprise and I think delight – and me not really knowing how to access [sic] this but knowing the scale, the colours, the textures were good and pleasing ... I felt a shared dance of team work and joy.

4 December. So began No 6. I've never had a week like this... I felt by now though high, calm and no 6 is a grey one, using floor rubbing of Kip's onto the same large paper only this time a vertical. A deeper grey tone over it and I feel alarmed as to whether I could handle this pronounced all over pattern of wood – rubbings from a box I think. Suddenly I was aware of a shadow shape from the silkscreen press handles on floor and thought beautiful, and we used it enlarged by using sponge on blocked red skin, a sort of foot shape and then we used a circle, the bin lid – firstly drawing around in deep red chalk – not right and then decided we'd paint the lid under a press – we'd been on the floor drawing the shadow and now I saw Kip painting the other bin lid this more orange red – and he pressed and turned it – we were on the floor again and I was elated, yet wanted to laugh, feeling we were like children. John saw it, [and] Stanley, Serena, that it was 'peaceful' 'spacious' 'calm' – the struggle of it all too. Printed in 4 colours (incl. grey) on Arches Moulin du Gue paper 36" x 48", edition of 20.

5 December. I am now writing these notes after the event and I have had time to reflect and consider what was happening in a way I could not at the time. For instance to run after shadows and bin lids is not something I could have done had Kip not been as he was, i.e. excellent in the co-operation and enjoyment of work ideas with the artists and being with it and in it. I could never have expressed, exposed, myself in such freedom. This is written a day after arriving in Scotland and regretful at the 'cut offness' in a flow of ideas ... We began No. 7, a white circle on blue with blue panel shadow taken from the purple one No. 2 ... but no – we stuck – now v. tired and it is possible failure, something set ourselves and difficulty so we left it.[46]

6 December. Last day ... It dawned on me what a week it had been, so 'very special' and that, tired as I was, sad it was completed, but as Kip said when we were saying our goodbyes 'it is a beginning'.

And so it was.

8 December. Can't come down to earth. Very affected by the week or 6 days of work at Cambridge on 6 silk screen ideas ... I've never really experienced a working week 'so special'. I find myself thinking of opera singers coming from different areas and taking part together, and see the pride of each others [sic] achievements [and] in held moments of that nowness hit something supreme. I think of Torvil and Dean.[47] The combined effort – the recognition of something a happening, something very special.

A few years later in an interview with Sheila Oliner she reflected on the whole experience:

I was absolutely overwhelmed with excitement at Curwen because of all the new technologies and so on and I probably rushed at it too much, making six prints. I was affected by my gouaches that looked [as if they] would make good silkscreens, but then when I started doing experimental prints I realised there was such a lot to learn and I went to the print exhibition in London at the Royal Academy, I think it was. I made notes about various textures, I asked Kip Gresham to come with me which he did and ... I realised it was such an exciting medium I wished I'd gone into this years ago.[48]

Barns-Graham returned briefly to Curwen Chilford in February 1992, to check the proofs of *Two Circles on Purple* (cat.23), but though there were discussions about a further visit to make prints, and Barns-Graham made some designs and separations during the winter of 1992–3, these eventually came to nothing.

Although their titles group these prints together as a series, they are very different from each other in appearance, even when they share a number of elements. *November II* is based on the two marks of *November I*, but is transformed by the purple which has been run over the top of the marks. The textured grounds of *November III (St Andrews)* and *November IV* were made from the same rubbing from the concrete studio floor, and this use of *frottage* can also be seen in *November VI*, which incorporates a rubbing of planks from a wooden floor. *November VI* also has the imprint of a dustbin lid to make the circular form.

While Barns-Graham found this experimentation liberating, it also helped her recognise what she did and did not want to achieve in printmaking. Over the next few months she looked at other artists' prints at exhibitions and museums: the Print Fair at the Royal Academy, a Tàpies exhibition at the Redfern Gallery, Andy Warhol and Jasper Johns at the Fitzwilliam Museum in Cambridge, Brice Marden at the Tate Gallery and Tàpies again at the Royal Cornwall Museum. She later commented on Tàpies's prints:

> I thought it was getting into another dimension, it was almost sculptural ... on the edge of other mediums. If I was doing silkscreen I would be concerned with colour – areas of colour and light and excitement ... I'm not sure that I'm so keen on getting a thick impasto on it and a mixture of etching on it ... Tàpies has done such inspiring work that they are almost paintings. Again it's almost on the edge of something else.[49]

In relation to her own prints, she knew that she wanted to make her own marks and not to make any further use of rubbings or found objects such as the dustbin lid.[50] She also, on cooler reflection, decided that she did not want the editioned prints released because of their experimental nature.[51] A few years later she wrote to Kip Gresham about *November VI*:

> You have PPs [printer's proofs] of the experimental works November VI (Floor Boards) grey. We have withdrawn this work from the series, and would not want it exhibited or sold ... As this was an experimental project we feel that any exposure of this work must be acceptable to us. To date we have only released 'November IV' and November V for exhibition and sale.[52]

However, carrying on the practice begun with the *Goat Series* (and which continued throughout her career) she made use of a number of the prints, in particular *November I, II* and *III*, as the basis for mixed-media works in gouache and acrylics. These re-appear with titles such as *Happening* and *Black Sun* (figs 16 and 17).

In 1994, Kip Gresham moved to his own studio at Duxford near Cambridge, and in October that year he visited Barns-Graham in St Ives to discuss further collaboration. Once again they decided to rework an existing painting rather than make a work conceived from the start as a print. A gouache from 1991 was chosen, 'the small "Untitled Acrylic 1991" ... colours of the work being Venetian Red, Ochre, Black and White over the black and a pinkish stripe down left hand side. Quite a small work'.[53] This became *Venetian Red* (cat.37). The printing required some experiments with paper. The choice of paper makes a difference to the final print and depends on the nature of the image, the sort of surface required and the technical demands of the print. When a print is made up of many layers the registration (getting one layer exactly on top of the previous one) is critical, and the paper has to be strong enough not to warp or stretch as the ink dries. The absorbency of paper is controlled by how it has been sized (or treated) during manufacture, with starch, gelatin or a synthetic finish.

Part of the experimentation with the *November Series* involved using a variety of papers of different weights and with different finishes (see cats 30–36). Barns-Graham's later screenprints made with Graal Press were printed with water-based materials. This necessitates the use of a very heavy, stable and quite hard paper, which will retain its original

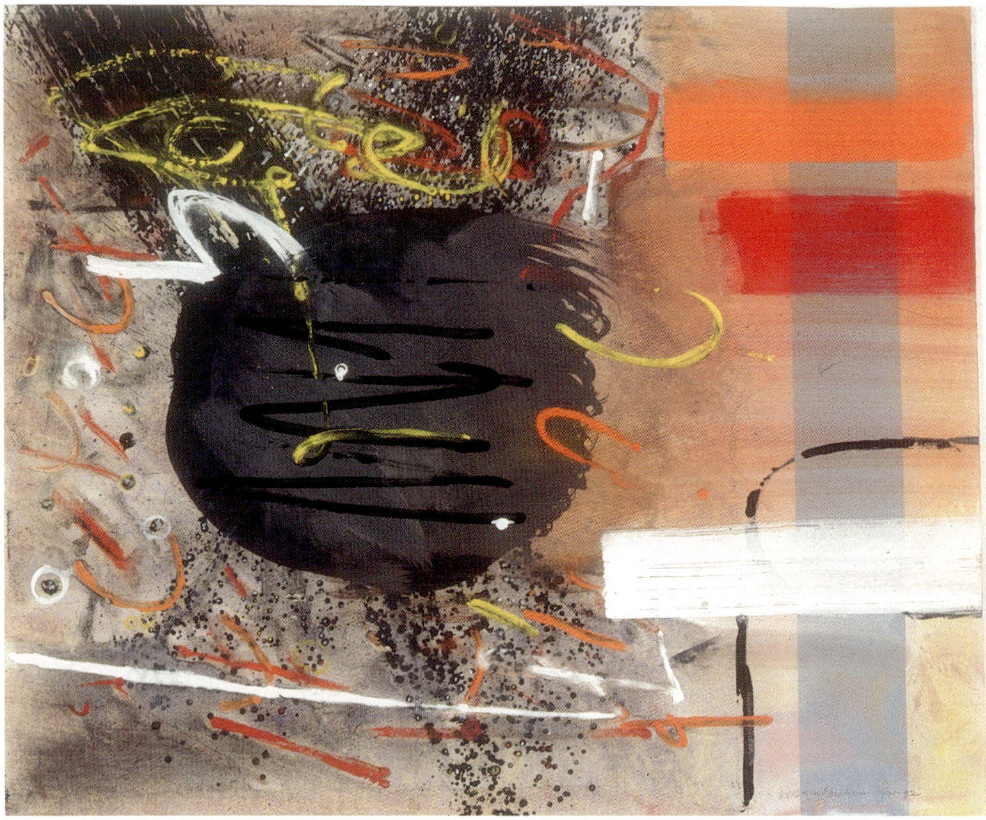

Fig. 16.

Happening, screenprint and acrylic mixed media, 1991. Barns-Graham used prints from the *November Series* as the basis for this image and fig.17.

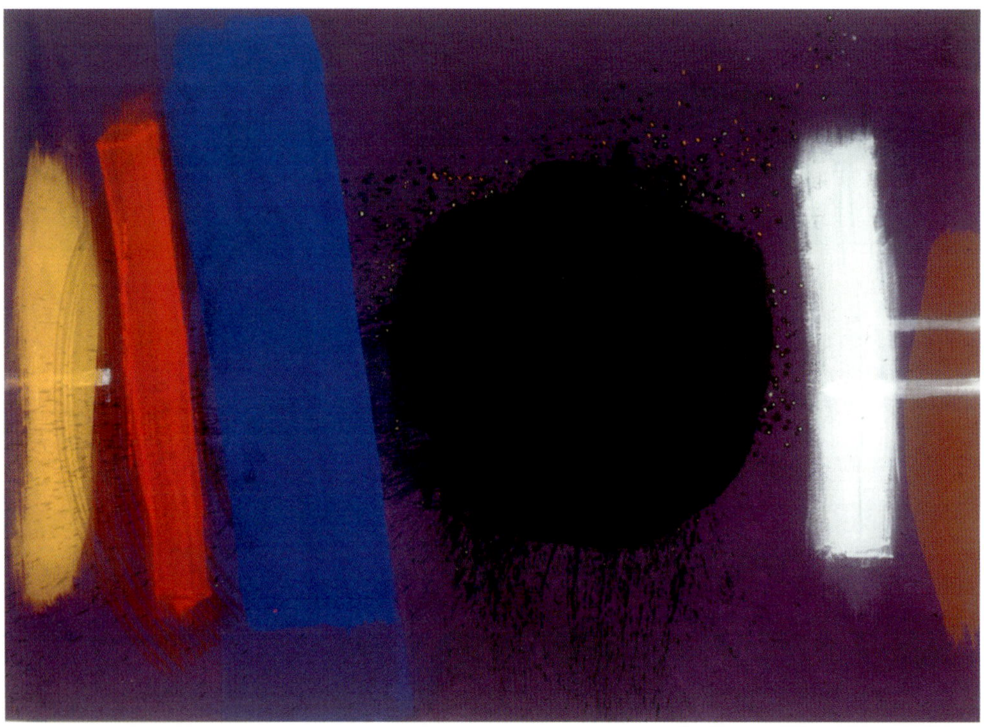

Fig. 17.

Black Sun, screenprint and acrylic mixed media, 1991–5.

dimensions throughout a process involving up to fifteen applications of paint.[54]

For *Venetian Red,* they finally opted for Moulin du Gué paper after some experimentation. This paper is unsized and therefore quite absorbent, and has a soft, pulpy texture. As Kip Gresham explains, 'The initial layers absorb into the paper and the subsequent ones begin to seal the paper and then stack up so a colour may be printed four or five times in order to get it to sit off the surface'.[55] Gresham pointed out to Barns-Graham that 'the surface adds interest to the flatter areas of the image while the linen content gives clean soft colour'.[56]

The project demonstrated some of the difficulties of this long-distance collaboration. Each proof had to be sent to Barns-Graham and then discussed over the phone or by letter, and changes had to be described in detail. For example, she wrote in January 1995:

> At least 2 of the separations had been missed ... when you examine the proof you will note that some of the reds (small marks) are missing, these are very essential notes of colour giving radiance ... The first brush stroke on the left needs a deeper tone, the lemon also lacks vitality, the horizontal brush stroke reading from the left has a grey tone meeting the red brush stroke ... more red to show of [sic] the black circle passing from under the white... [57]

To expand her knowledge and achieve a more conducive working relationship, she needed to work directly with people who had the necessary expertise, but for a proper partnership she needed people closer to home. In the autumn of 1996 she collaborated with Rachael Kantaris at Porthmeor Printmakers. This organisation was set up in 1992 in the refurbished Penwith Print Workshop studio, offering courses, the use of equipment and printing services.[58]

Over a period of several weeks Barns-Graham and Kantaris worked together on three prints. The first was *Eight Lines I* (cat.16). In the space of twenty years, Barns-Graham had made many versions of this image as drawings, and had one in black chalk hanging in her home: 'It's eight lines ... of sand dune or wave movements, very simple, starting with a straight line and then building up into waves crisscrossing, just in line.'[59] She continued to produce the image in a variety of media, as thick white gouache lines on blue background (fig.18), in terracotta chalk and in pen and ink. It proved to be a very popular image; as she said in an interview: '... many people said to me, "Is this an etching?" and I said, no, it was a line drawing, pen-and-ink and I thought [it was] a pity I hadn't done [it] as an etching [because] so often people wanted the one I'd sold.'[60]

The pen-and-ink version is the most simplified of these drawings, and made an ideal image for transition into an etched line. Once more the diaries chronicle the progress of the print:

> 24 September. Using copper plate and hard ground as against [Rachael Kantaris's] suggestion of soft ground (she thought I wanted the chalk effect like my [drawing] but I wanted the crisp hard [traditional] etching line for contrast to my drawing. I enjoyed the 3 hours.
>
> 25 September. 2nd day at print shop. Took a rough pull of the 8 line etching – a bit thin in places. Began work on 2 large steel plates for my colour etching from one of my acrylic works on paper – not copying but the same idea. My plate on the large size for their equipment.
>
> 27 September. Stop-out again on 8 lines and [leave] to dry. Nitric acid dip plate 2 and 3. Very interesting and exciting and unpredictable.
>
> 1 October. We worked again on 8 lines etching on copper, burnishing, re-putting into acid and [made] a rough print. Also worked on one of the steel plates (3) for colour etching – putting the sugar coating into acid and cleaning off the stop-out etc getting more depth of shape. An interesting morning.

This colour etching was to be *Scorpio I* (cat.17). At this time,

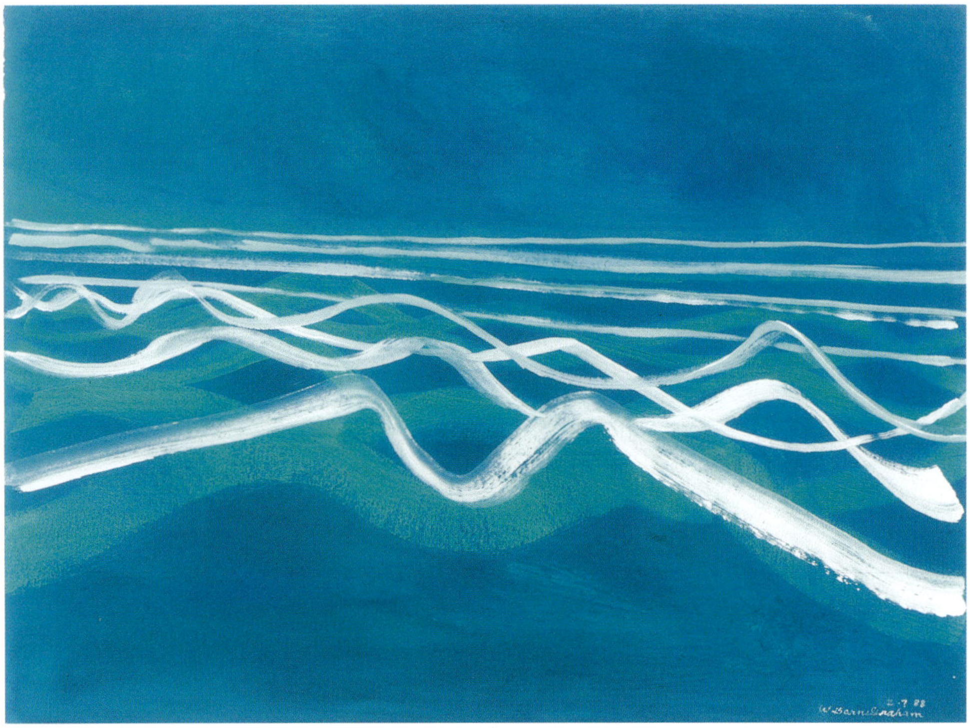

Fig. 18.

Eight Lines (White on Blue), acrylic, 1988. This is one of many variations on this theme that Barns-Graham returned to repeatedly. These works always sold quickly, and the popularity of the image was one of the reasons she used the motif for an etching.

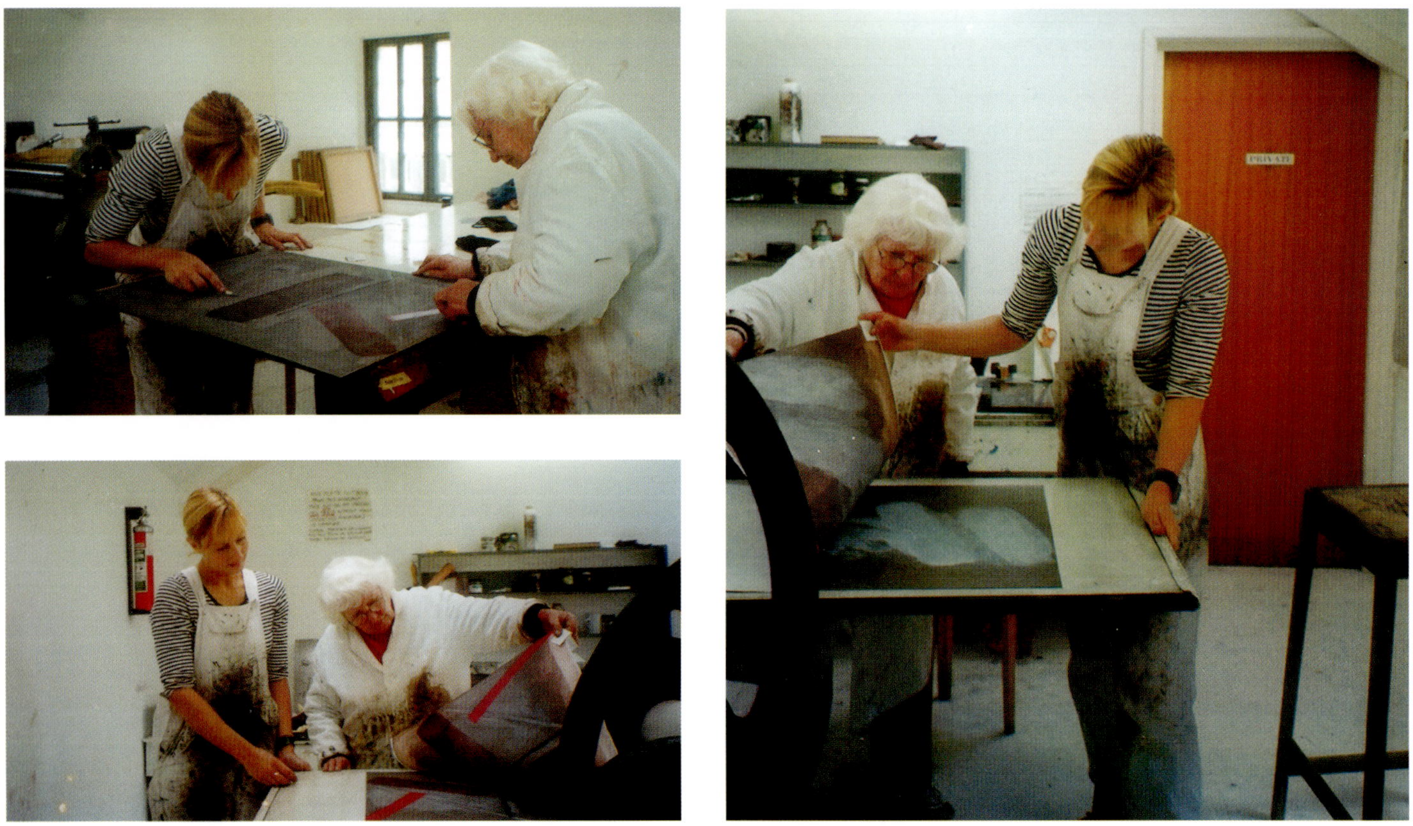

Fig. 19.

Wilhelmina Barns-Graham and Rachael Kantaris working together on *Scorpio I* at Porthmeor Printmakers, St Ives, 1996.

Barns-Graham was working on the second of her *Scorpio Series* of paintings. The artist described these paintings, begun in 1995, as being

> entirely abstract. An orchestration of brush strokes, mainly upright – a vibration of colour, like a song. The brush strokes vary in size and width, in texture and weight. Some over, or under lapping or both. The weight and size of the brush strokes is important, whether it is heavy, light, thick or liquid; or painted deliberately calm; swift or assertive, and those taking a deliberate risk. Sometimes, another form is introduced, a circle, curve or dots. The series may be a development from my theme of many years 'Things of a Kind', and frequently they take weeks to complete.[61]

She needed a print technique that would replicate her brush marks in all their variety, and was also interested in learning about colour etching. *Scorpio I* was made on three steel plates and was printed in five colours. *Scorpio II* (cat.18) also used sugar-lift, from two copper plates using ten colours .

In the technique of sugar-lift etching, the image is painted onto the plate with a sugar solution. This is then covered in stop-out and plunged into a bath of boiling water. The sugared areas dissolve and lift, exposing the brush marks, which can then be etched in acid. In *Scorpio I*, the burgundy brush mark was textured with aquatint shaken on by hand before the etching process.[62] To make these many-coloured prints from two or three plates, several colours have to be applied on one plate by careful inking.

Barns-Graham's diary entries again record the process and her emotions:

> 2 October. My 6th ½ day at the print room. This time working all 3 steel plates for colour etching – burnishing, stopping out ... [for] the brown print, the deeper background and stripes, white, black/brown, wine and red. Very interesting but very tiring.

> 3 October. Interesting working on smaller plate, transferring black forms on to paper and on to 2nd plate to see where forms go ... it's a different way of working ... [put] the 3rd plate (steel) in acid and the other, copper, in ferric chloride – learning new things but pain and tiredness hit me [and] I had to stop at 1.30 ... Rachael has done a lot of work now printing 4–5 of the Eight Lines which are delicate and some movement if a bit less variation than I intended. Also checked on the Black/White on chocolate ground with red in it.

> 18 October. Work ... was [at an] exciting stage as colour pulling on no. 3 ... I see now my 9 days is [an] introduction. One needs weeks or years [of] experience and then continually 'finding out'!

> 6 November. Rachael arrived with ... 8 lines and 3 of the other two colour etchings and signed PP copies ... They really are quite exciting for first efforts ... she thought them remarkable for 6 weeks work.

These three prints were produced in small editions of only 25. *Eight Lines* proved to be so popular that when Barns-Graham began to work with Graal Press she decided to make a new print of this image with Robert Adam (*Eight Lines II*, cat.20) in an edition of 75. This was followed by *Six Lines* (cat.21).

The year 1998 was a very busy one in terms of printmaking, as Barns-Graham noted in her diary at the end of the year, listing new prints and new collaborations:

> Summary of the Year
> I have worked hard – produced 2 new silk screens [sic] prints [at] Dundee with Alastair [sic for Alasdair] Currie ... 'Summer' [and] ... the other, 'Spring' based on walking up the rock garden path [at] Balmungo ... but in the Autumn, working once a week with Carol Roberts [sic for Robertson] [I] learnt much more about grounds and textures and sent before that designs for small colour etchings so all that

> was new! to Hugh Stoneman ... so its been a reasonably 'hard work, stick at it, go slow' a fairly productive year, with joys and some sadness of deaths, and uneasy awareness maybe my time left is short?[63]

She also began work on another print with Kip Gresham for a portfolio and spent some time looking into the technique of making carborundum prints. In addition, she was getting work ready for an exhibition in Brussels for the following year which, for the first time, would include a large number of her prints.

Early in 1998 Barns-Graham was in Scotland, returning to Dundee Printmakers to produce some screenprints. She worked with artist Alasdair Currie for three days a week, over two months, and made two works, *Spring* and *Summer* (cats 38 and 39). Not having made a screenprint herself since 1991, she first had to remember the techniques, working on a small design and then moving onto something larger to 'let loose and be less formal (but I hate too much complication for silk screen) but I'll try and have a go ... we spent some time discussing medium, different to Cambridge 1991, now water-based medium, cleaner, safer, no awful stinks and much easier to clean up'.[64] The idea for the first print came from a painting she had recently done in St Ives 'of lemon yellow, yellow, orange – blue – red stripes in various widths of one each and worked on the new film paper for separations to take with me ... tomorrow'. Unfortunately she had made the separations in blue, the one colour that does not block ultraviolet light, and so she 'had to go over with the brown sticky stuff, solidly for the shapes that are to be solid pure colour'.[65]

The diary entries for the following days record the printing of the grounds, a yellow ochre and white mixed for transparency and lightness; the next layer was 'a sort of sunshine yellow, tint of red and white lemon and cad[mium]'. Getting the colours as she wanted them was a challenge, and they had to make white grounds to go under the coloured bars. They also had to take the proofs first to the window and then out of doors to check the colours in daylight, the orange mark in particular giving trouble. The red shape was straightforward, 'a good positive vermilion slightly yellow in it so not too dark', but the ultramarine shape was a struggle, requiring three coats to cover the colour of the red where it crossed over. After three weeks she started on the second print, *Spring*, making the separations at home. The swinging loose grey/black brush stroke gave her particular trouble, and she tried eight versions at home and several more in the print studio before she was happy with it. She already had the colour scheme in mind, but a walk round the garden gave her the first idea for a title:

> Went up garden with R. feeding the hens. The daffodils, white now [as] well as yellow, are becoming fields of yellow, a few cillas [sic] in off-side corners and buds and birds are active. I realise going up rock garden path, looking up the greyish under branches crossed with bigger black, on my right was the path of snowflakes, on my left the yellow of the daffodils and but for the ground I am describing my 2nd acrylic for silkscreen so I think I will call it the one word 'Balmungo'![66]

The print had two grounds, one a light lemon yellow followed by a second, slightly warmer and darker. Both the curved grey-black brush mark and the solid black line had a little lemon yellow added, which helped to harmonise the colours.

One important lesson for the future that Barns-Graham learned from this experience was that once she and the printmaker had reached a certain level of trust and understanding, she could let go; it was unnecessary for her to be there constantly, checking each print as it emerged from under the screen. This was just as well, as she returned to St Ives before the editioning was complete. They were made in small editions of 20 for *Summer* and 30 for *Spring*. Both prints were exhibited in Cornwall, *Spring* at the Newlyn Society of Artists summer exhibition and *Summer* at the Penwith Society autumn exhibition.

It is clear that by now screenprinting was the print technique best suited to her working methods. In many ways it mirrored her painting practice, working on several images at once. However, for the time being her interest in other print techniques continued. In May she visited Sheila Oliner's studio in St Ives to look at carborundum techniques.[67] Later in the summer she made contact with Hugh Stoneman. Stoneman was an etching specialist who had set up and run the Print Centre in Covent Garden, and then Islington, in London. Terry Frost had worked with him on some of his most ambitious printmaking projects. In 1995 he relocated his print workshop from London to Madron near Penzance in Cornwall, as Stoneman Graphics.

Barns-Graham's contact with him was almost certainly prompted by a visit in the summer of 1998 from the McGearys, father and daughter, who ran the McGeary Gallery in Brussels and who wanted to put on an exhibition of Barns-Graham's work the following spring. She showed them some work including prints, which they particularly liked. Her diary notes that 'they need about 25 works. I need to make 8 new small prints'.[68] The next day she contacted Stoneman to discuss their working together. He explained that he specialised in woodcuts and etchings, not screenprints, but they made arrangements to meet.[69]

In September Stoneman visited her to look at her work and then she visited his studio, taking some separations she had made based on one of her existing paintings, though she was aware that what she knew about was screenprinting. At his studio he talked to her about colour etching and showed her various films they used with different mediums and textures. She did not begin working on ideas for etchings until late October in Scotland, working directly on the film. She was worried that she was working too much with screenprinting in mind, recording her concerns over several days:

> Worked on film paper for idea for etching ... I felt I was loosening up a bit.
> I am not quite sure if working too much as silk screen. Took me all day to find satisfactory design with what I have done but needs translating into black ... Once I understand the method apart from silk screen I am away!
> I think I am getting into the mind of etching as against silkscreen but I suspect my ideas are more suitable for silkscreen and I think more that way but I must plod on... [70]

Notes she wrote for a phone call to Stoneman to check that she was working correctly describe how she built up each image:

> I made sheets of colour for grounds ... The whole design in black I put over it. I coloured shapes or panels placing under the black design ... I landed myself with several problems. Just want confirmation that my procedure is correct.
> - Make a separation for each colour but painted in black starting with ground not to [sic] dense
> - All one design but separated into each colour separation Using the darkest colours as final separation.[71]

By November she had sets of separations for five images, which she sent to Stoneman with colour charts. They decided to do one print to start with, *Eclipse* (cat.19). She had already done some paintings of this subject, anticipating the total eclipse of the sun that was due to occur the following year. (Cornwall was to be one of the best places to witness the eclipse; her diary for 26 September 1998 records the purchase of a guide to the eclipse, though in the event she was in Scotland when it occurred.) The image consists of three circles and four bars floating in a mysterious and slightly ominous blue space. The arrangement of the four bars draws the eye across the space in the same way that the dark semicircle of the moon entering from the right would move across and cover the sun, already veiled in blue shadow.

In June 1999 she received a quote from Stoneman for making a further etching, but nothing came of this. But early 1999 saw her also working again with Kip Gresham. In late 1998 he had contacted her to invite her to contribute a print for the *King's College Portfolio*, which was commissioned to raise funds for an Arts Centre at King's College, Cambridge. There was to be an edition of 100, and each artist would receive ten copies of their own print and one copy of the complete portfolio. The portfolio includes works by Peter Blake, Sandra

Blow, Stephen Buckley, Alan Davie, Jane Dickson, Anthony Frost, Antony Gormley, Anthony Green and Patrick Procktor.

Barns-Graham worked on designs for this print in December 1998 and by January 1999 *Blue Light, Summer* (cat.40) was at the proof stage.[72] The separations were made so that each colour was printed on the white of the paper rather than building up in layers over the coloured ground and the lower marks. Gresham told her: 'We have allowed most of the colours to print onto white paper which has added vibrancy to the orange and permitted the lemon yellow to fire strongly.'[73] This method keeps each colour and mark discrete, and meant that the lower marks did not interfere with the surface colour or finish. However, Barns-Graham really preferred to have all the marks printed in full, as they would be in a painting, so that the layering and interweaving of lines and bars and circles was real as well as apparent.

A second proof came in three versions, with two choices of blue ground. Gresham wrote:

> We have also made a second version with the ground colour printed twice on the right hand side, to repeat the divisions between the ochre/blue of the first proof. We did this for two reasons; firstly it allows you to see what happens when the ground colour is stronger and, secondly it allows you to compare a flat area with the critical (but invisible) crossover under the red/white intersection.[74]

A third version was included, with a yellow ground. This was editioned separately from the portfolio as *Summer (Yellow)* (cat.41).

Barns-Graham's projects with Stoneman and Gresham demonstrate the difficulties of this kind of long-distance working. She was never quite sure if she was using the correct techniques. Stoneman wanted separations painted in black pigment, whereas Gresham would take colour separations and make photographic negatives from these. Either way, she could not be closely involved in the process and proofs could not be checked with both printmaker and artist looking at the same work together. However, December 1998 saw the commencement of a printmaking partnership with Carol Robertson that developed into a close working relationship. This would allow Barns-Graham to become familiar enough with the screen-printing process to recognise how to exploit it fully.

The first three prints resulting from this collaboration were included in an exhibition early in 1999 which, for the first time in Barns-Graham's career, included a substantial number of prints, made in the preceding eight years with a variety of printmakers. This was *The Wilhelmina Barns-Graham Exhibition* in the McGeary Gallery in Brussels, which ran from 22 April to 12 May 1999. Of the 26 works exhibited, twelve were prints: *Untitled April 1991* and *Two Circles on Purple* and *November IV* from Curwen Chilford; *Venetian Red* made with Kip Gresham; *Scorpio I*, *Eight Lines I* and *Scorpio II* made with Rachael Kantaris in St Ives; *Spring* and *Summer* made at the Dundee Printmakers Workshop; and *Beach*, *Quiet Time* and *Orange and Lemon Playing Games* made with Carol Robertson. A further work – *Happening '91* – was a mixed-media work, based on the screenprint *November I* and overpainted with gouache. The exhibition was therefore both retrospective and prospective, looking back at Barns-Graham's printmaking thus far, and giving intimations of developments to come as she moved on to work exclusively with Robertson.

NOTES

1. Wilhelmina Barns-Graham Archive (hereafter WB-G Archive), 'Tit Bits Book', compiled 1998.
2. Tate Gallery Archive, TV South West transcript, 8613, p.300.
3. Tamsyn Woollcombe, The British Library Sound Archive, National Life Story Collection (hereafter NLSC): 'Artists' Lives', *Wilhelmina Barns-Graham*, Tape Numbers F4747–4751, June 1994.
4. Letter from Jim Whitlock to the author, 20 March 2006.
5. Lynne Green, *W. Barns-Graham: A Studio Life*, Lund Humphries, 2001, p.267.
6. WB-G Archive, letter from Bernard Leach, 29 January 1974.
7. WB-G Archive, letter from Bernard Leach, 14 May 1974. The cottages referred to were bought to extend the space of the Penwith Gallery.
8. The artists were Barbara Hepworth, Ben Nicholson, Peter Lanyon, Robert Adams, Alan Davie, Duncan Grant, Henry Moore, F.E. McWilliam, Bernard Leach, Merlyn Evans, Michael Rothenstein and John Piper. Another portfolio, *A Spring Collection*, was published by the Penwith Society in 1978 and in 1990 a portfolio was published to raise funds for the Tate St Ives appeal.
9. WB-G Archive, diary entries, March–April, 1976.
10. WB-G Archive, notes from etching class: 'My first plate was on hard ground. Wave drawing, Line drawing … Repeat process of hard ground on v. small zinc plate drawing on with needle hard ground as with plate (1) of waves on zinc. Stopping out. Aquatint.'
11. Letter from Ivan Polley to the author, 1 October 2006.
12. WB-G Archive, diary, October 1977, various entries.
13. In Sheila Oliner, taped interview with Barns-Graham, 16 September 1993.
14. She was invited to work with Edinburgh Printmakers in 1988. Robert Livingston, who had once been director of the Crawford Art Centre in St Andrews, was then director of the print workshop and he proposed a print project.
15. Email from Norrie Colston to the author, 6 November 2006.
16. In Sheila Oliner, taped interview with Barns-Graham, 16 September 1993.
17. Though there is no documentary or circumstantial evidence to support this, Carol Robertson, in a conversation with the author, remembered Barns-Graham talking about this print in relation to her etching classes at the Dundee Printmakers Workshop.
18. WB-G Archive, diary entries, various dates, November 1982.
19. WB-G Archive, diary entry, 20 December 1982.
20. Walter Chamberlain, *Etching and Engraving*, London, 1981, now in the WB-G Archive.
21. WB-G Archive, diary entry, 11 March 1983.
22. The Trustees of the Barns-Graham Charitable Trust have decided to have a small number of prints made from this plate (cat.7).
23. The artists were Barns-Graham, Ruth Beardsworth, George Donald, Carol Dunbar, Alexander Fraser, Elspeth Lamb, William Littlejohn, Tom Mabon, Alex Nisbet, Susie Patterson, Cameron Ross and Gill Tyson.
24. WB-G Archive, diary entry, page for August 25 but written 23 September 1988.
25. Email from Fergus McLachlan to the author, 10 November 2006.
26. See Green, *W. Barns-Graham*, p.239, fig.162, for a chalk drawing of a child with a skipping rope.
27. WB-G Archive, diary entry, 18 May 1990.
28. WB-G Archive, diary entry 31 July 1991.
29. Illustrated in Green, *W. Barns-Graham*, p.173, fig.95.
30. WB-G Archive, letter from Gresham to Barns-Graham, 9 September 1991.
31. WB-G Archive, letter from Gresham to Barns-Graham, 17 October 1991.
32. WB-G Archive, letter from Barns-Graham to Stanley Jones, 4 March 1992.
33. WB-G Archive, draft of a letter to Stanley Jones, 27 January 1992.
34. WB-G Archive, letter to Serena Castle, 7 October 1992.
35. Sheila Oliner, taped interview with Barns-Graham, 16 September 1993.
36. WB-G Archive, diary entry, 23 September 1991.
37. WB-G Archive, diary entries for 1991, 1 October: 'Began experimenting with print materials onto tracing paper with polished back – based on the feather design – exciting and expanding'; 2 October: 'Worked short time on printing materials No 2 design'; 3 October: 'Working on the printing mediums left me, mostly playing around No 3 sheet "Sacrifice".'
38. WB-G Archive, diary entry, 29 September 1989: '… returned to draw the 3 goats that never kept still.'
39. WB-G Archive, diary entry, 27 November 1991.
40. WB-G Archive, letter to Serena Castle, 7 October 1992.
41. WB-G Archive, diary entry, October 18 1991.
42. WB-G Archive, diary entry, October 22 1991.
43. WB-G Archive, diary entry, October 24 1991.
44. WB-G Archive, diary entry, October 19 1991.
45. The motif of the continuous brush stroke embracing three sides of the image, and the green colour scheme, relate this work directly to a group of paintings made after the death of Barns-Graham's friend, Margaret Christie, in 1988.
46. Only about five prints were made of this image and there are none in the Barns-Graham collection. One was sold from The New Academy Gallery Business Art Gallery, London. See WB-G Archive, letter dated 23 February 1995, about the sale of November prints, including *November VII*, numbered 3/3.
47. The then British ice-dance World and Olympic Champions.
48. Sheila Oliner, taped interview with Barns-Graham, 16 September 1993.
49. ibid.
50. Author's interview with Carol Robertson and Robert Adam, 29 May 2006.
51. WB-G Archive, diary entries, February–May 1992.
52. WB-G Archive, letter to Gresham, 9 January 1995.
53. WB-G Archive, letter from Barns-Graham to Gresham, 9 November 1994.
54. See Robert Adam and Carol Robertson, *Screenprinting: The Complete Water-based System*, London, 2003, pp 142–6. Almost all the Graal prints were made on Arches 400gsm paper.
55. Author's interview with Kip Gresham, 9 November 2005.
56. WB-G Archive, letter from Gresham to Barns-Graham, 18 January 1995.
57. WB-G Archive, letter from Barns-Graham to Gresham, 24 January 1995.
58. In 1990, as a fundraising effort to help raise money for Tate St Ives, the St Ives Tate Action Group (STAG) commissioned a portfolio of ten etchings which were printed at Hawthorn Prints. Those who had taken part went on to form Porthmeor Printmakers. See Cornwall County Council Art Collection Online, www.cornwall.gov.uk/index.cfm?articleid=8397.
59. Woollcombe interview, NLSC, June 1994.
60. Sheila Oliner, taped interview with Barns-Graham, 16 September 1993.
61. WB-G Archive, statement by Barns-Graham about the *Scorpio Series*, July 1998.
62. WB-G Archive, undated notes from Rachael Kantaris.
63. WB-G Archive, diary entry 1998.
64. WB-G Archive, diary entry, 24 February 1998.
65. WB-G Archive, diary entry, 2 March 1998.
66. WB-G Archive, diary entry, 22 March 1998.
67. WB-G Archive, diary entry, 20 May 1998.
68. WB-G Archive, diary entry, 28 July 1998.
69. WB-G Archive, diary entries, September–November 1998.
70. WB-G Archive, diary entry, 23–30 October 1998.
71. WB-G Archive, notes for a phone call, 30 October 1998.
72. WB-G Archive, letter from Gresham, 22 January 1999.
73. WB-G Archive, letter from Gresham, 27 January 1999.
74. ibid.

3

GRAAL PRESS AND SCREEN-PRINTS 1998–2004

Detail of *Beach*, 1999 (cat. 42).

THERE WAS A TIME WHEN IT WAS POSSIBLE TO WRITE OF screenprinting that 'compared with other printing processes it is relatively crude, since the mesh of the screen does not allow much fineness in drawing', and that artists 'striving for autographic qualities find that the medium has little to offer them'.[1] Or again, 'Lithography is adept at reproducing painterly nuance; screenprinting, on the other hand, is an art in which painterly touch is irrelevant'.[2] However, for some artists, Richard Hamilton for example, this was a positive quality of screenprinting: 'The medium has a certain appeal ... because it is less autographic than etching or litho – it hasn't their dependence on the hand of the artist. In that sense it is a modern printmaker's medium.'[3] Writers on printmaking, such as Pat Gilmour, felt that lithography was the medium for artists 'whose vitality resides in gesture; the artist who is a sensual or subtle colourist rejoicing in transparent inks; the artist who wants one studio in which he may juxtapose the hand-drawn and the mechanically processed'.[4]

That these assertions are no longer true is amply borne out by the work that Wilhelmina Barns-Graham made in collaboration with Carol Robertson between 1998 and 2003. In fact, the delicate subtlety of the medium as it has developed in recent years means that it can be difficult now to distinguish between screenprints and lithographs.

In 1998 Carol Robertson and Robert Adam set up Graal Press to research and develop new approaches to printmaking. They met while studying at the Slade School of Art in 1986, and at that point began to work together with the aim of making etching and screenprinting both physically safer and more creative. Later they introduced their working methods to Edinburgh Printmakers Workshop (where Adam had become director and Robertson was a studio artist), and to artists and educators from all over the world through seminars held at the Workshop. In 1992 Robertson brought these techniques to Edinburgh College of Art, where she was a lecturer, and in 1998 they taught their methods at Wimbledon School of Art.

Most printmaking techniques have historically involved a variety of hazardous chemicals. The use of acids, tars, rosins and toxic solvents for making plates, printing inks and cleaning materials meant that print studios contained poisonous, flammable and volatile substances which have often had a serious effect on the health of printmakers. Counteracting these hazards as much as possible involved installing expensive and space-consuming fume cupboards and proper extractor and ventilation systems. In recent decades many printmakers have worked to develop systems for printmaking that would eliminate these dangerous materials. Robertson and Adam found from their research and experimentation that other benefits emerged in addition to improving the safety of printmaking, and they went on to develop a whole range of materials and working methods for screen- and intaglio printing.[5]

Their screenprints are made with high-quality artists' paints in acrylics, gouaches and liquid watercolour, and with hand-made paints created with the finest-quality pigments and acrylic painting aids rather than printing inks. The very finely ground pigment particles can pass through the finest mesh screens, allowing a much greater range and variety of mark-making and finishes than had been possible previously. These paints are available in the whole colour field rather than the more limited palette offered by commercial printing inks, and can be adapted with painting aids to generate a variety of finishes. This allows for great subtlety in the layers of grounds, in the movement and activity beneath the surface marks, and in the play of matte

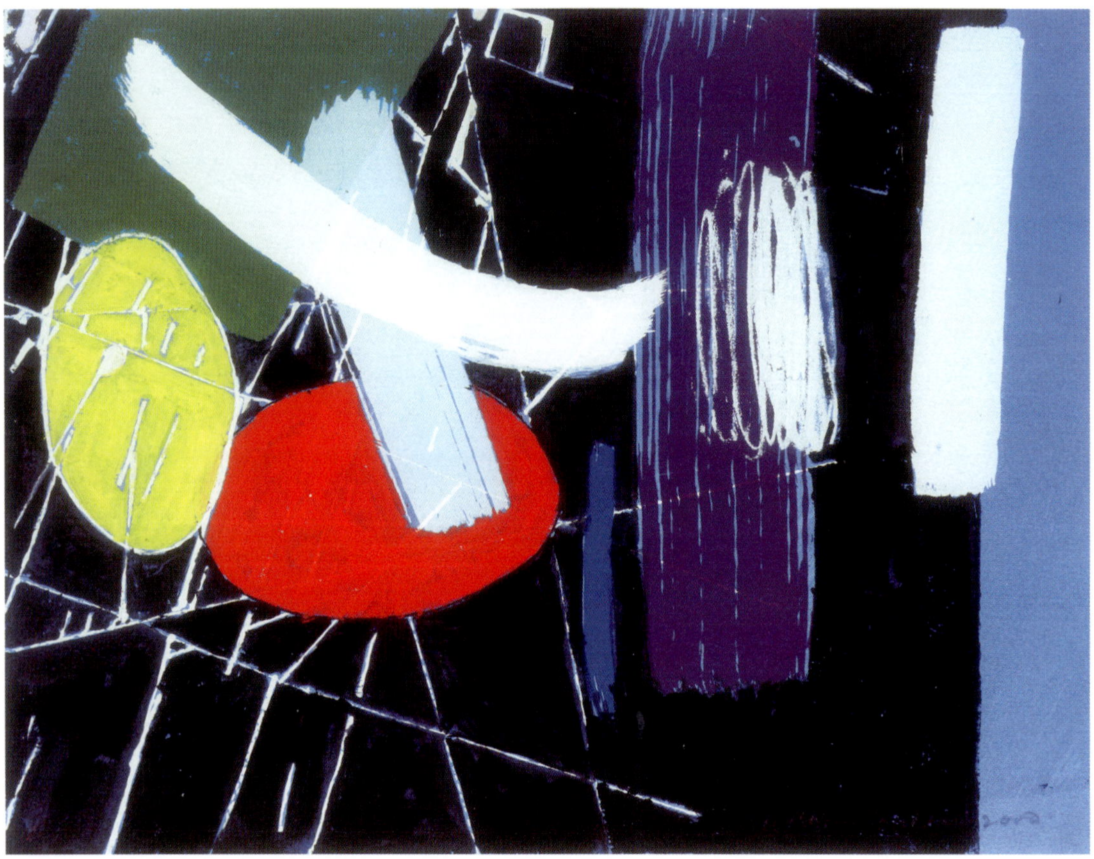

Fig. 20.
Millennium Series, mixed media, screenprint and acrylic, 2000.

Fig. 21.
Examples of textures and effects made with a variety of tusche mixtures.

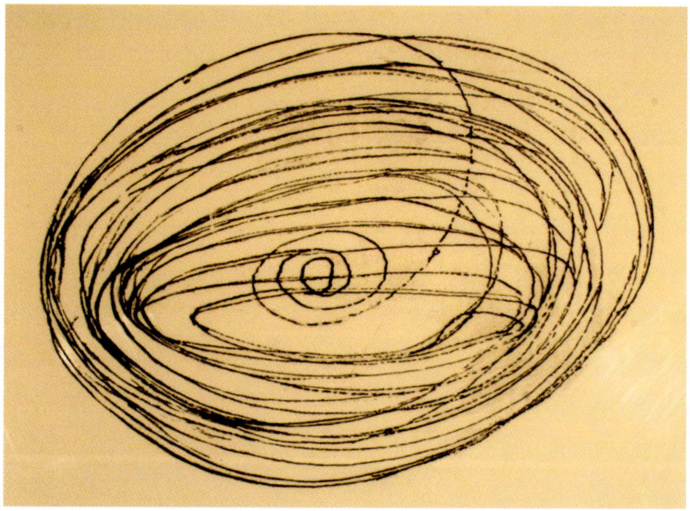

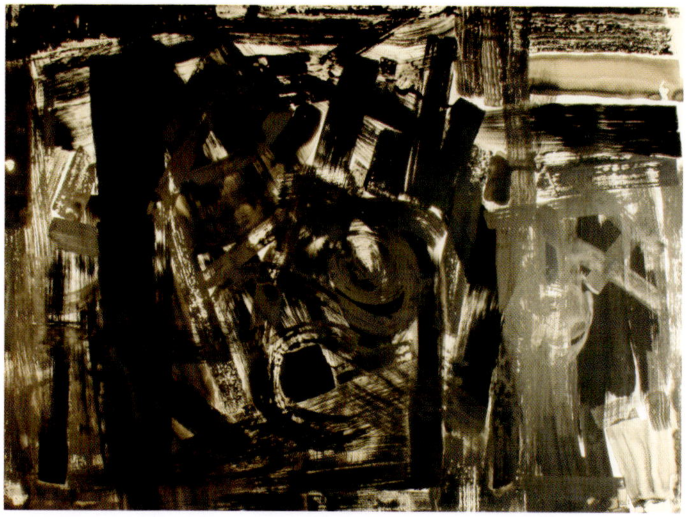

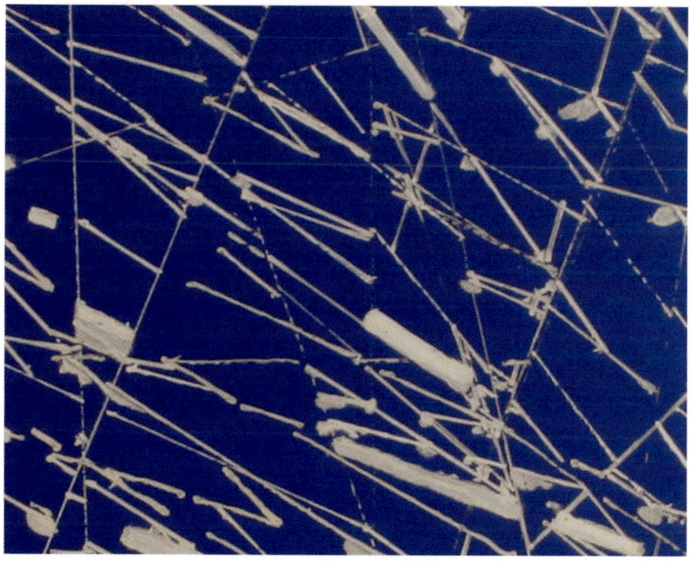

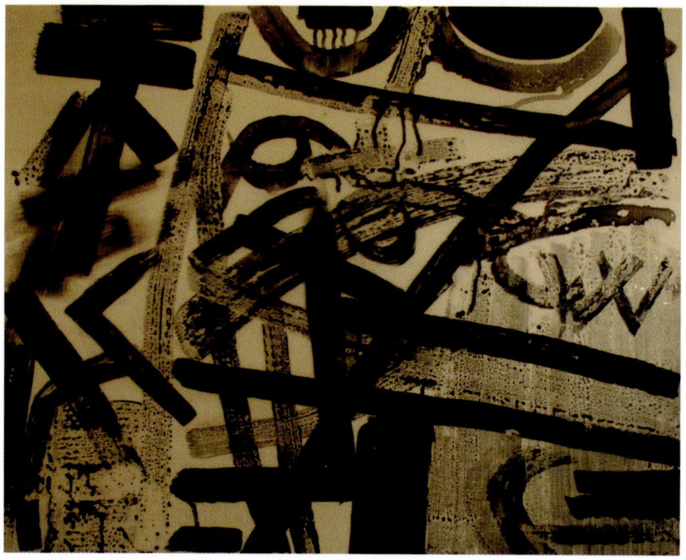

against sheen, translucency against opacity, grittiness against smoothness or velvetiness – as seen for example in *Millennium Series Red* (cat.61).

Robertson and Adam also developed a range of tusches (the opaque drawing and painting materials used to make the positives or separations), which take advantage of this fine printing. These tusches allow the marks made on the separation sheets to be as varied and complex as those made for lithography, from solid marks to delicate and transparent washes built up in layers (fig.21). These can provide all sorts of effects like those of soft-ground etching, lithography, gouache, monotype and airbrush, and can capture the artist's gesture, the autographic mark-making, in a very immediate way. The many different combinations of tusches, fine and coarse screen meshes, and acrylic and gouache paints now allow for a huge number of possibilities and variables in each print. These technical advances mean that screenprinting is an infinitely more sophisticated method than it was in the past.

The screenprints Barns-Graham made with Graal Press constitute the largest and most consistent body of her printed work, and the most illuminating in terms of the partnership between artist and printmaker.[6] Between December 1998 and Barns-Graham's death in January 2004, 44 prints were editioned and a further 17 were ready in proof form. She also made two etchings. These printed images also have their counterparts in her paintings, as her studio practice continued to inform her printmaking and vice versa.

The artist and printmakers first met on 20 November 1998 at Balmungo to discuss working together. Robertson showed Barns-Graham some of the original prints they had made with other artists such as Eduardo Paolozzi and Barbara Rae, as well as the variety of materials available and what could be done with them. Robertson explained her concept that screenprinting can be thought of as 'painting in slow motion', and that 'at the moment the artist hesitates or desires to change the movement of the brush it was often the time to put that positive aside and start another'.[7] With this concept in mind, Barns-Graham painted with tusches onto clear sheets of PVC with different sizes of brushes to make positives which could be printed in layers to create grounds. She admitted in her diary that she was nervous to begin with, but that as the possibilities emerged both she and Robertson got excited.[8] There followed an intense period of work for both of them. Barns-Graham spent the next few weeks learning how to use the materials and working on designs.

Her diary entries bear witness to her engagement in this work. On the second visit to Balmungo, she and Robertson made some more positives to be used as layers for grounds and a couple of individual brush marks. Barns-Graham was not happy about the design, but wrote, 'I am learning about mediums [sic] etc and it all takes time'.[9] They then decided to fine-tune their communication by using a painting as a starting point in the same way as one would work from a sketch. They made a set of separations based on a painting done in 1998.[10] It was, Barns-Graham wrote, 'on grey ground, blue cobalt circle, tan stripe LHS and black and white and dark grey RHS to try separations for silk screen. Difficulty getting paints on to film – tried different things and using acrylic medium. 8 separations; 2 grounds, 2 blues, tan 2 grey blacks and white.'[11]

Over the next days she continued working on different ideas: 'more than 8, half yellow blue, large blue circle and uprights blues, red, black, white and terracotta ... After lunch put a purplish red on 2 grounds and over 3 small designs – beginning another idea.'[12]

When Robertson and Adam returned to Balmungo on 11 December they brought a proof of the grey print (cat.82). The reaction was positive: 'Excellent! We then reworked on the small orange and some fresh separations and I made 2 grounds for dark one. Title for grey being "Quiet Time", going to edition 60. A successful morning.'[13] Barns-Graham then began work on a small design for what became *Orange and Lemon Playing Games* (cat.68): 'Somewhat messily did 3 separations for small lemon orange and black ovals design – in black acrylic ... and acrylic varnish.'[14] And the next day she was doing

> another version of 'Quiet Time', 'Another Time' perhaps using red [cat.78]. Long talks and [Carol had] done a print of the small orange with yellow and white line under black horizontal broad band RHS, sand ground and white and black stripes LHS. Began moving around the 2nd small one, part of an idea for etching she took away ... I think I'll prefer the 2nd on lemon ground, cad[mium] yellow stripe LHS and black oval, right hand orange band horizontal and over a line oval and ½ a one.[15]

This refers to *Beach* (cat.42) and *Orange and Lemon Playing Games*. Within a month of their first meeting, they had started work on five prints and begun two series.

At the beginning, it was necessary for each of them to develop an understanding of the other's working methods. Barns-Graham explained in detail how she worked on several paintings at once. She would make up diluted colours in a series of small Pyrex bowls. Each painting was built up in many layers, each layer having to dry before the next marks were added. Even the grounds were made of several layers, the accumulation of washes giving a different effect than if the same colour was put on in one thick layer. Into each ground wash, she would put small amounts of the other colours she was going to use, so that the ground colour carried within it the information about the colours to come. For example, an ultramarine wash would have a little red in one layer, a little yellow in another and a little violet in the third; each of these grounds would pick up the colours of the marks on top.

Although she had already moved beyond the limited techniques of her 1972 screenprint *Vermilion Discs onto Turquoise Square* (cat.25), Barns-Graham still had a restricted notion of the possibilities of screenprinting. She had enjoyed the collaborations at the Curwen Chilford studio and at Dundee, and at the latter she had noticed the fresher atmosphere in the studio, where they were also using a water-based system.[16] But from what she had seen she still thought screenprinting would produce prints with a quite flat solid finish. So first Robertson showed her how she could use the range of brown tusches on clear plastic sheets and the different effects that were possible, including making soft, complex washes. The layers of separations could be built up in the same way that she constructed her paintings. After their first meeting, Robertson took some separations away to her studio and returned with prints to show what could be achieved.

One print that demonstrates the relationship between Barns-Graham's printmaking and her painting methods particularly well is *Walkabout Time* (cat.85). The grey ground is made up of five layers, each one a translucent version of each of the coloured bars. A translucent mustard is followed by a translucent purple, then a translucent green and so on. These finally combine together to make the grey ground. The colour theory which this demonstrates meant that Robertson had to have unerring faith in the way that the image was assembled because, until the last coloured bar was printed, the relationships would not balance and the image would not 'sing'.

Barns-Graham was quick to understand the benefits of using the same paint for painting and screenprinting, the possibilities offered to her by this way of working and the way it dovetailed with her own painting methods. Robertson encouraged her to move away from thinking in terms of making 'separations', and instead to make positives to hold different brush marks, drawn marks and washes for grounds. She explained that once the brush marks had been made onto the clear sheets they could be kept and reused in different combinations and arrangements, allowing the artist to work easily on a series of themed prints. These positives collectively formed a visual dictionary of personal marks. The knowledge that her marks were preserved and safe was liberating for Barns-Graham, enabling her to experiment without wasting energy.

This was particularly important in view of Barns-Graham's age. She was 86 when she and Robertson started working together, and not physically strong. She was worried that as she grew older she would lose the balance and vigour and effort needed to make the strong gestural marks in her paintings. It required courage to make the last brush stroke in a painting when she was unsure that she still had the control and strength to place it exactly in the right place, with the requisite force and energy. Robertson screenprinted marks from the 'dictionary' in a range of colours onto sheets of clear PVC so that Barns-Graham could experiment with building new compositions (fig.22). The artist found that she could take advantage of the screenprinted shapes, not only to allow images for her prints to change and grow in an organic way, but also to help with her paintings. Instead of having to get a mark right first time, she could use the screenprinted brush strokes to position and re-position each mark, and also decide on the colour, opacity or transparency she wanted before committing herself in irreversible paint.

Having the shapes printed like this also allowed artist and printmaker to work as a team. Robert Adam noted that Barns-Graham

> would sit perched on a chair, with Carol at her feet carefully moving and adjusting individual printed brushmarks and fragments on coloured grounds ... it seemed like a fast-moving kaleidoscope as the coloured brushstrokes were discarded and replaced, until each element was perfect and playing in harmony with the others ... Carol would be instructed to place a sheet of clear plastic over the composition and carefully note the components.[17]

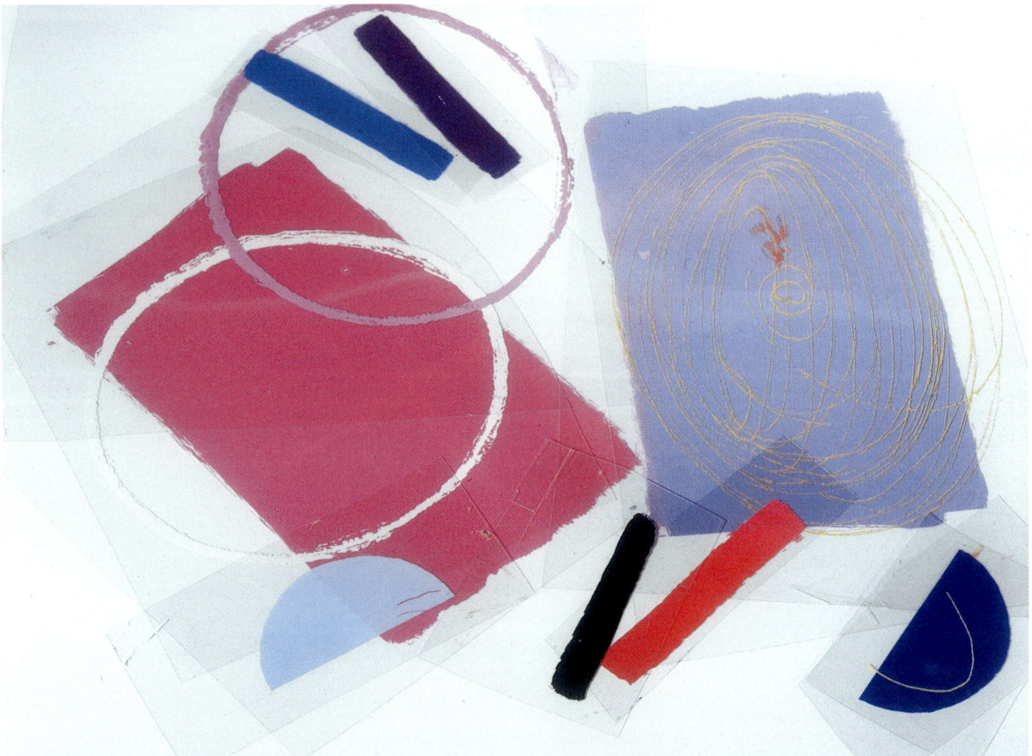

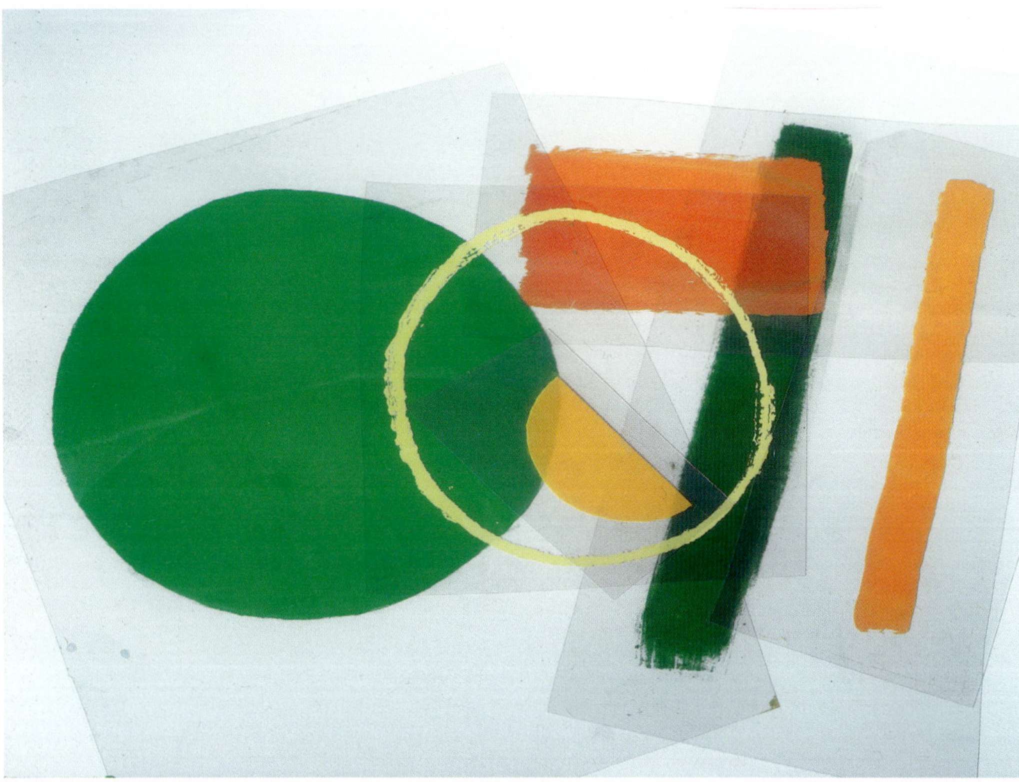

Fig. 22.

Two examples of individual brush marks screenprinted in colour on clear acrylic sheets.

Fig. 23 (opposite).

Assemblage showing, clockwise from lower left, screenprinted brush marks, a map showing elements of an image, a screenprint made from the map (*Cobalt and Pink Playing Games*) and the development of a further image.

Carol Robertson recalled how

> After these active sessions Barns-Graham would call Rowan James and Adam up to the studio and would ask them to comment on the compositions made that day. The group would view the work from all directions and individually describe feelings evoked by each piece. She would want to know how each person's eye travelled around the image as the spaces that were created between the brush strokes and other shapes were as important as the marks themselves. She was also interested in the perceived halos of colour which were induced by the juxtaposition of specific colours. Barns-Graham would gauge everyone's reaction with great care, scolding anyone who became too literal. She would then make further decisions and instruct the nearest person to move the elements fractionally. I would then make a new map of the composition.[18]

As this collection of marks grew, it became possible to move the marks around and use them in other combinations. For instance, the *Sunghrie* prints (cats 75–7) use the same elements and marks in altered positions and printed in different colours.

During the proofing stages the components of each colour would be weighed and noted so that even in poor light conditions an exact colour could be re-created for the edition. An unusual problem arose in the printing of the *Earth Series* (cats 56–60). The connecting colour between these prints is

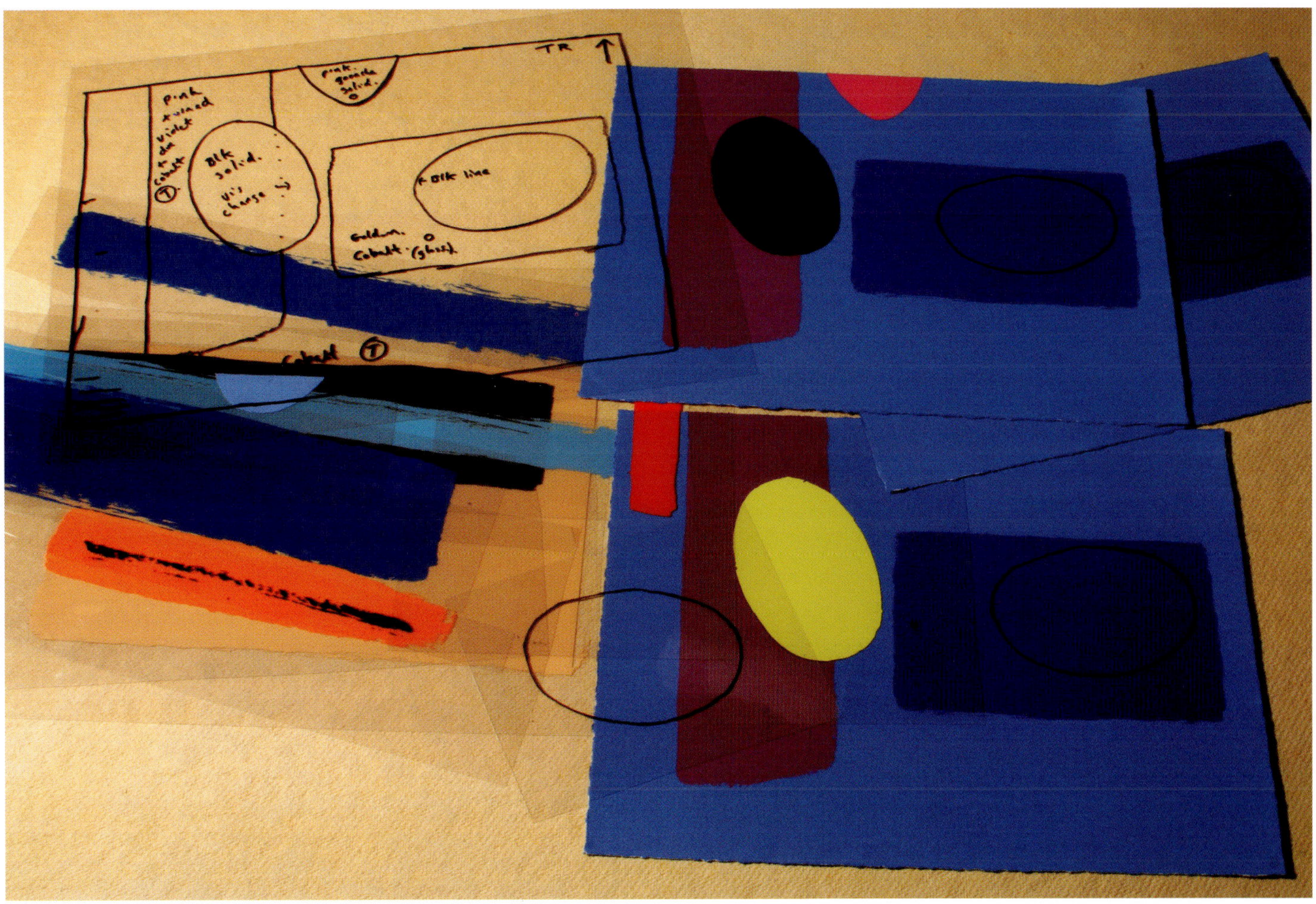

made from an iron oxide pigment powder. More pigment had to be ordered to complete the series, but the colour that arrived was different. It transpired that the iron oxide came from a quarry in Germany; the seam from which the original pigment was made had run out and the new seam was a slightly different colour. Robertson had to alter the colour with artists' paints to get it as close as possible to the original.

Once the collaboration became established, Robertson would travel to Balmungo, sometimes on a weekly basis when Barns-Graham was in Scotland, taking proofs, experiments and variations to discuss. Eventually the artist was creating new work too fast for the printmaker to keep up. Barns-Graham would approve a proof for printing and then move swiftly on to a variant in the series, or to another image altogether. Having finished one idea, she was impatient to start another and would say, 'Oh, you can print that when I'm dead'.[19]

Much of the success of this partnership lay in the trust that developed between Robertson and Barns-Graham as they each learned to respect, understand and communicate with each other. This was a symbiotic relationship of equal partners, with Robertson exemplifying Pat Gilmour's description of 'the creativity of the printer in this collaborative situation, whose role is analogous to a conductor interpreting a composer's music, or an actor living the part in Shakespeare'.[20]

The relationship also afforded Robertson an insight into the creative process, which for Barns-Graham was normally a very private activity. They would discuss at length the way moving one shape in an image impinged on all the others, creating tension between elements or upsetting the balance. Moving even the smallest details or accents could change the formal shape of a composition and affect the way the eye travelled over and read the image. Often when separations or proofs were spread out around the studio, the artist would suddenly point out a relationship between her images and a shadow or a paint spill on the rug, or marks in two adjacent prints. Sometimes she would take all the coloured marks, throw them up in the air and see how they fell. Back in the print studio, Robertson 'could try something ... and take it back and [Barns-Graham] would say "Oh, that's the relationship we saw in the studio"', and incorporate it. An example of this is the sandy colour and rough, textured ground in *Water Dance (Porthmeor) No. V* (cat. 97), which derived from the floor covering in the studio. Barns-Graham was also keenly aware when something was wrong. Early in their relationship, Robertson arrived one day with a new print, one of the *Orange and Lemon Playing Games Series*. The artist could hardly bear to look at it, saying she could 'never have made such a depressed oval'. Robertson found that the mark had been inadvertently reversed, and although the difference was very small, it did completely change the mood of the work.[21]

Barns-Graham was stimulated by the way a work could take her by surprise; an accidental arrangement or a fleeting glimpse was an important way of seeing which allowed the artist to discover unexpected relationships. One day when she and Rowan James were looking at some proofs of the *Earth Series*, she recorded:

> Carol had sent a print of white shapes, touch of yellow on terracotta, designed 2 years ago ... and this one I disliked and suggest 2 white shapes should be greyed or blushed. She'd made a pastry yellow and sweet pink ... by chance when R. threw [it] on [the] ground I saw it upside down and it was a fresh idea and the pale pink worked as a shape 'going out'. What Relief.[22]

Later when she was signing and numbering the completed *Earth Series*, she was unhappy with the fourth in the sequence.[23] The prints were stacked up in the studio and as she moved around she saw the print upside down. Once more, it seemed to work. *Earth Series IV* and *Earth Series V* (cats 59–60) became inversions of the first three in the series, and they were signed in that orientation, which explains why the Graal Press blind stamp appears upside down in the top left corner of these two prints.

Robertson gradually developed an intuitive understanding of Barns-Graham's creative thought processes, which sometimes enabled her to help the artist work through difficulties. The print *Homage to Johnny* (cat.46) was particularly problematic. It belongs with a series of paintings entitled *Goodbye Johnny* made after the death in 2000 of Barns-Graham's friend and St Ives contemporary, the artist John Wells. It was very important to Barns-Graham that she should get it right, but after trying a large number of variants something was not working, and she could not describe what the problem was. Robertson remembers asking her:

> Is the feeling like seeing a sky lark in the sky, and listening to it and listening to it, and then looking for it and seeing it flying higher and higher until it becomes so small that it seems to disappear? And she said 'That's exactly it'. I went home and re-printed another twenty. Now we don't really know what was different, but what was different was that I understood and it worked.[24]

These prints also bear witness to Barns-Graham's acute sensitivity to colour:

> In common with a select group of distinguished artists she had the unusual gift of synaesthesia. This meant that sensations she experienced were translated intuitively into specific colours with attendant harmonies and discords. I remember going through the alphabet with her once, and her telling me ... the particular colour she associated with each letter.[25]

This could lead to problems sometimes, as for example on one occasion when she bought a book about Kokoschka by mistake, instead of one about Kandinsky. She was distracted by her perception of the 'K' which she saw as yellow, and did not read the name properly.[26] But her sensitivity went much deeper than this. As she and Robertson built up a way of communicating about their work, a vocabulary involving all the senses developed to describe what they were doing and seeing. They would talk about colours in terms of sounds and tastes, describing something as being sharp and tangy like lemon or deep and rich like cocoa. They began to work with a new material, Lascaux Resonance Gouache, which had been developed according to a theory relating to resonance patterns and electromagnetic waves.[27] The paints contain oil of sage and bioinformation:

> By means of biophysical techniques, highly structured frequency waves – resonance-patterns – have been developed. They are obtained from plants, precious stones, metals, minerals, trace elements, as well as from precious gases, fermenting processes, etc. Transposed to suitable carrier materials such as tinctures or essences, and in this case added to a colour formula, they beneficially support the human energy field, specifically aimed at addressing individual potential.[28]

The sharp aroma of the mixture adds the sense of smell to the experience of working with these paints, though it is not apparent to the observer, but Lascaux asserts that the addition of bioinformation means that 'the colours obtain a specific resonance capacity, which has a beneficial effect on the painter as well as on the observer'.[29] Barns-Graham felt that these additives rendered literal her feeling that there might be a therapeutic quality to her art.

Colour and sound were also closely connected. In her mind a print would 'sing' when shapes and colours were in perfect harmony. The musical analogy extended to the structure of her compositions; the underlying geometry often involved very accurate measurements and clever inversions. Each colour was a note that built up with the next into a chord, each shape a measured beat in the overall rhythm. In view of the fugue-like patterns in many of her prints, with shapes and colours interweaving and reiterating, it is not surprising to discover that she enjoyed listening to the music of Bach.

Artist and printmaker also needed a shared vocabulary to describe the various marks that were used in the prints. Brush marks were Barns-Graham's principal means of expression, so the brushes she used were important to her, and she used only one make in a variety of sizes. A mark would be described as a bar, stroke, arc, oval, line oval, half oval, oblong, ground, panel, slash, quick stroke, big drop, spiral, circle, stripe, strip or line, with the orientation described as upright, diagonal, down, across, RHS and LHS (right-hand side and left-hand side). She also used conté crayons, markers and pens for lines, particularly relishing the 'stuttering' line obtained from a white typing correction pen which echoed the broken and textured lines of her early offset drawings of glaciers. This can best be seen in the delicate tracery of white lines in the *Vision in Time Series* (cats 88–92), images which were partly inspired by seeing cracked ice on a puddle during a winter walk.[30]

These names are purely to do with their shape, and do not evoke any representational associations. To give names to shapes such as the central motif in the *Earth Series*, or the soft-edged oval in *White Circle Series I* (cat. 99), would have been too explicit, imposing an external meaning and interfering with the creative process. This discipline not to name things extended also to the titles of Barns-Graham's works. The titles are not explained, and she did not like them to be too literal or descriptive. Titles were usually given after the making of the image. As Lynne Green has written, works were named 'not for the initial inspiration, [but] in response to the resonance the finished image has for her: the association, feeling or visual sensation it generates'.[31] Barns-Graham took a keen interest in politics and world events; her diaries contain many entries commenting on the news, and works sometimes refer to what was going on at the time (for instance her paintings with titles related to the Queen's Silver Jubilee in 1977, the Olympic Games in Barcelona in 1992, the conflict in Bosnia in 1994, the total eclipse of the sun in 1999 and the Millennium). Some titles may hold multiple meanings. 'Sunghrie' was the name of one of the Siamese cats that she and Rowan James both loved, but was also thought by Barns-Graham to be the name of a Tibetan river.[32] She had long been interested in Tibet and Buddhism, and though it is only speculation to identify conscious overtones of this belief in the vibrant yellow colour scheme of the *Sunghrie Series* (cats 75–7), it seems a reasonable interpretation.[33]

For the *Time Series* (cats 78–89), Barns-Graham made a long list of over sixty time-related expressions, such as Ancient Time, Show Time, Counting Time and Dream Time; clearly in that respect the series could have continued indefinitely.[34] *Tango* (cat.48) was not the first name for this image, though it seems most apt, as the crossed-lines motif in some strange way evokes the swing and staccato movements of the dance. *Xmas Card* and *Untitled Brown* were tried out as titles, and a painting from 2002 which incorporates the same white-line motif was entitled *Confrontation*, a mood which also resonates through the dance. The title of *Beach* (cat.42) stuck, in spite of Barns-Graham's instinctive distaste for the name. It was inspired by the view from her St Ives studio which looks directly onto Porthmeor beach, and relates in both its colour and its shapes to representational works she made of the beach covered with swimming towels and wind screens (fig.24). *Water Dance (Porthmeor)* is possibly the most evocative and descriptive of the titles (cats 93–8). Again, the motif is related to the view from her studio window, recalling the appearance of sparkling sunlight reflected off moving water.

Barns-Graham had always worked with themes and series in her paintings, using them to explore ideas thoroughly, and now she could develop prints in this way, too. Themes could be developed over time, but the frequent visits by Robertson and Adam to Balmungo meant there was a continuity that had been lacking in her other printmaking endeavours. Sometimes a series would develop from a concept she was working on in her painting, but often images from one series of prints became a starting point for the next series, evolving through slight variations in shapes and relationships, through nuanced colour changes or through the introduction of a new element which took the image off in a new direction. This movement of ideas and motifs through a succession of series is illustrated by a number of prints. The *Time Series* (cats 78–85) began with *Quiet Time,* based on an existing painting. The main elements of this, a large circle and a number of vertical and slanting bars, are repeated through many colour combinations. An extra element, an energetically drawn spiral, gives a sense of movement to *Walkabout Time* and *Runabout Time*. The circle and bars re-appear in *Celebration at 90* (cat. 44), but the circle is enlivened with swirling marks reminiscent of the artist's paintings based on the firework display from the opening of the Barcelona Olympics, which she had watched on television. And another motif, full of downward rushing movement, lies beneath the circle. This came from the central motif in the *Earth Series* (cats 56–60). The motif appears again in *White Circle Series III* (cat.101). The underlying basis of this print is *Celebration at 90*. Making use of an early proof, Robertson ran

Fig. 24.
Summer Painting, 1986, gouache. This beach scene shows the view from the artist's studio in St Ives.

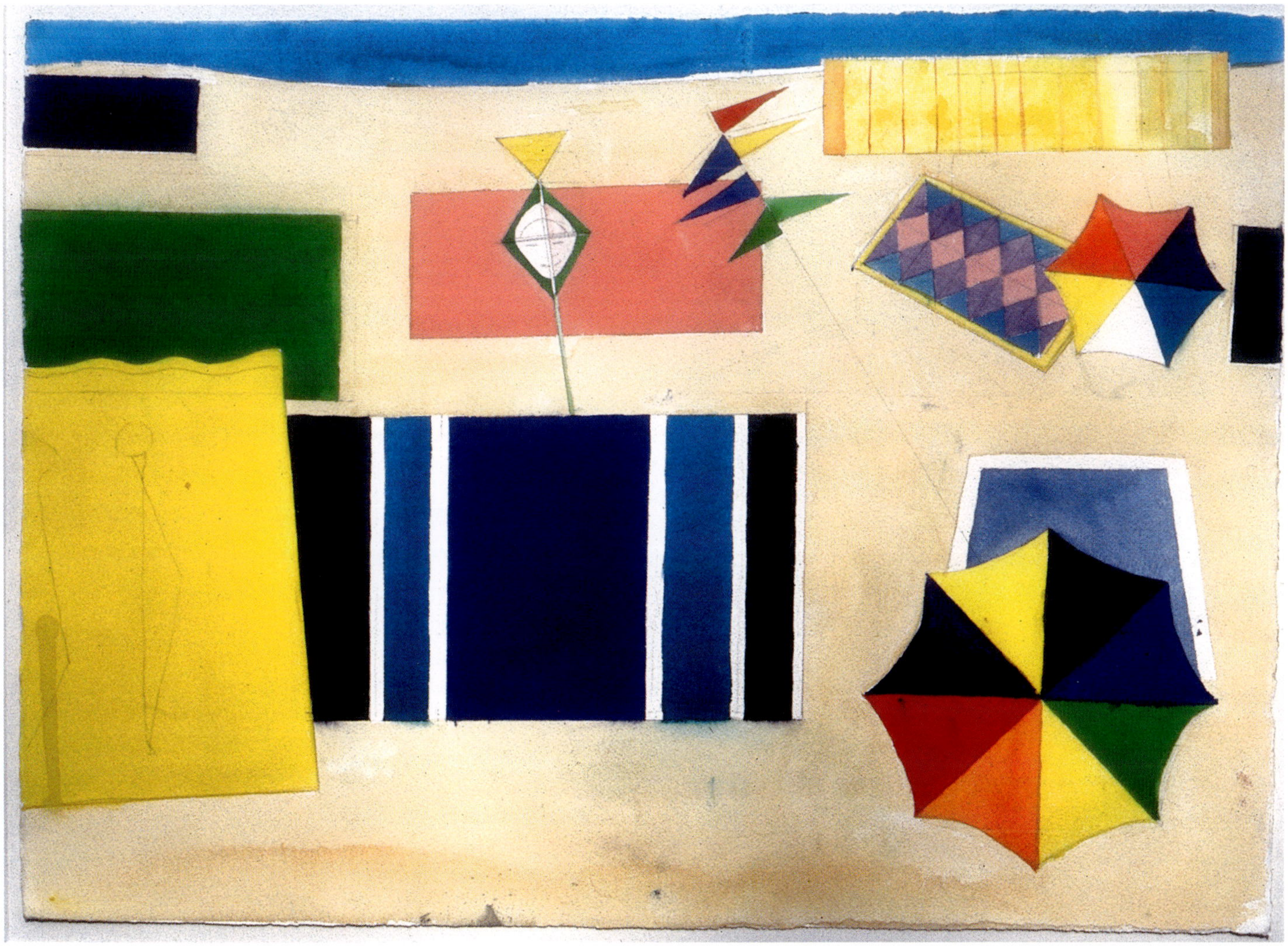

a flat layer of translucent ultramarine over the whole image, producing a metamorphosis from earth and fire to something subaqueous and mysterious. The magenta line on the left side of *Celebration* became an intense blue. The dusty quality of the earlier print is transformed to a smooth, silky sheen.

The three *Playing Games Series* (cats 53–5, 68–70 and 71–4) express explicitly Barns-Graham's life-long exploration of colours. The titles invite the viewer to contemplate the varied interplay and reaction of colours with one another, and the way a slight change in shade, tone or hue affects the colour next to it. The *Orange and Lemon Playing Games* prints consist of four main elements: a slanting bar, a horizontal rectangle and two ovals, some solid and some in outline. A half-oval appears in two of the images. The first print in the series sizzles with bright shades of yellow and orange, while the second and third are altogether more restrained. The shapes of solid and outlined ovals are repeated in the *Red Playing Games Series*, with a more complex interlayering of bars and panels. The strong, almost astringent yellow also reappears in this series, and becomes a link to the final series, *Cobalt Playing Games.* In *Cobalt and Pink Playing Games* (cat. 54) the blue of the title is easily apparent, but in *Cobalt Playing Games* (cat. 53) it seems as if the only blue is the half-oval entering from the left. However, it is a translucent glazed rectangle of cobalt pigment that transforms the hot yellow and orange to cool green and pink.

The same elements appear again in the more complex images of the *Millennium Series* (cats 61–7). This is a series of six small prints, plus a further and smaller version made specially for the limited edition of Lynne Green's book, *W. Barns-Graham: A Studio Life*. The dominant motif of the series is made up of two brush marks intersecting to make a cross shape in the upper left of the image. A variety of vertical marks, oval shapes both solid and in outline and a scribbled vertical mark appear in all versions of the series, in differing orientations and numbers. Each print in the series has its own character. *Millennium Series Green* and *Millennium Series Brown* use opaque matte colours, where others use more transparent and reflective finishes. The final layer of *Millennium Series Blue I* is a faintly coloured gloss, while *Millennium Series Blue II* has a more complex ground than the others, using a quarter-section of a swirling ground made for the *Vision in Time Series* (cats 88–92).

The last few months of Wilhelmina Barns-Graham's life were as prolific as any previous period of it, and were largely taken up with printmaking activities. Throughout the summer of 2003 she was busy creating several new series, and even through the autumn, when she was ill, she was still able to look at and discuss the proofs as Robertson brought them to Balmungo, and to sign editions as they were finished.

Once again the diaries document her progress. On 7 August 2003 she recorded a

> successful and enjoyable visit. [Carol] took away 4 v. small ones to enlarge 3, and experiment with the pale blue pillar abstract, the white circle with black and streak of purple, black in white circle on blue, brown with red, white and black, touch of red at top, being small [one] done before Xmas, the Russian influenced one Apr. or May. To do a [illegible] of the red background to the white oval spiral and white brush stroke done this week on old sheet with dry red panel!

Some of these became the *White Circle Series* (cats 99–101), and one became *Tango*. The printmakers returned a week later, and Barns-Graham thought that Robertson had 'been "carried" away with this little ultramarine circle and done certain variations on the enlarged square ... I didn't feel it was a good design but why? we discussed thinning the white circle which I will do'.[35] The next day she went to the studio and 'thinned proportion of 2 White Circles. Not satisfactory. After lunch played with red and white spots on a blue square one and one Carol had played experiments on and we found we had two possible exciting prints. Hope I think so on later viewing as one can fluctuate'.

That evening Rowan stuck down the small 'satellite' spots on the separations for *White Circle Series I* and *III* and Barns-Graham's reaction was: 'They look exciting prints to be, I think, then I blow cold and think they are too romantic? but I am at present a bit against all my efforts.'[36] On 21 August, she recorded:

> Another enjoyable occasion with Carol and Robert. Showed Carol what had been done since last Thursday and she brought over more experiments and had tackled a brown small one with black and white mark and white lines and red narrow form coming in at the top. Selected one of these and kept some sheets for working on. She liked enormously what I had done to the white circle 2 on blue with black and the large experiment of this one on Celebration birthday print.[37]

Fig. 25.
Homage to Johnny, mixed media screen print and acrylic, 2003.

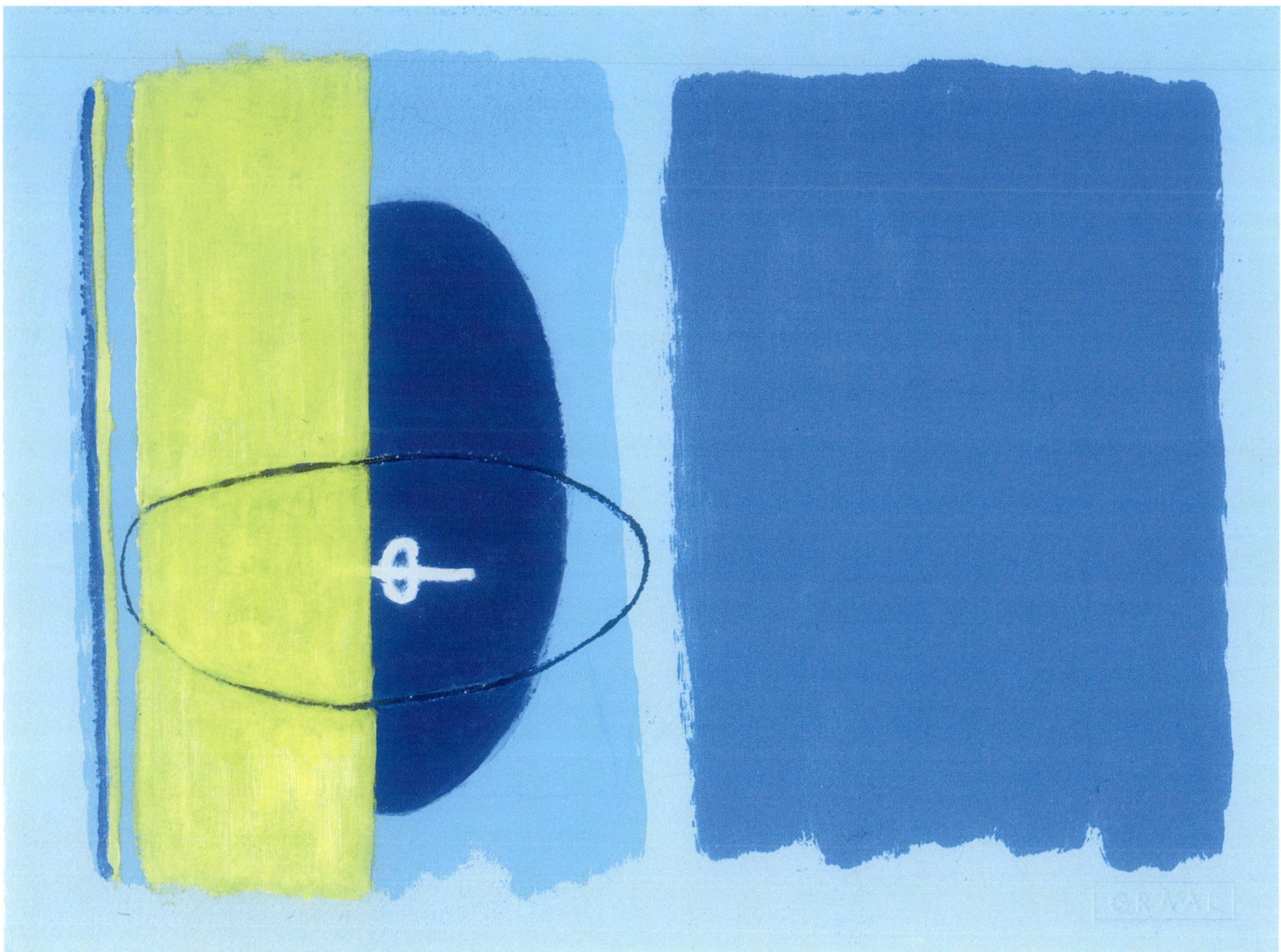

Unusually, the prints in the *White Circle Series* are different shapes and sizes. The first and second in the series are simple images with few elements, whereas the third is complex, incorporating the elements from *Celebration* beneath the blue. But all share the rich, dark and indeed romantic mood that slightly worried the artist; perhaps she felt that romance was not serious enough. However, when Robertson brought the final proof for *White Circle Series II*, 'she just saw it and beamed'.[38]

Several prints had not been editioned at the time of Barns-Graham's death, though almost all had been seen by her at the proof stage. Four of the *Time Series* and three of the *Vision in Time Series* had been set aside when she moved on to a new series, intended to be editioned at some later date. There were also single prints, some relating to themes in her paintings. *Construction Series I* (cat.45) is clearly based on the *Firth of Forth Series*, inspired by the iconic red railway bridge.[39] *June* (cat.47) initially looks similar to these works in its colour and elements, but it also has strong echoes of the 1996 *June Painting*, repeating the black arcs of a boat shape.[40]

Throughout her working career, Barns-Graham constantly referred back to her earlier work, revisiting themes and images, and in some respects her prints had brought her full circle. At the end of *A Studio Life*, Lynne Green records a telephone conversation in which the artist described a new painting, *Gaia Series (Mars) I*: 'There is movement, a lot of space, simplicity, and construction – this is something I've been trying to achieve for years.' She continued, 'That painting in the Tate [St Ives] show [*Black Oval*, 1957–9] is a key: what it said is *very* much what I am doing now'.[41]

These remarks could just as easily apply to her last prints, for the black oval was precisely what she was doing. The soft-edged, cloudy black shape that Green describes as a unique image in 1957 had prefigured her late work and re-emerged in the *White Circle Series*. And the movement, space, simplicity and construction of *Gaia* she also found in *Water Dance (Porthmeor) No. III* (cat.95) The first two in this series are square, and the brush marks fill the space. Robertson printed the third on an oblong sheet, meaning to cut it down to square. When Barns-Graham saw the print, she said, 'That is what I have always been trying to do'.[42] (See cat.95.) The sparkling lines have a space to dance into, giving a sense of potential change, and yet there is an immanent quality to this image which is in perfect equilibrium. The *Wind Dance* and *Water Dance (Porthmeor) Series* (cats 102–6 and 93–8) are joyful works of art, but there is also an austerity in their apparent simplicity that is made manifest in *Water Dance (Porthmeor) No. VI*, the final print in the series and the only one Barns-Graham did not see in proof (cat.98). There is a strange irony in the fact that the last work by this supremely colourful artist should be in restrained monochrome tones of black, white and grey. But it is restrained only in hue – the textures and finishes of the print are rich and tactile, the velvet-black ground contrasting with the creamy, glossy whites.

However, despite the artist's assertion that in *Water Dance (Porthmeor) No. III* she had reached some kind of completion, it is certain that she would soon have set off in some new direction. For instance, *Three Elements* and *Two Elements* (cats 49 and 50) exhibit bold and monumental new shapes. In the summer of 2003, Barns-Graham had once again sorted through her artist's proofs to use for experimental mixed-media works, a practice that took some of the risk out of painting; if it did not work there were several more prints that could be played with. But this activity had often also been productive of new ideas. The *Millennium Series* and *Homage to Johnny* had proved particularly fruitful in this respect (see figs 20 and 25). Had she lived a little longer this interconnection between her painted and printed work would have achieved a new union. According to Robertson, the next project was to have been screenprinting onto painted canvas. Rather than utilising the multiplied image and transforming each one into a unique painting, Barns-Graham would have used the controlled freedom of the repeatable screenprinted marks to make unique prints. Having started her printmaking with monotypes, perhaps she had come full circle after all.

NOTES

1. Antony Griffiths, *Prints and Printmaking: An Introduction to the History and Techniques*, London, 1980, pp.110–12.
2. Susan Tallman, *The Contemporary Print from Pre-Pop to Postmodern*, London, 1996, p.60.
3. Richard Hamilton, quoted in Pat Gilmour's introduction to *Kelpra Studio, The Rose and Chris Prater Gift, Artists' Prints 1961–1980*, exh.cat., Tate Gallery, London, 1980, p.25.
4. Pat Gilmour, *Lithographs from the Curwen Studio: A Retrospective of Fifteen Years of Printmaking*, exh.cat., Camden Arts Centre, December 1973 – January 1974 (in the Tate Archive).
5. See Robert Adam and Carol Robertson, *Screenprinting: The Complete Water-based System*, London, 2003.
6. Much of the content of this chapter is based on an interview by the author with Carol Robertson and Robert Adam, 29 May 2006.
7. Email from Carol Robertson to the author, 11 January 2007.
8. Wilhelmina Barns-Graham Archive (hereafter WB-G Archive), diary entry, 20 November 1998.
9. WB-G Archive, diary entry, 27 November 1998.
10. Robertson always refers to these clear plastic sheets as 'positives', whereas in her diaries Barns-Graham always refers to them as 'separations'.
11. WB-G Archive, diary entry, 1 December 1998.
12. WB-G Archive, diary entry, 2 December 1998.
13. WB-G Archive, diary entry, 11 December 1998.
14. WB-G Archive, diary entry, 18 December 1998.
15. WB-G Archive, diary entry, 19 December 1998.
16. WB-G Archive, diary entry, 24 February 1998.
17. Robert Adam, 'Willie Barns-Graham – a personal appreciation', in *Wilhelmina Barns-Graham 1912–2004. A Tribute: Recent Paintings and New Prints*, exh.cat., Art First, April–May 2004, pp 38–9.
18. Email from Robertson to the author, 11 January 2007.
19. Author's interview with Carol Robertson and Robert Adam, 29 May 2006.
20. Pat Gilmour, *The Mechanised Image: An Historical Perspective on 20th Century Prints*, London, 1978, p.96.
21. Author's interview with Carol Robertson and Robert Adam, 29 May 2006.
22. WB-G Archive, diary entry, 24 July 2003.
23. WB-G Archive, diary entry, 10 August 2003.
24. Author's interview with Carol Robertson and Robert Adam, 29 May 2006.
25. Adam, 'Willie Barns-Graham – a personal appreciation', p. 40. See also http://www.uksynaesthesia.com: 'In its simplest form [synaesthesia] is best described as a "union of the senses" whereby two or more of the five senses that are normally experienced separately are involuntarily and automatically joined together. Some synaesthetes experience colour when they hear sounds or read words. Others experience tastes, smells, shapes or touches in almost any combination.'
26. WB-G Archive, diary entry, 3 November 1996.
27. For a full description of the theory and of the pigments see the Lascaux website, www.lascaux.ch.
28. ibid.
29. ibid.
30. Author's interview with Carol Robertson and Robert Adam, 29 May 2006.
31. Lynne Green, *W. Barns-Graham: A Studio Life*, Lund Humphries, 2001, p.266.
32. Author's notes from an undated conversation with Rowan James, 2004. Barns-Graham referred to the prints in her diaries variously as 'Sunghrie', 'Sungari' and 'Sunghari'. I have been unable to identify a Tibetan river with this name but the river Sunghari or Song Hua flows out of Mongolia in northeast China.
33. In her diary for 8 September 1974 she recorded a list of books she was reading about Tibet and wrote, 'Wish I could have visited Tibet before the communists took over.' A few days later (on September 14) she also wrote that she found 'reading Buddhist books [a] great help to maintain quiet'.
34. WB-G Archive, miscellaneous notes.
35. WB-G Archive, diary entry, 14 August.
36. WB-G Archive, diary entry, 16 August.
37. WB-G Archive, diary entry, 21 August.
38. Author's interview with Carol Robertson and Robert Adam, 29 May 2006.
39. See Green, *W. Barns-Graham*, p.265, fig.187.
40. See *Wilhelmina Barns-Graham: Movement and Light Imag(in)ing Time*, exh.cat. Tate St Ives, St Ives, 2005, illus. p.47.
41. Green, *W. Barns-Graham*, pp 273–4.
42. Author's interview with Carol Robertson and Robert Adam, 29 May 2006.

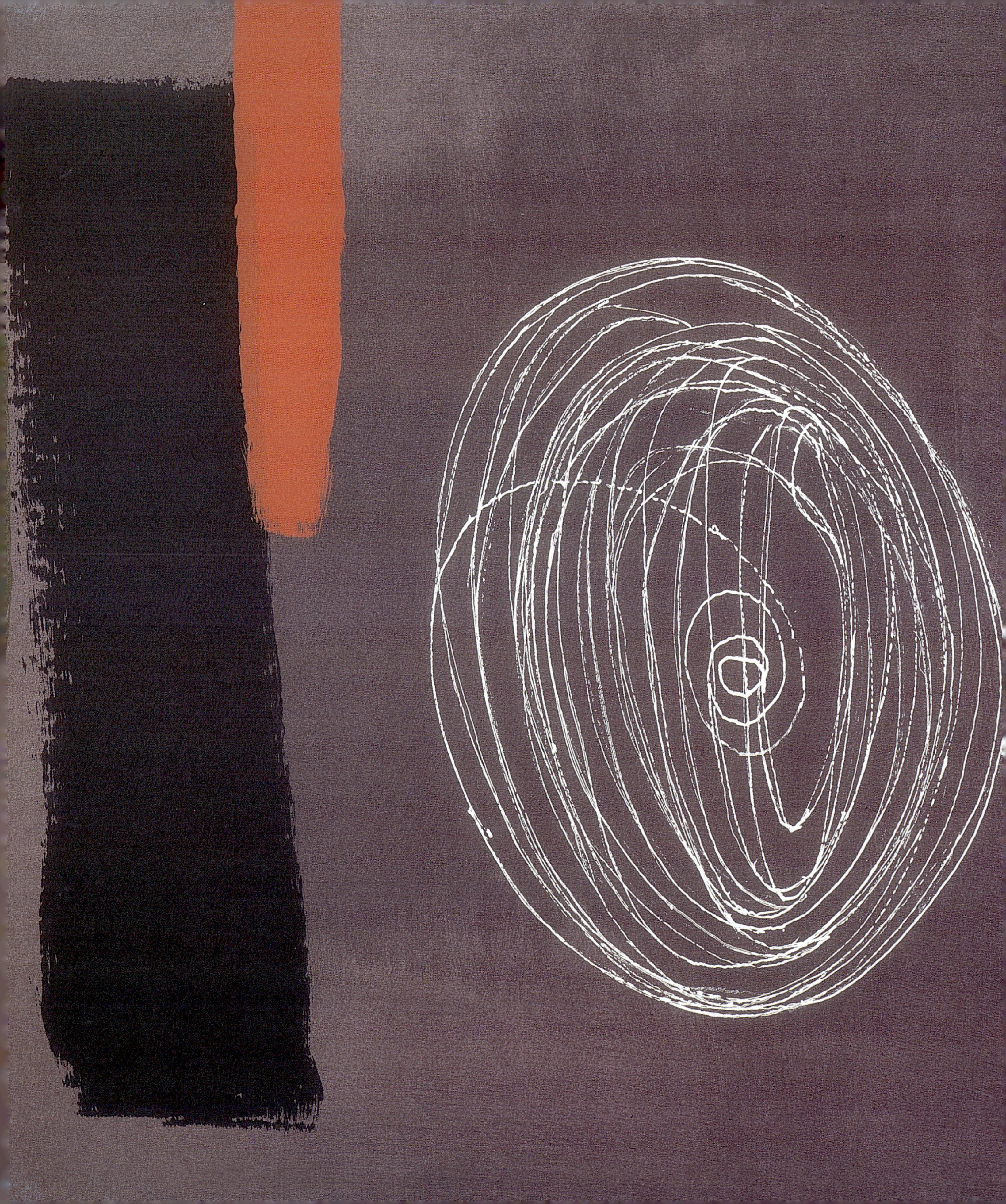

CATALOGUE OF PUBLISHED AND UNPUBLISHED PRINTS

Detail of
Walkabout Time, 1999
(cat. 85).

THE CATALOGUE IS DIVIDED INTO PUBLISHED AND UNPUBLISHED prints and, within those groups, by medium and then by date (except for the Graal Press prints). Two of the unpublished etchings have been reprinted posthumously in very small editions. So, too, has one engraving which had never been proofed and which existed only on the plate (cat.9), and one screenprint which existed in separations (cat.51).

The prints that Barns-Graham made with Graal Press are arranged alphabetically by series, preceded by single images that were not part of a series.

Details of printing plate, number of colours and separations and make of paper are included where known. Dimensions are in centimetres. The number of artist's proofs has not been included in each catalogue entry. For most of the published prints there are five artist's proofs (A/P) and usually two printer's proofs (P/P). The artist's signature has been transcribed here as she wrote it, omitting the hyphen in Barns-Graham.

The prints that were editioned posthumously are numbered in pencil, lower left, and stamped with a statement of authentication on the reverse.

UNPUBLISHED PRINTS

Cats 7, 8 and 9 have been editioned posthumously and published by the Trustees of the Barns-Graham Trust, in a small edition of 25 by Robert Adam of Graal Press.

ETCHINGS

Cat.1

Glacier, 1952

Etching

Six states

14.7 x 23.4 (plate mark)

Size of paper: various

Mounted A/P signed and dated, lower right: *W Barns Graham 1952*; lower left: *Artist's Proof*; inscribed, verso: *Print taken by Bouverie Hoyton*

One copy of State 6 inscribed, verso: *Print taken by John Wells*

One copy of State 6 inscribed, verso: *Print taken by WBG*

Penzance School of Art

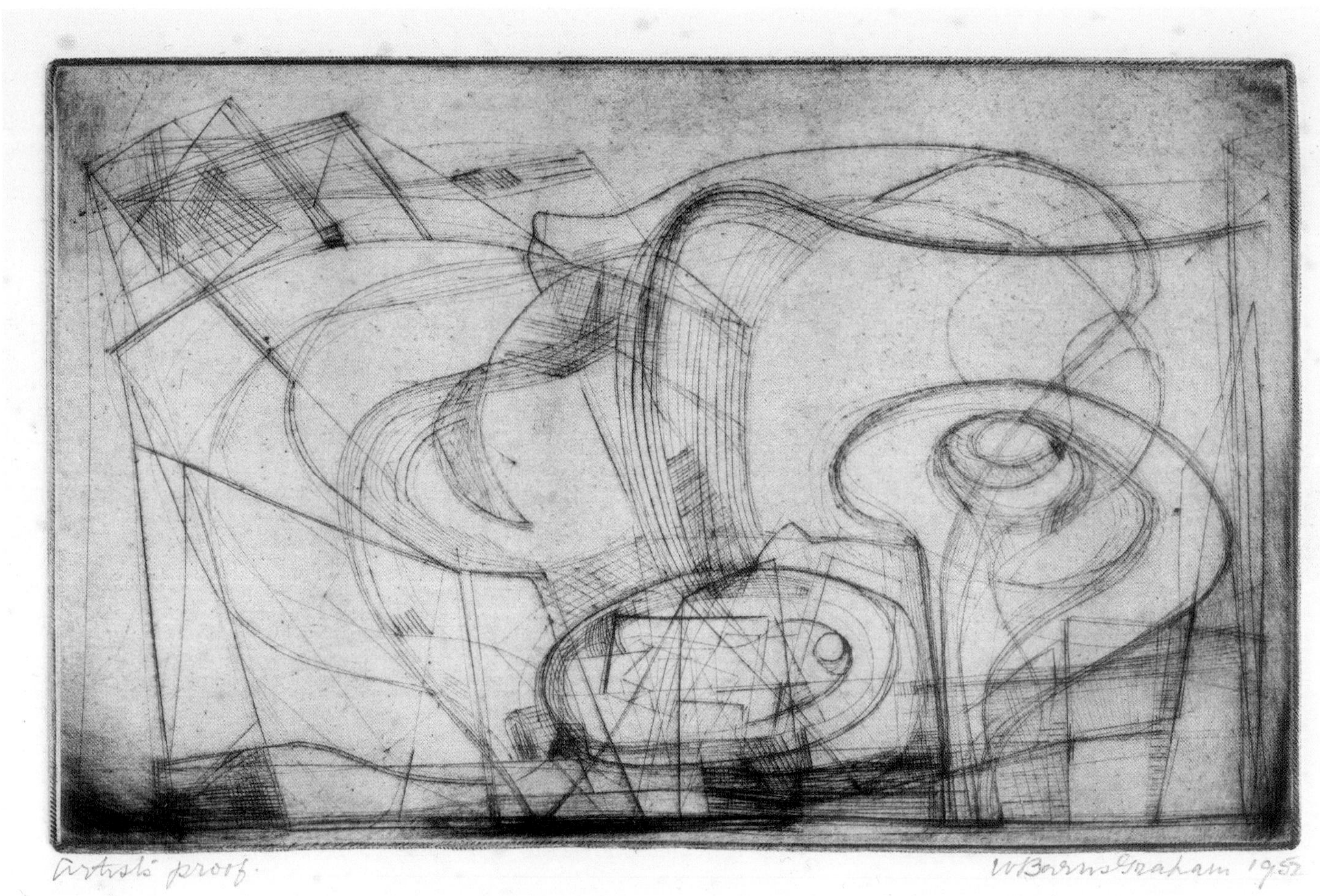

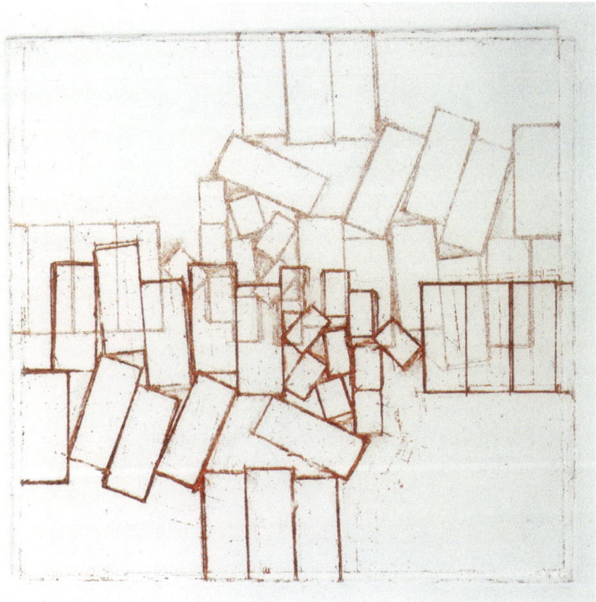

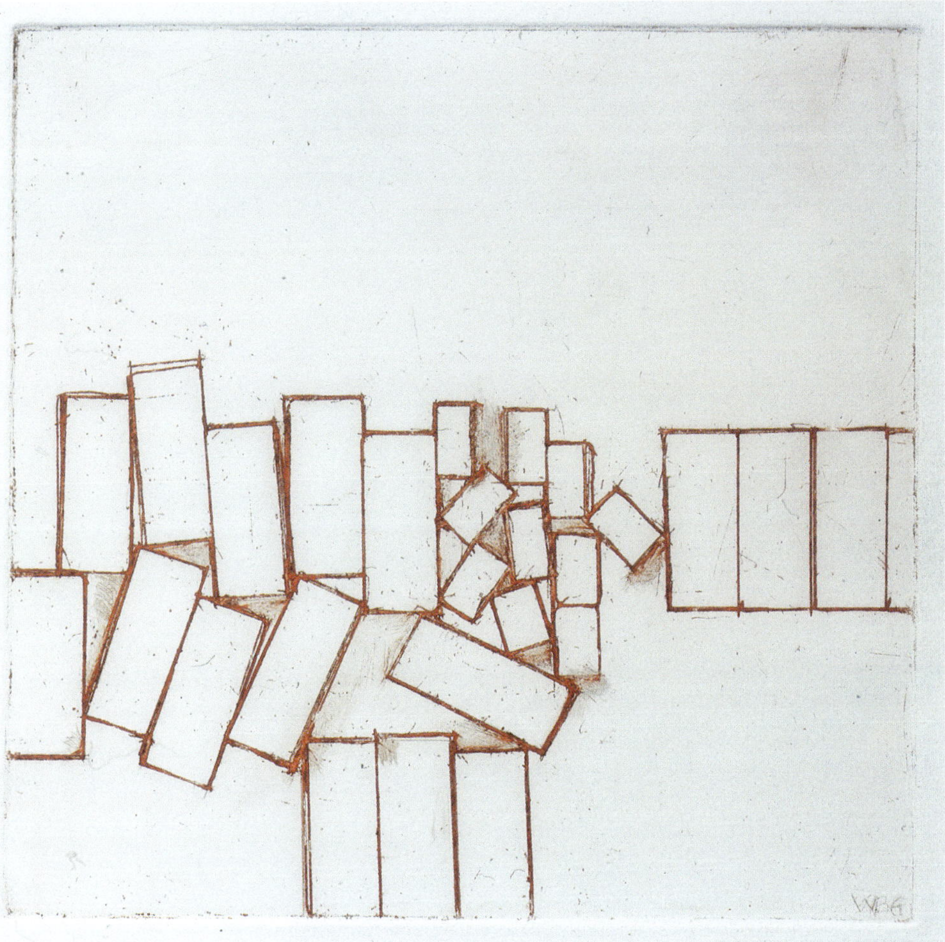

Cat.2

Untitled, 'Things of a Kind', 1971–2

Etching

Sixteen copies of an experimental print in four states, various colours, some printed as a double image, one overdrawn with red and black ballpoint pen

18.7 x 19.5 (plate mark)

Size of paper: various

States 2 onwards inscribed in plate, lower right: *WBG*

Note: The etching plate is wrapped in a newspaper dated 24 November 1971.

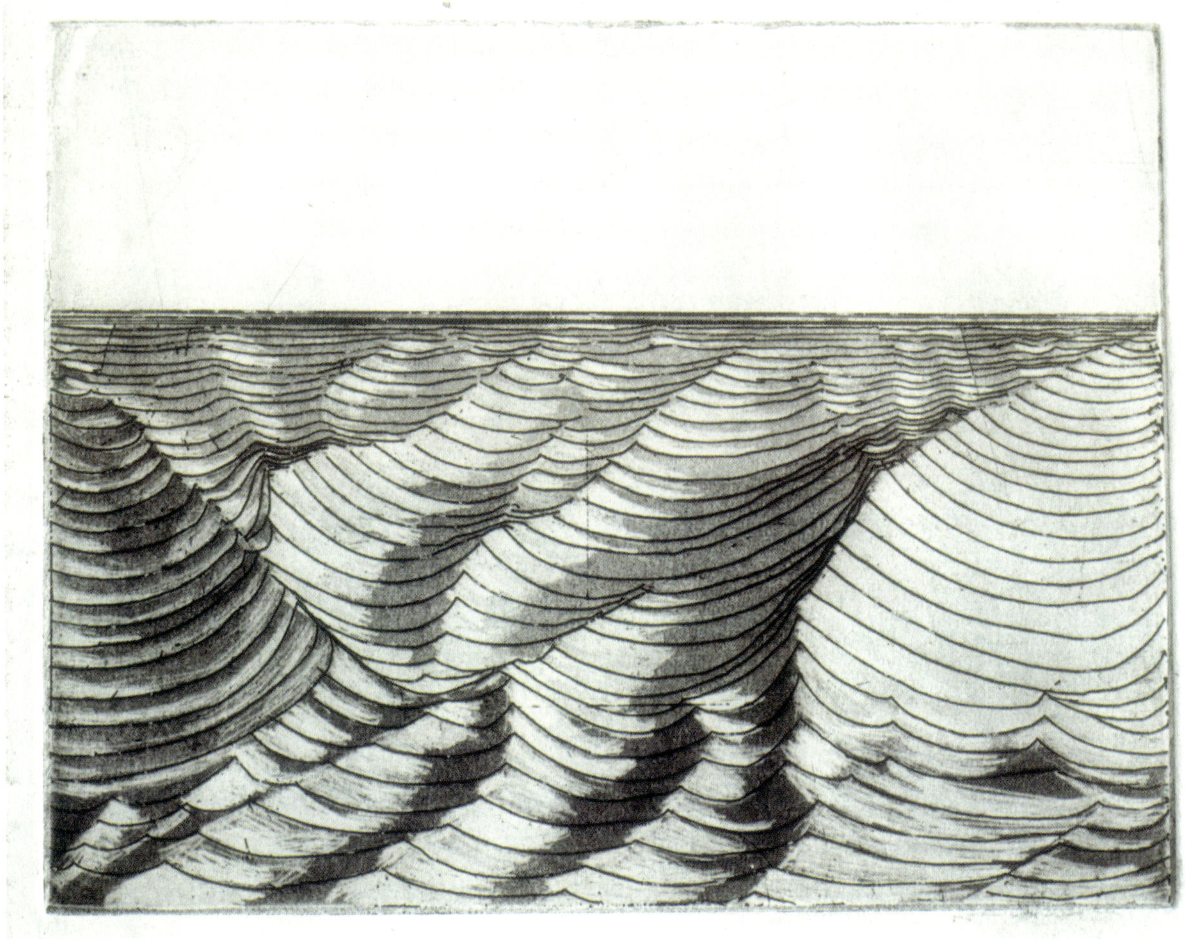

Cat.3

Wave, 1976

Etching and aquatint on zinc plate

Six states, some with aquatint ground

13.0 x 16.3 (plate mark)

Size of paper: various

One copy inscribed: *hard*

Note: Probably done at etching classes with Roy Walker at Penwith Print Workshop.

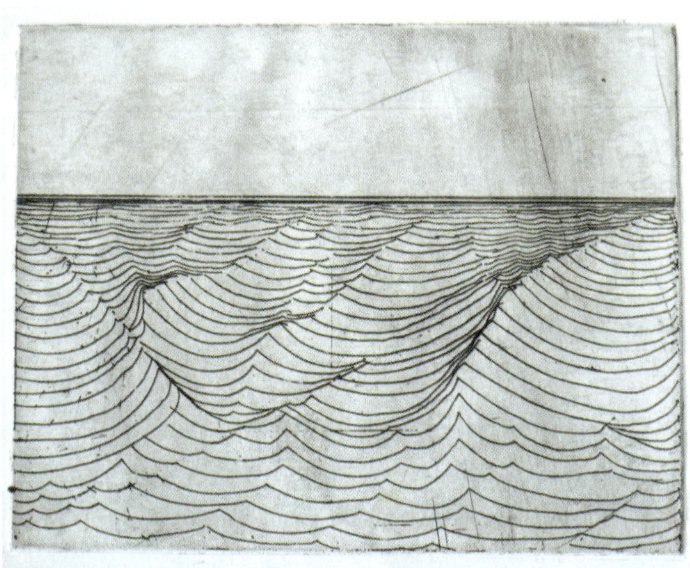

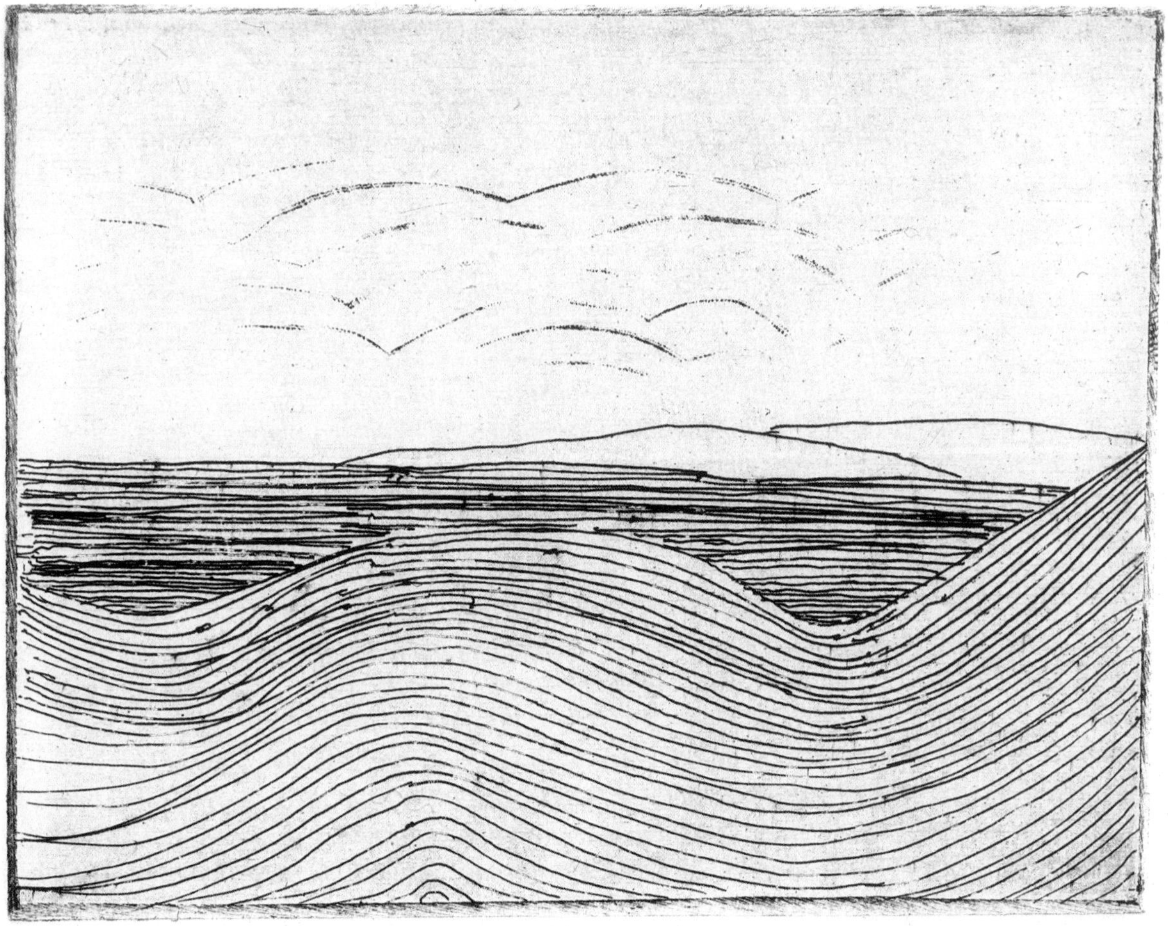

CAT.4

Small Wave, 1976

Etching

9.0 x 11.2 (plate mark)

19.5 x 26.2 (paper)

Note: Probably done at etching classes with Roy Walker at Penwith Print Workshop.

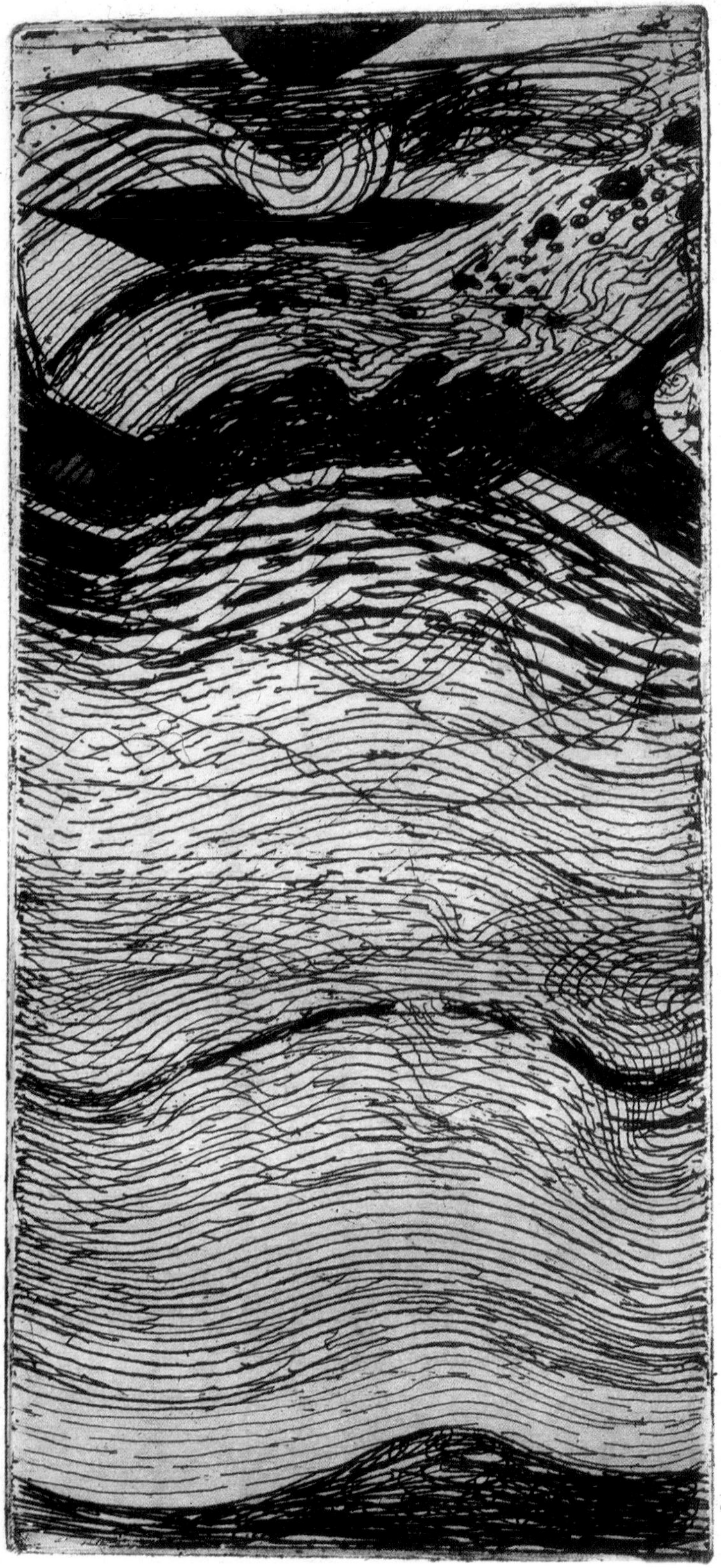

Cat.5

Wave, 1982–3

Etching and aquatint

Two states, one with lines only, one with aquatint and deeper bite

16.5 x 7.5 (plate mark)

Size of paper: various

Dundee Printmakers Workshop, Andrew Hambleton

Note: The states are not inscribed, and the print is dated from the circumstantial evidence of the plates being stored with leaflets from Dundee Printmakers Workshop, one being a membership form dated September 1982 – August 1983, and the other a page about the etching course and how to prepare a plate.

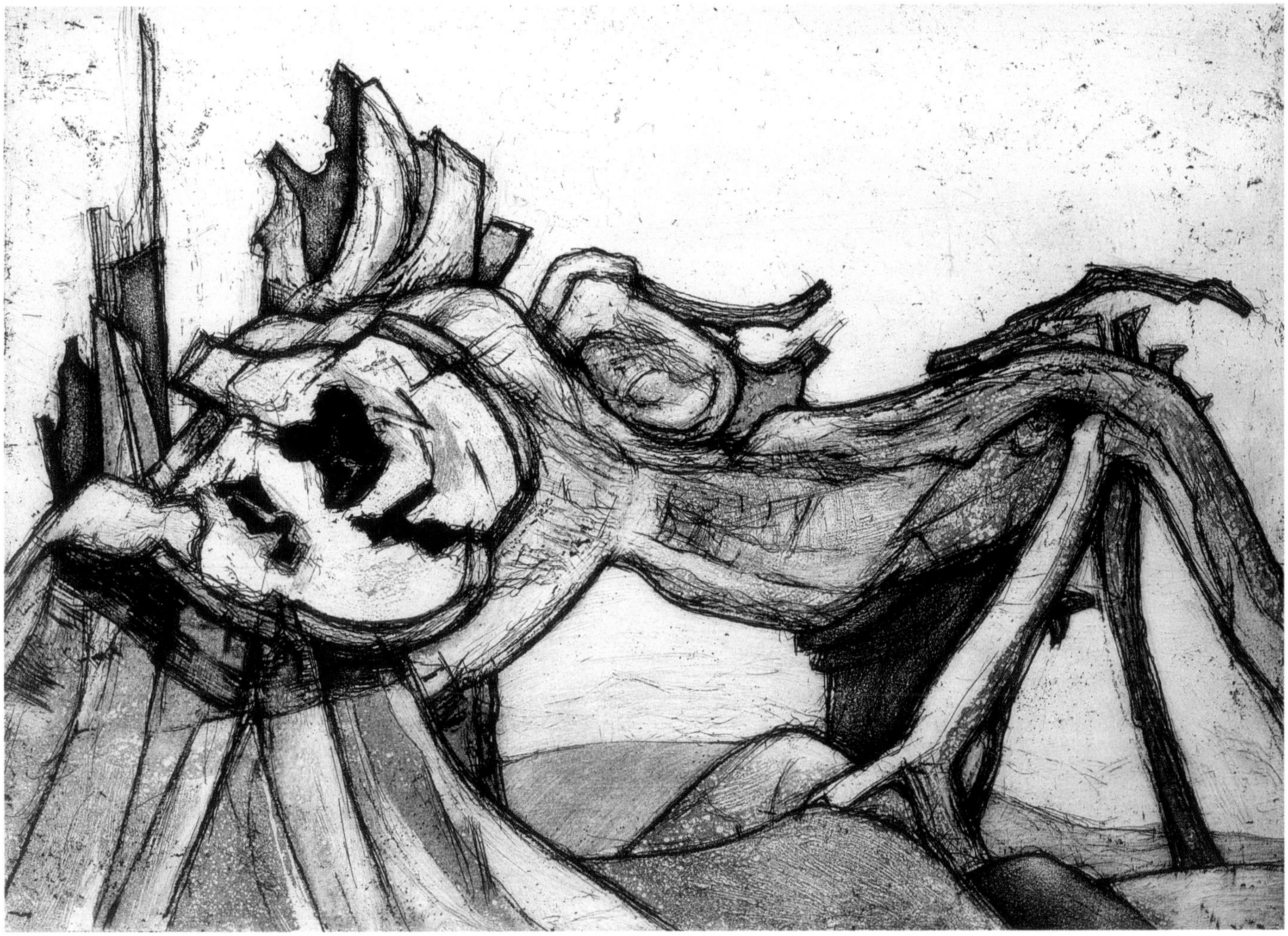

Cat.6

Tree Freak (Small), 1982

Etching and aquatint

Thirteen states, some with aquatint, some with overpaint

21.8 x 29.9 (plate mark)

38.7 x 51.8 (paper size)

Each state inscribed with state number, lower left, for example: *Stage 13*

Dundee Printmakers Workshop, Andrew Hambleton

Lit.ref.: Sheila Oliner, 'It's a beginning', *Printmaking Today*, vol.3, no.4 (Winter 1994), pp 8–9

Note: Based on a drawing made in 1979.

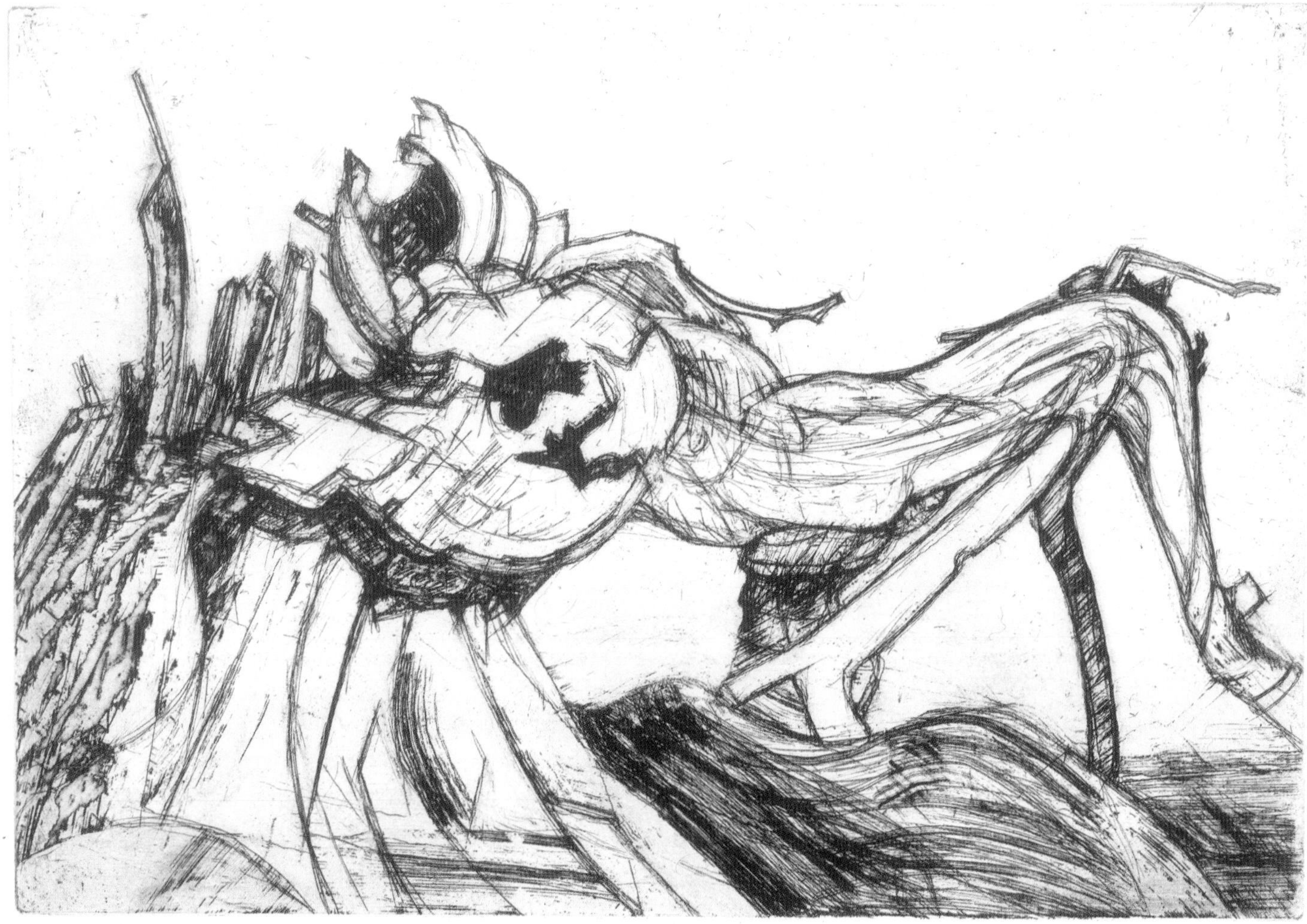

Cat.7

Tree Freak, 1982

Etching

Eight states

27.3 x 38.7 (plate mark)

38.2 x 51.8 (paper size)

Each state inscribed with state number, lower left, for example: STAGE I

Dundee Printmakers Workshop, Andrew Hambleton

Note: Edition of 25 editioned posthumously in 2006 by Robert Adam at Graal Press on Arches Velin Blanc 400gsm, 58.0 x 76.0.

Cat.8

Fish and Circles, date unknown, possibly 1982

Etching

Nine states including one consisting solely of an open-bitten circle, printed in orange ink

27.0 x 34.9 (plate mark)

Size of paper: various

Note: Edition of 25 editioned posthumously in 2006 by Robert Adam at Graal Press on Arches Velin Blanc 400gsm, 58.0 x 76.0.

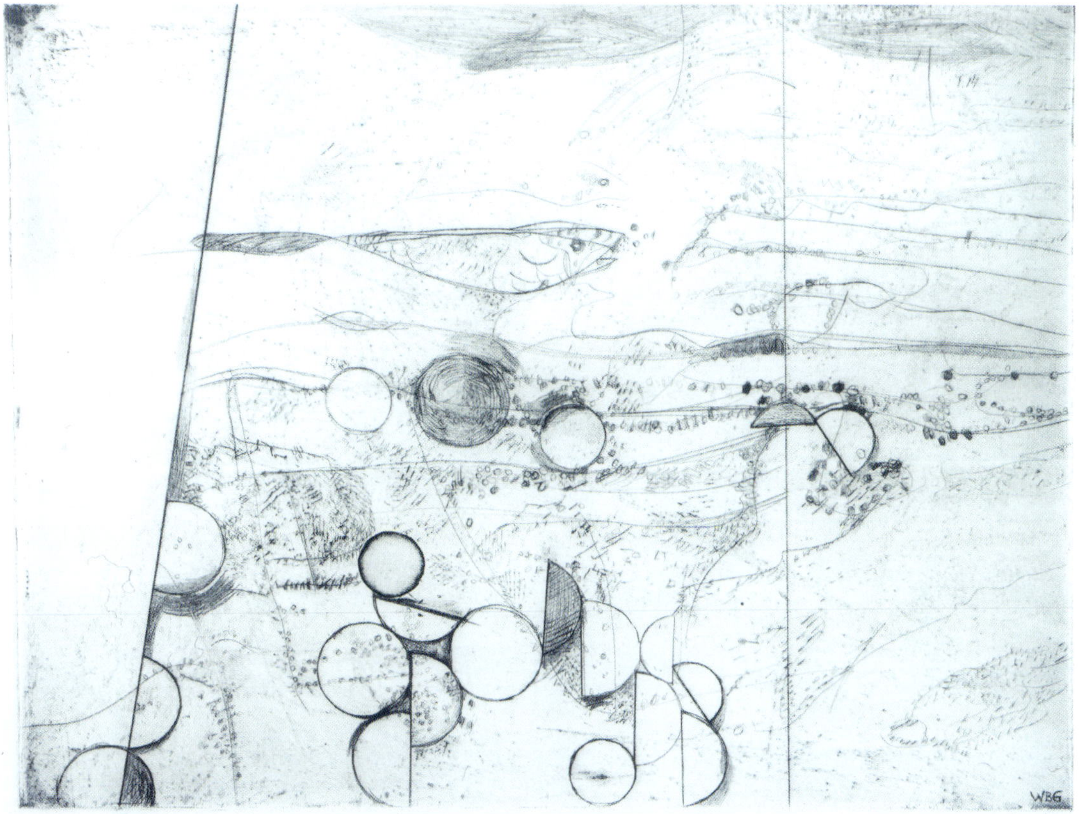

Cat.9

Landscape, date unknown

Engraving on plastic sheet

24.0 x 39.2 (plate mark)

58.0 x 76.0 (paper size)

Arches Velin Blanc 400gsm

Note: This was never printed even as a proof during Barns-Graham's lifetime. Edition of 25 editioned posthumously in 2006 by Robert Adam at Graal Press.

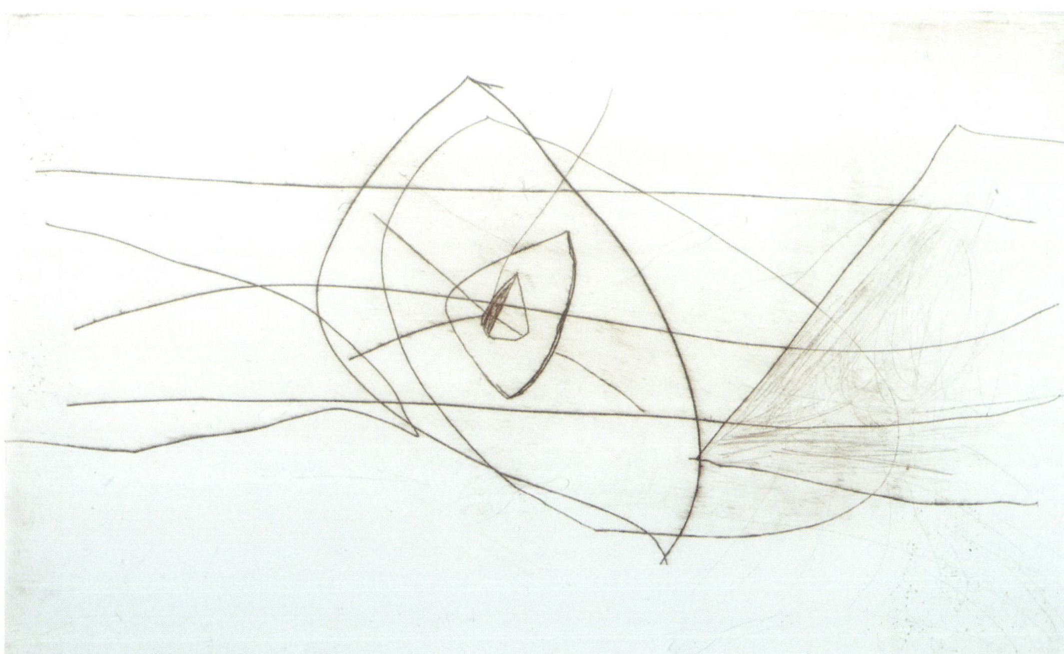

LITHOGRAPHS

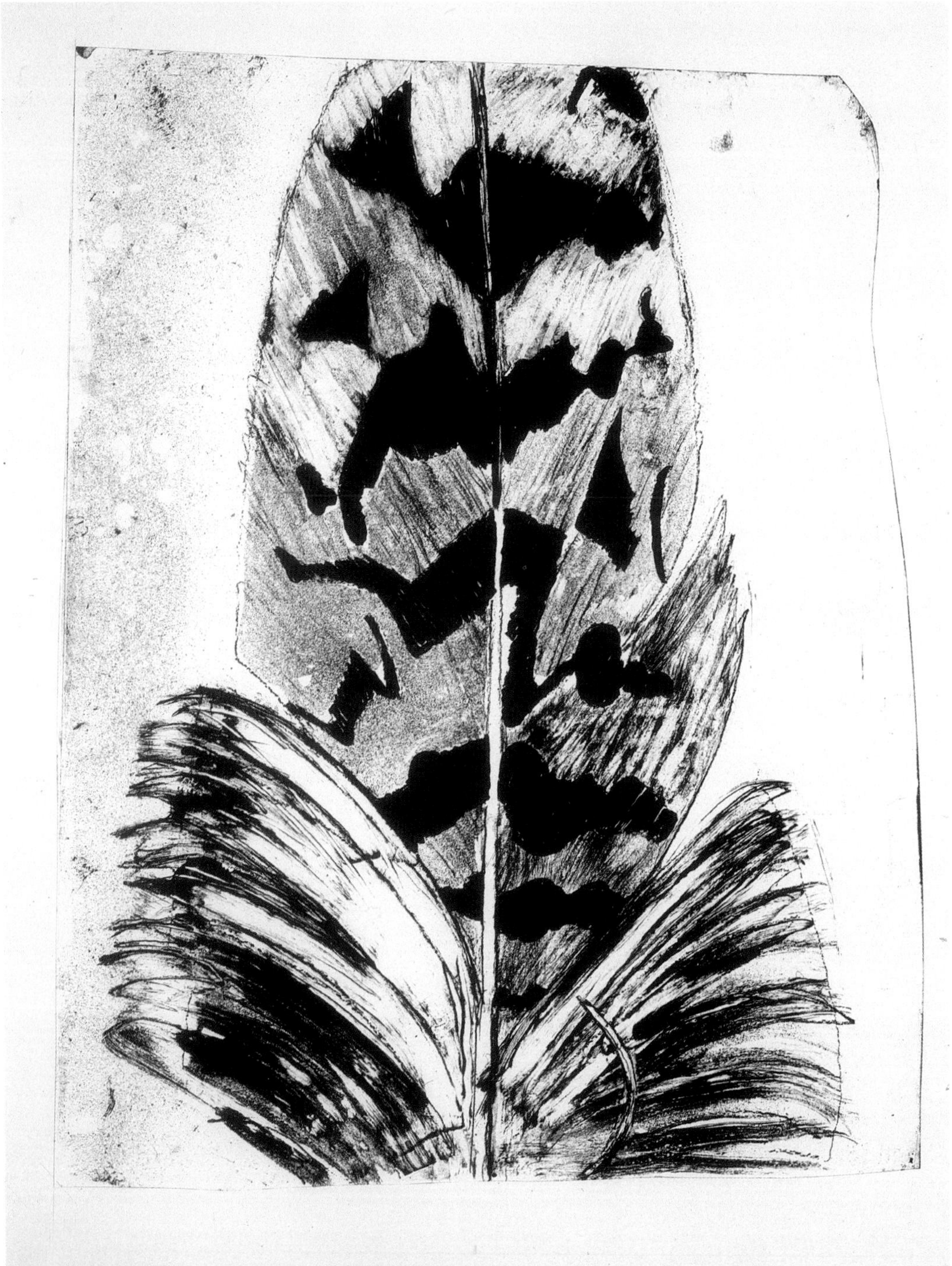

Cat.10

Gull Feather, 1992

Lithograph

54.0 x 42.0 (image size, irregular)

74.0 x 54.8 (paper size)

Various trial proofs printed in black or brown or both

Serena Castle, Curwen Chilford Studio

Note: Not signed or dated, proofs printed on verso of another artist's print.

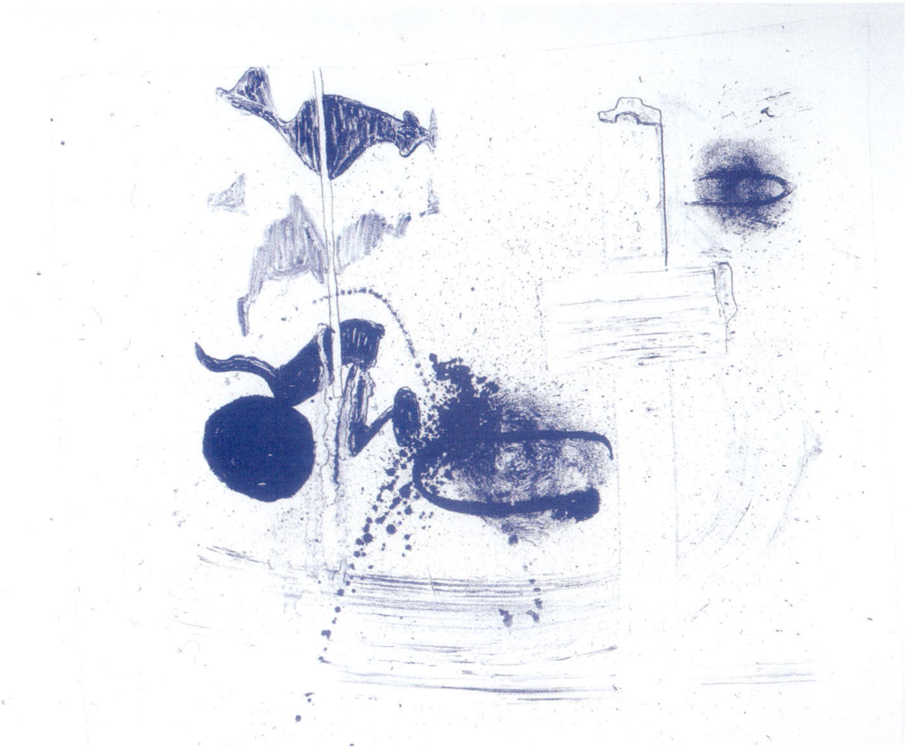

Cat.11

Goat Series, 1992

Lithograph

65.5 x 56.3 (image size, irregular)

83.3 x 64.5 (paper size)

Arches Velin Blanc

Printer or press: Serena Castle, Curwen Chilford Studio

Note: Two designs were printed as one in error. Several trial proofs exist with inscriptions relating to colours. Some were used as a basis for mixed-media paintings, *Goat Series I* and *Goat Series II*.

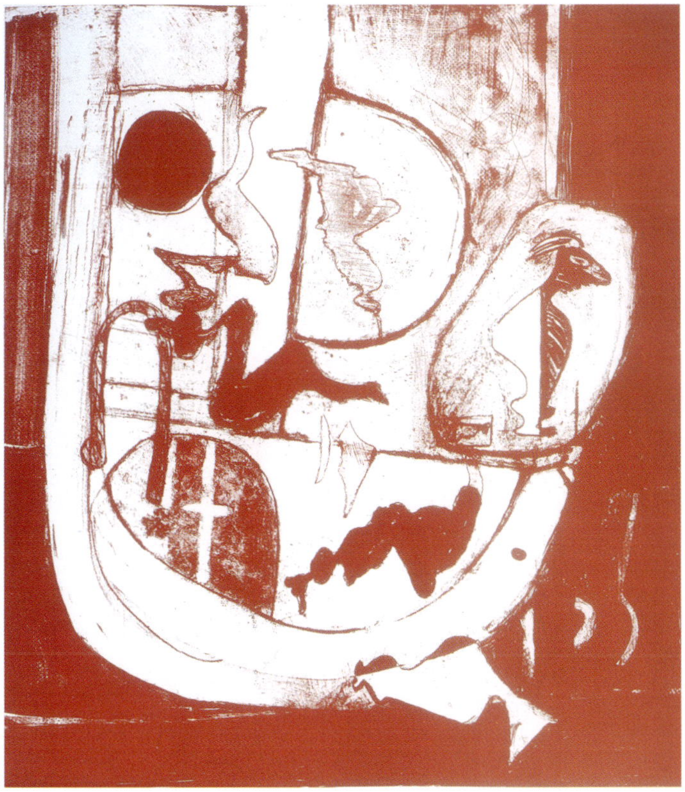

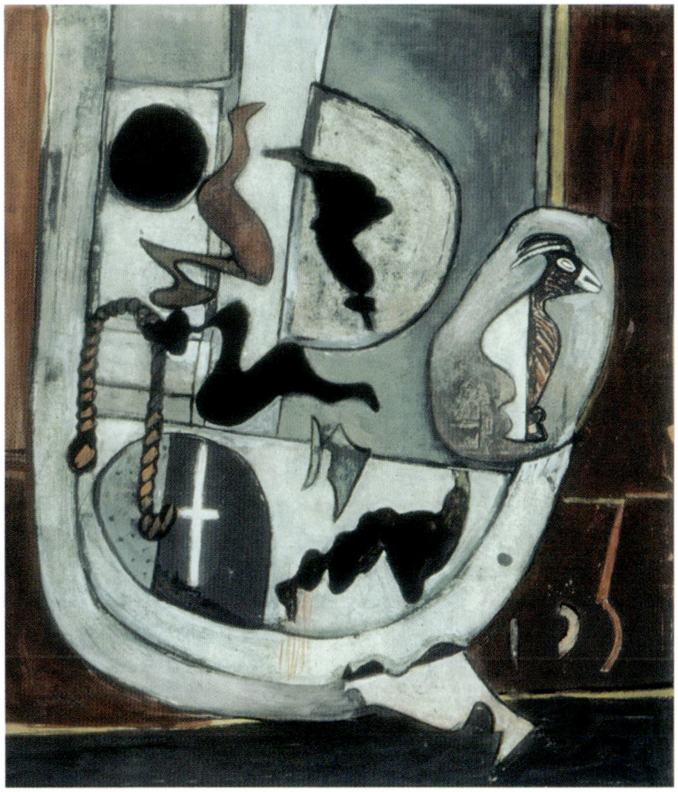

PUBLISHED PRINTS

LINOCUTS

These linocuts were not published in numbered editions but they are included amongst the published prints as they were distributed, some probably as Christmas cards, and copies of *Night in Venice* were mounted for exhibition.

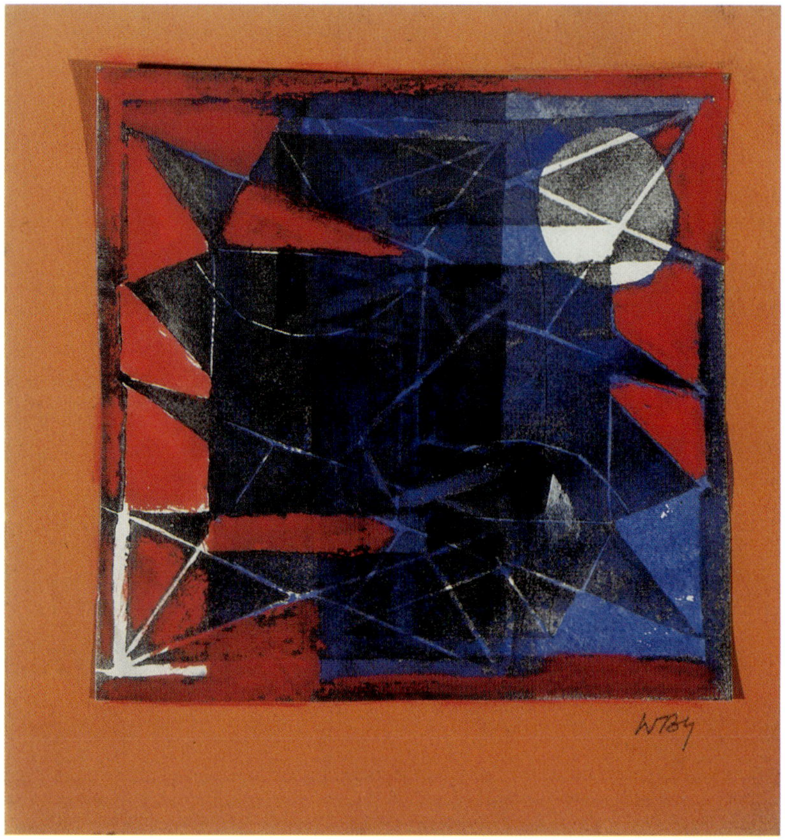

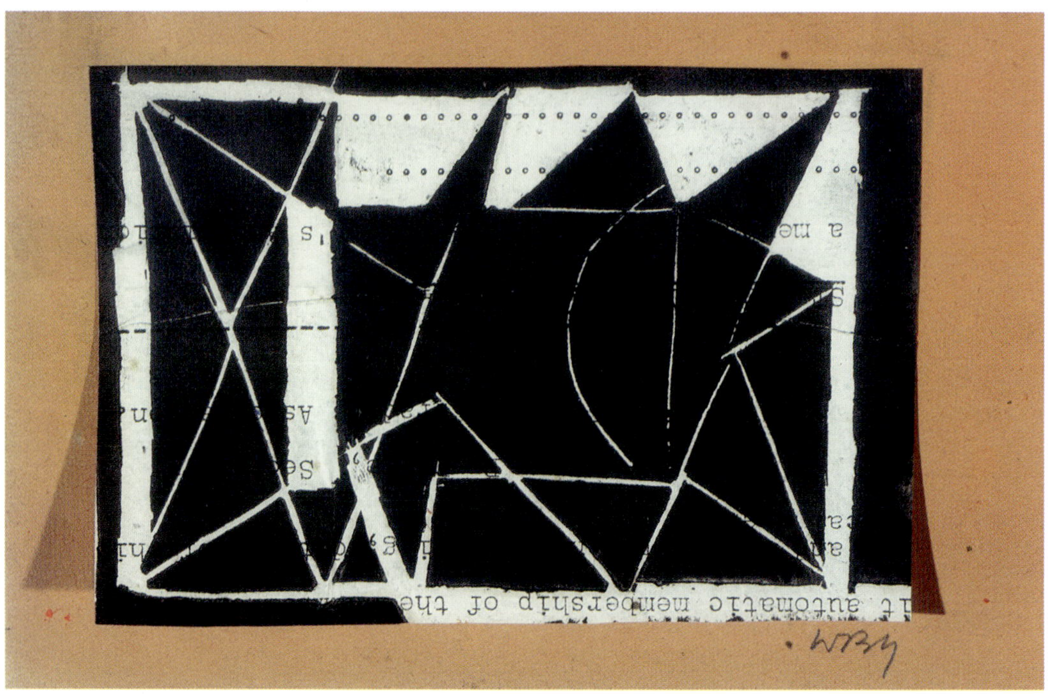

CAT.12

Rock Forms, 1953

Linocut, black ink with hand-colouring

8.6 x 12.5 (image)

Size of paper: various

One copy signed lower right: *WBG*; a second copy signed and dated: *W Barns Graham 1953*

Note: The archive contains four versions mounted on folded card, some with hand-painting, one doubled image and one printed on a typed form.

Cat.13

Rock Forms, 1953

Linocut, black ink with hand-colouring

14.5 x 19.8 (image)

Size of paper: various

One copy signed and dated: *W Barns Graham 1953*; a second copy inscribed: *Rock Forms*

Note: The archive contains three versions, one as a single image, one printed double one way, one printed double in the opposite direction. Some are mounted on grey card.

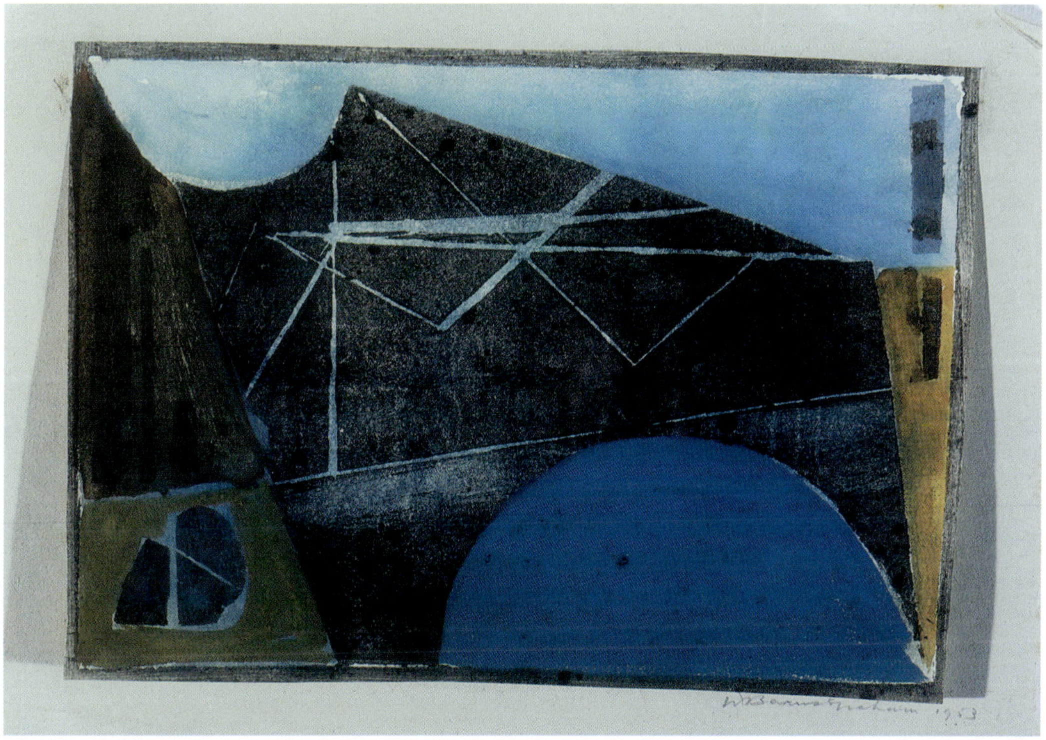

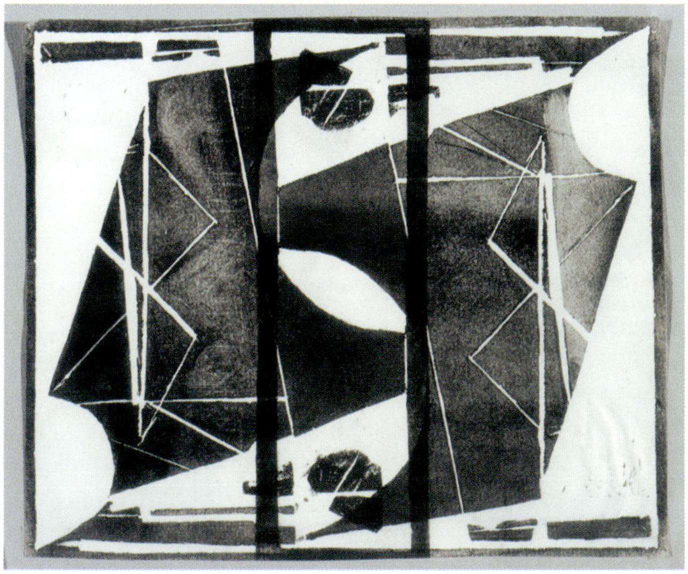

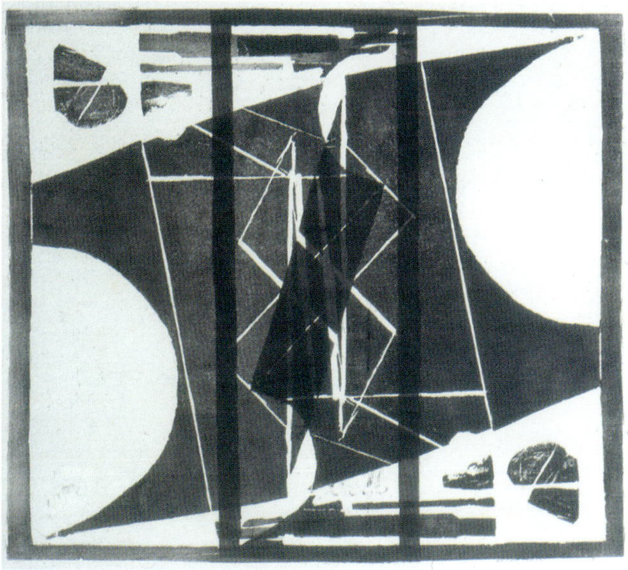

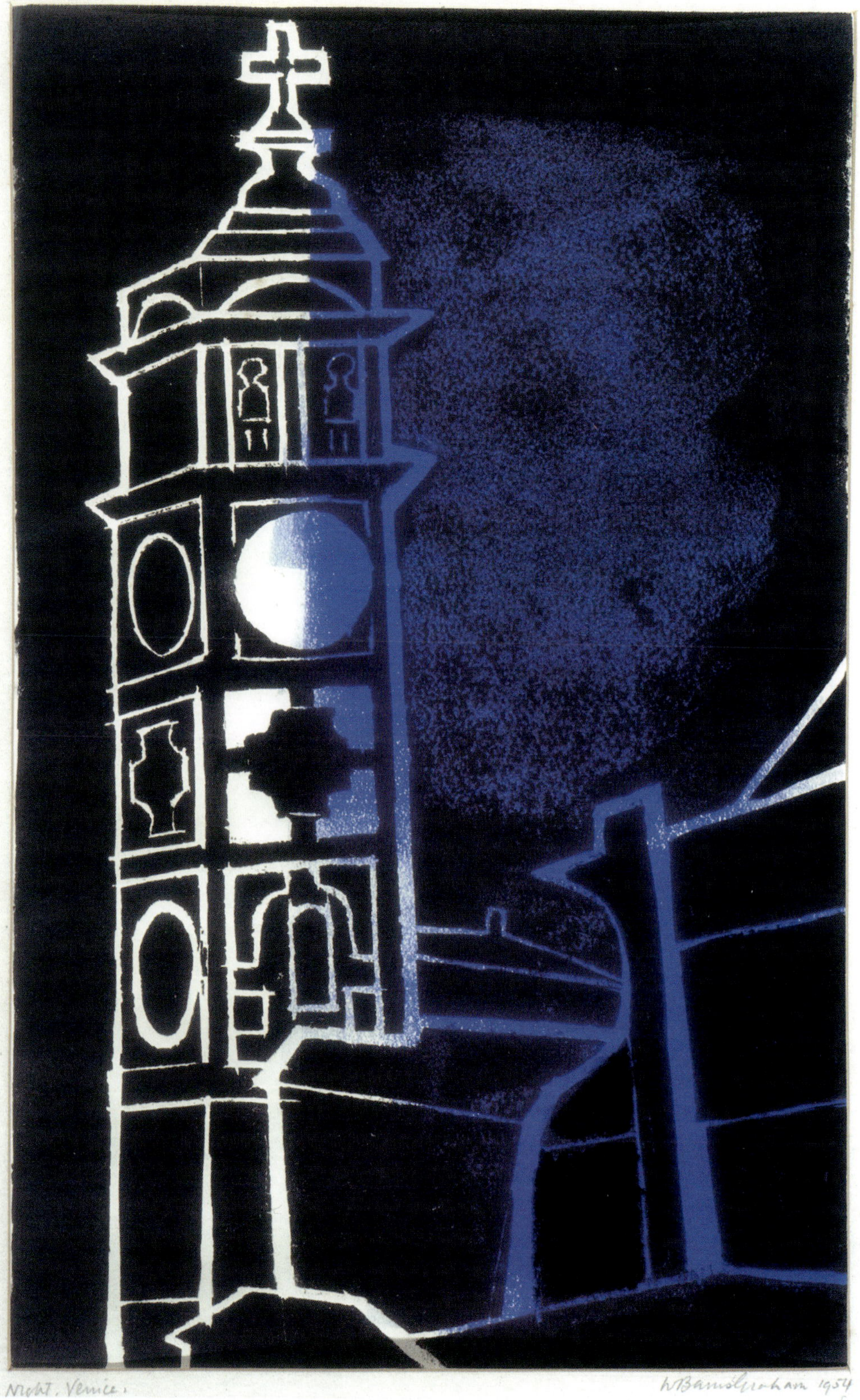

Cat.14

Night in Venice, 1954

Linocut, black ink with hand-colouring

30.3 x 18.6 (image)

Size of paper: various

Signed and dated, lower right, on mount: *W Barns Graham 1954*; lower left: *Night in Venice*

Note: The archive contains ten versions, some uncoloured, some with blue and some with brown hand-colouring.

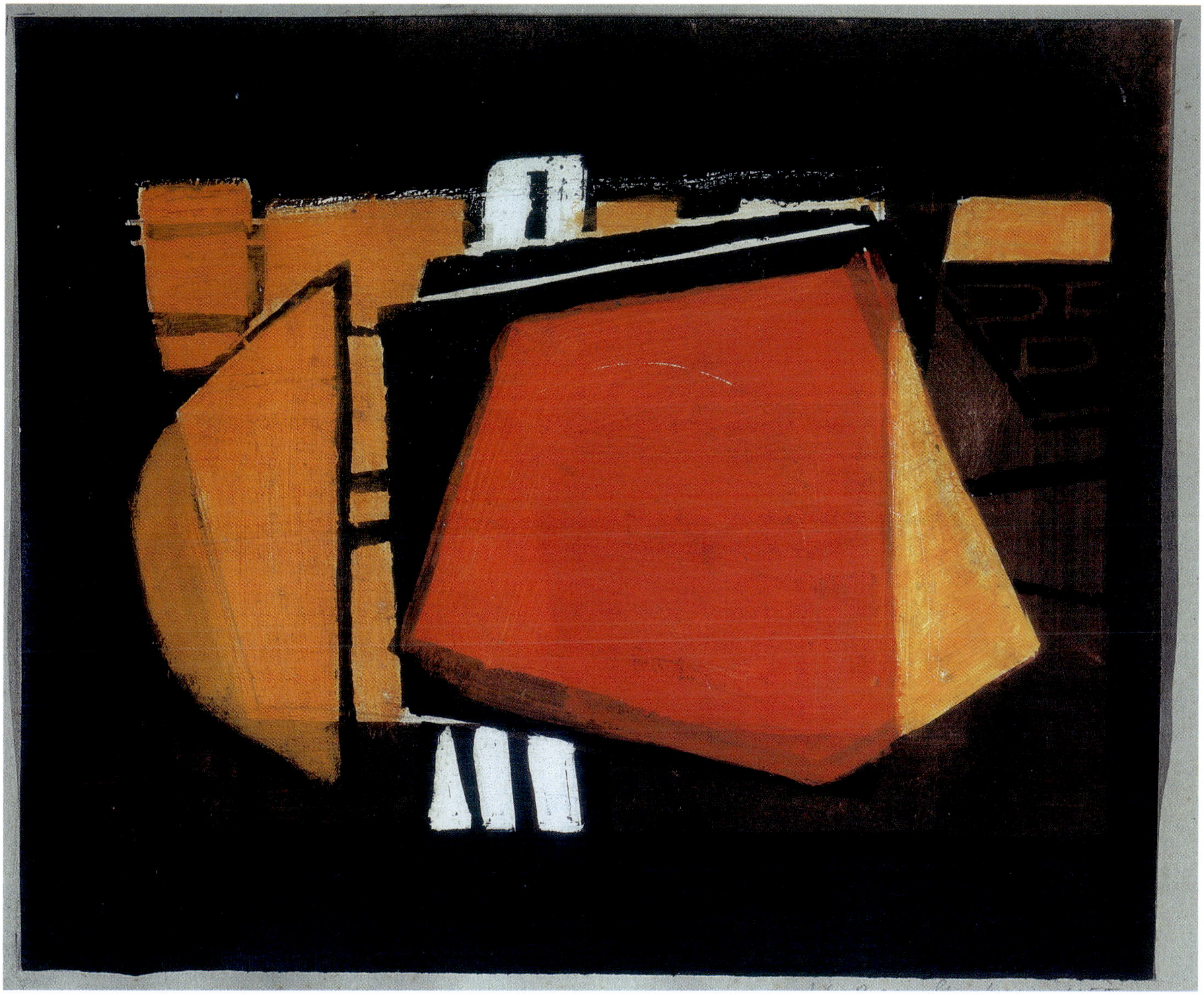

Cat.15

Untitled Abstract, 1955

Linocut, black ink with additional hand-colouring

19.1 x 22.5 (paper size, trimmed to edge of image)

Signed and dated, lower right: *W. Barns Graham 1955*

Note: Only one print exists in the archive. The design is based on the *Geoff and Scruffy Series* of paintings dating from 1954 to 1956.

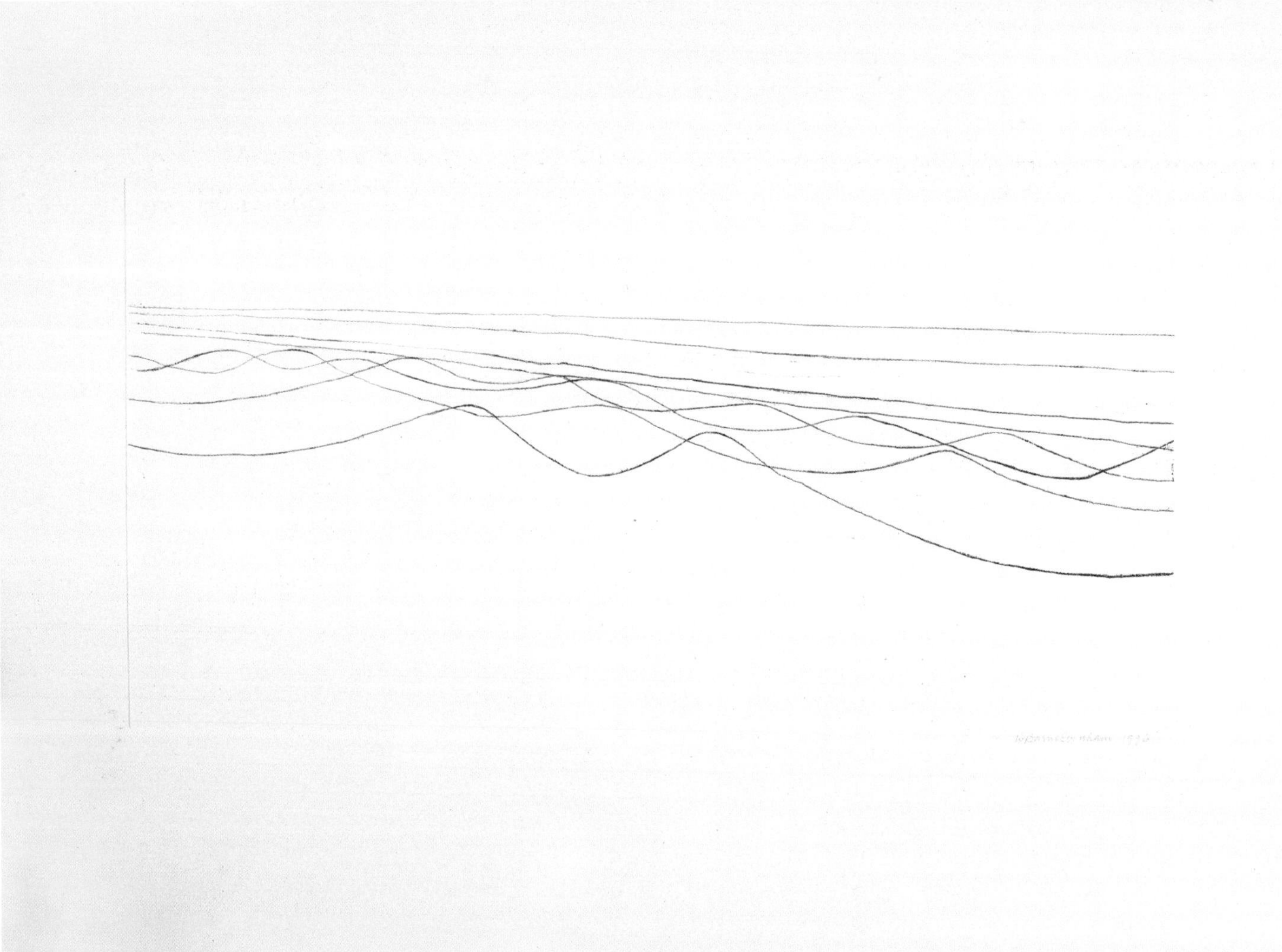

ETCHINGS

Cat.16

Eight Lines I, 1996

Soft-ground etching on copper plate

32.0 x 60.6 (plate mark)

57.5 x 75.5 (paper size)

Signed and dated, lower right: *W Barns-Graham 1996*; numbered, lower left

Edition of 25. Rachael Kantaris, Porthmeor Printmakers, St Ives

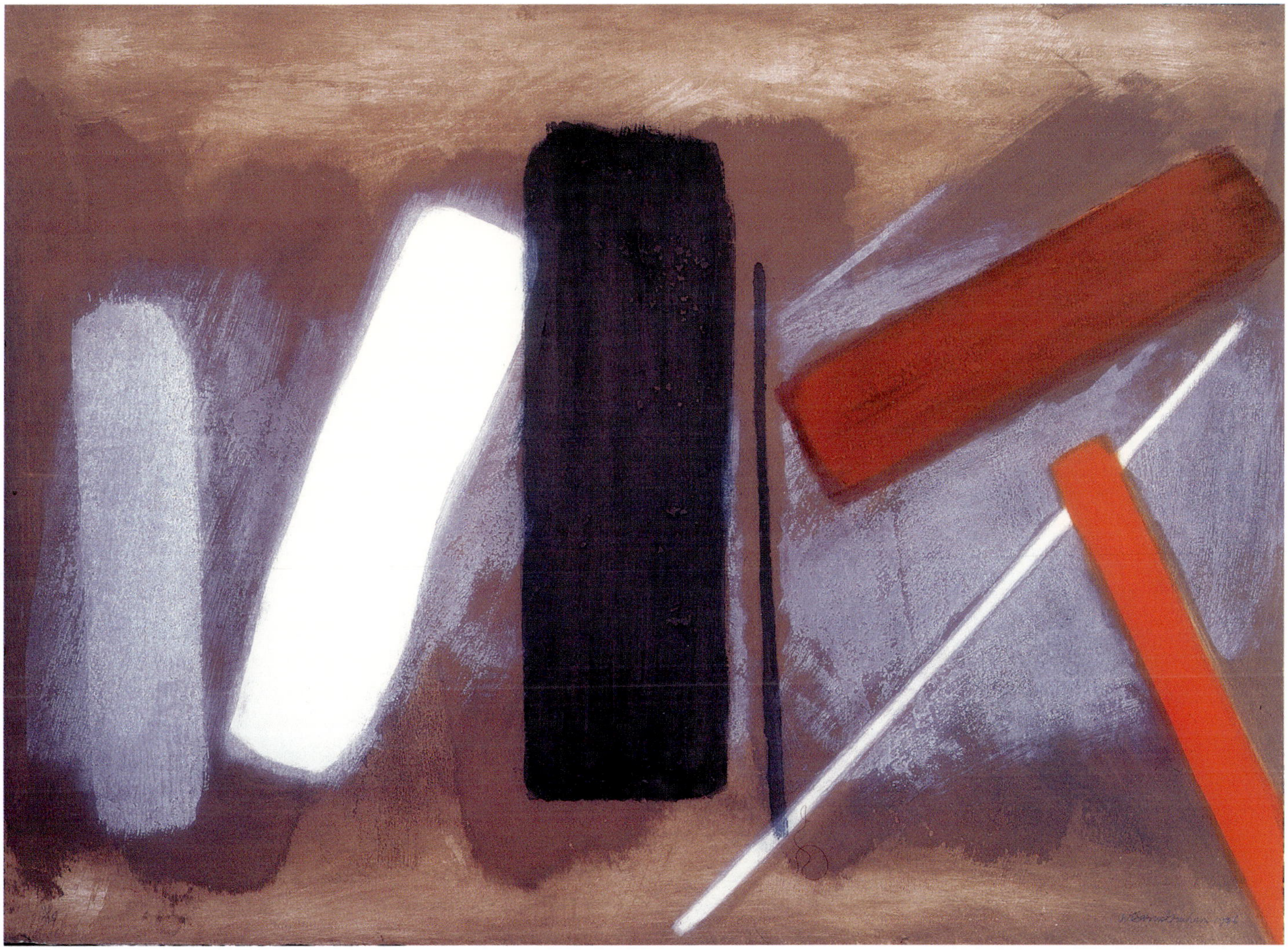

Cat.17

Scorpio I, 1996

Sugar-lift etching and aquatint, five colours on three steel plates

56.0 x 76.0 (image and paper size)

Signed and dated, lower right: *W Barns Graham 1996*; numbered, lower left

Edition of 25. Rachael Kantaris, Porthmeor Printmakers, St Ives

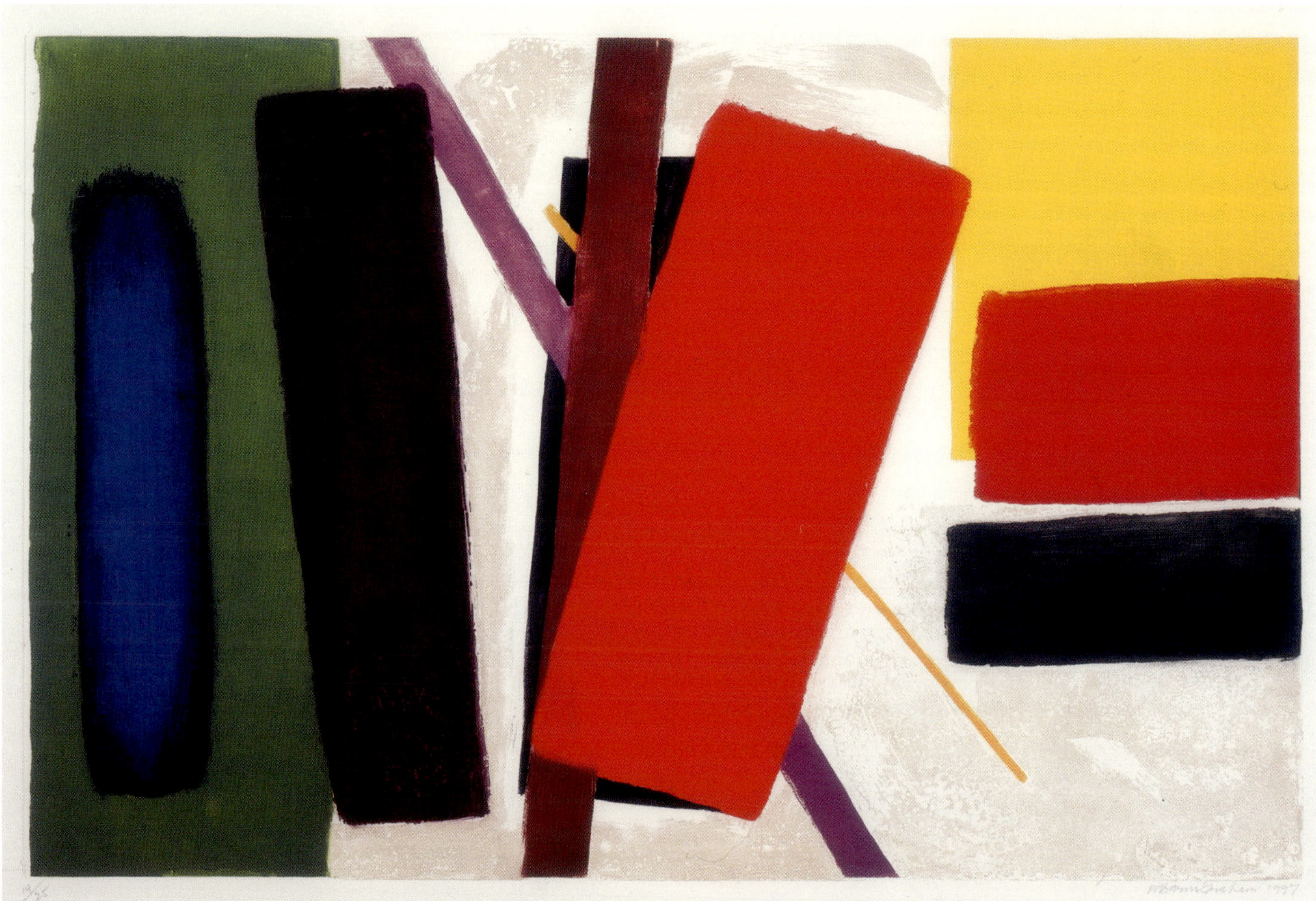

Cat.18

Scorpio II, 1997

Sugar-lift aquatint, ten colours on three copper plates

40.0 x 60.0 (plate mark)

57.0 x 75.0 (paper size)

Signed and dated, lower right: *W Barns Graham 1997*; numbered, lower left

Edition of 25. Rachael Kantaris, Porthmeor Printmakers, St Ives

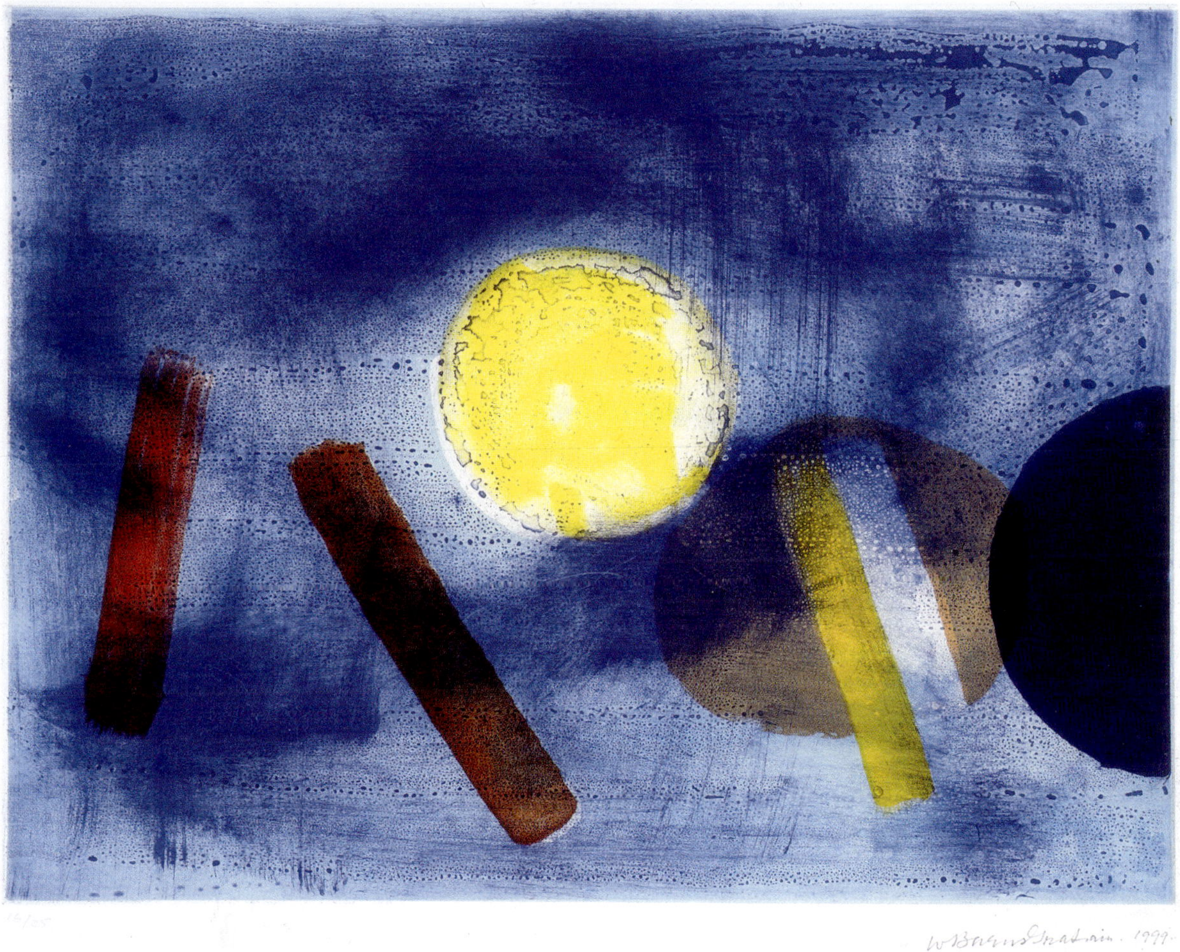

Cat.19

Eclipse, 1999

Colour etching

28.7 x 36.9 (plate mark)

55.8 x 65.5 (paper size)

Signed and dated, lower right: *W Barns Graham* 1999; numbered, lower left

Edition of 25. Hugh Stoneman, Stoneman Graphics, Madron, Penzance

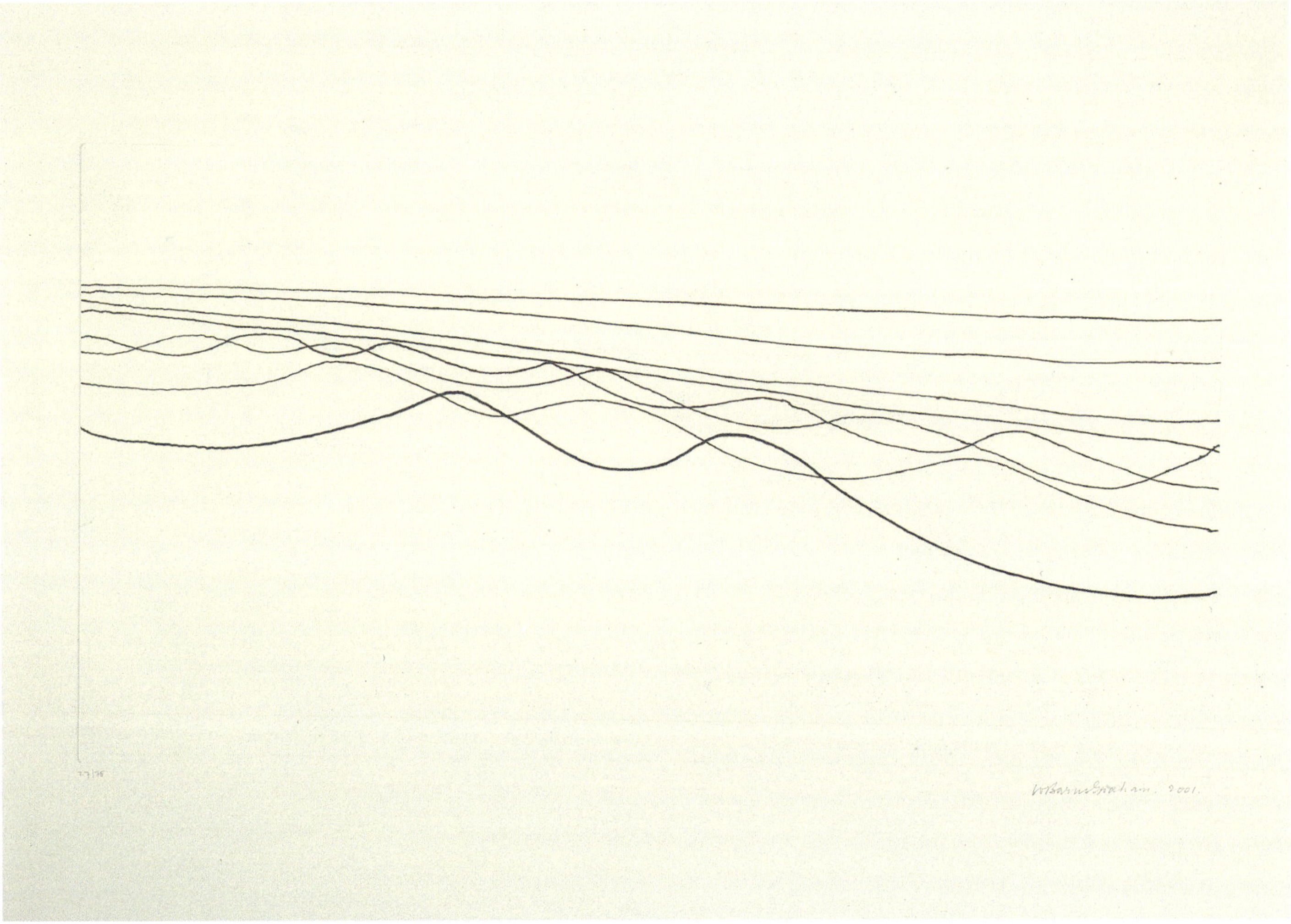

Cat.20

Eight Lines II, 2001

Etching

33.2 x 61.0 (plate mark)

57.5 x 76.0 (paper size)

Signed and dated, lower right: *W Barns Graham 2001*; numbered, lower left

Edition of 75. Robert Adam, Graal Press

Note: Barns-Graham wanted this print to be completely white except for the black lines, an effect very hard to achieve with conventional oil-based printing inks. A special water-based intaglio ink was hand-made for this edition incorporating acrylic painting aids.

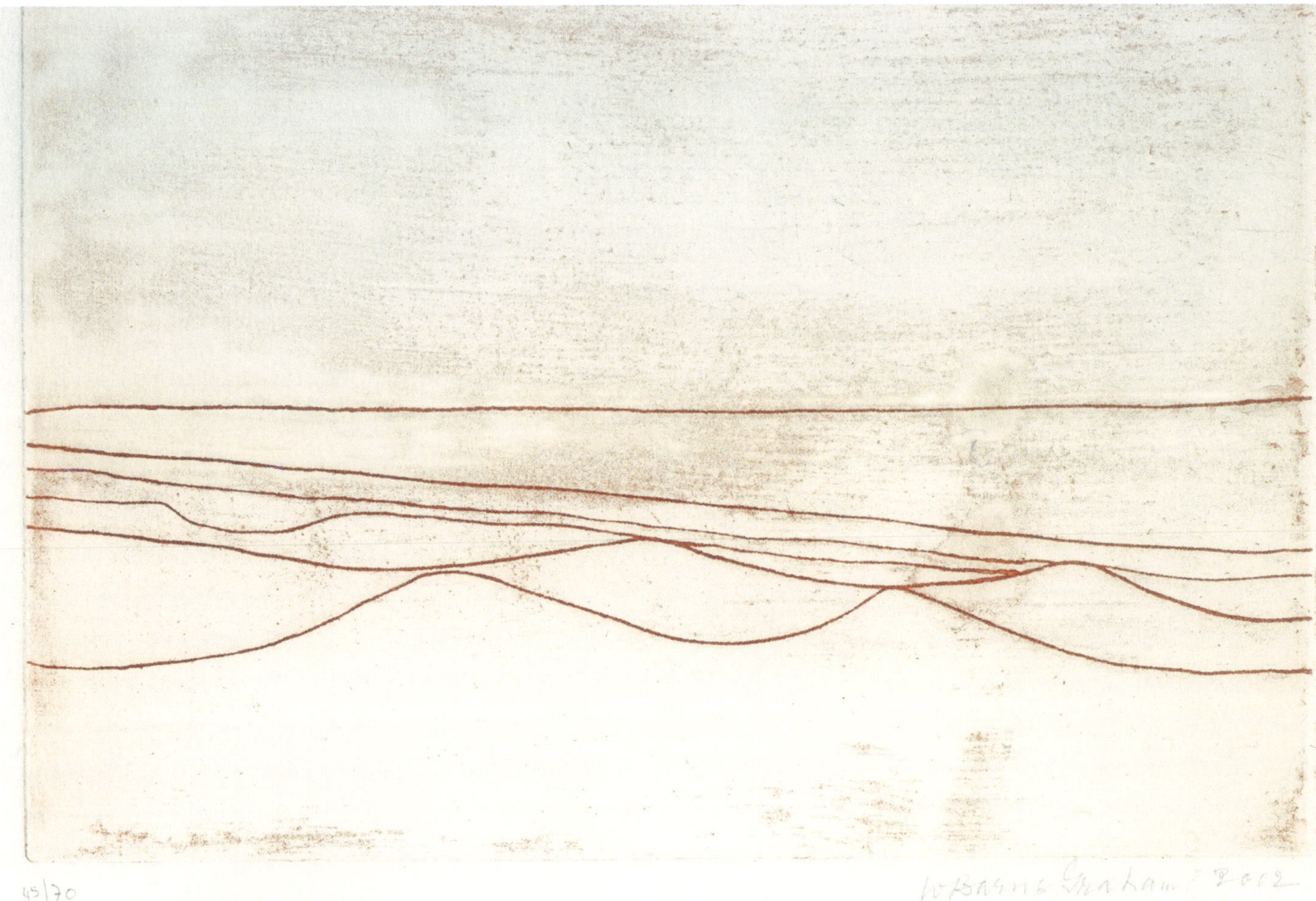

Cat.21

Six Lines, 2002

Etching, printed in sanguine

19.7 x 27.0 (plate mark)

37.7 x 57.6 (paper size)

Signed and dated, lower right: *W Barns Graham 2002*; numbered, lower left

Edition of 70. Robert Adam, Graal Press

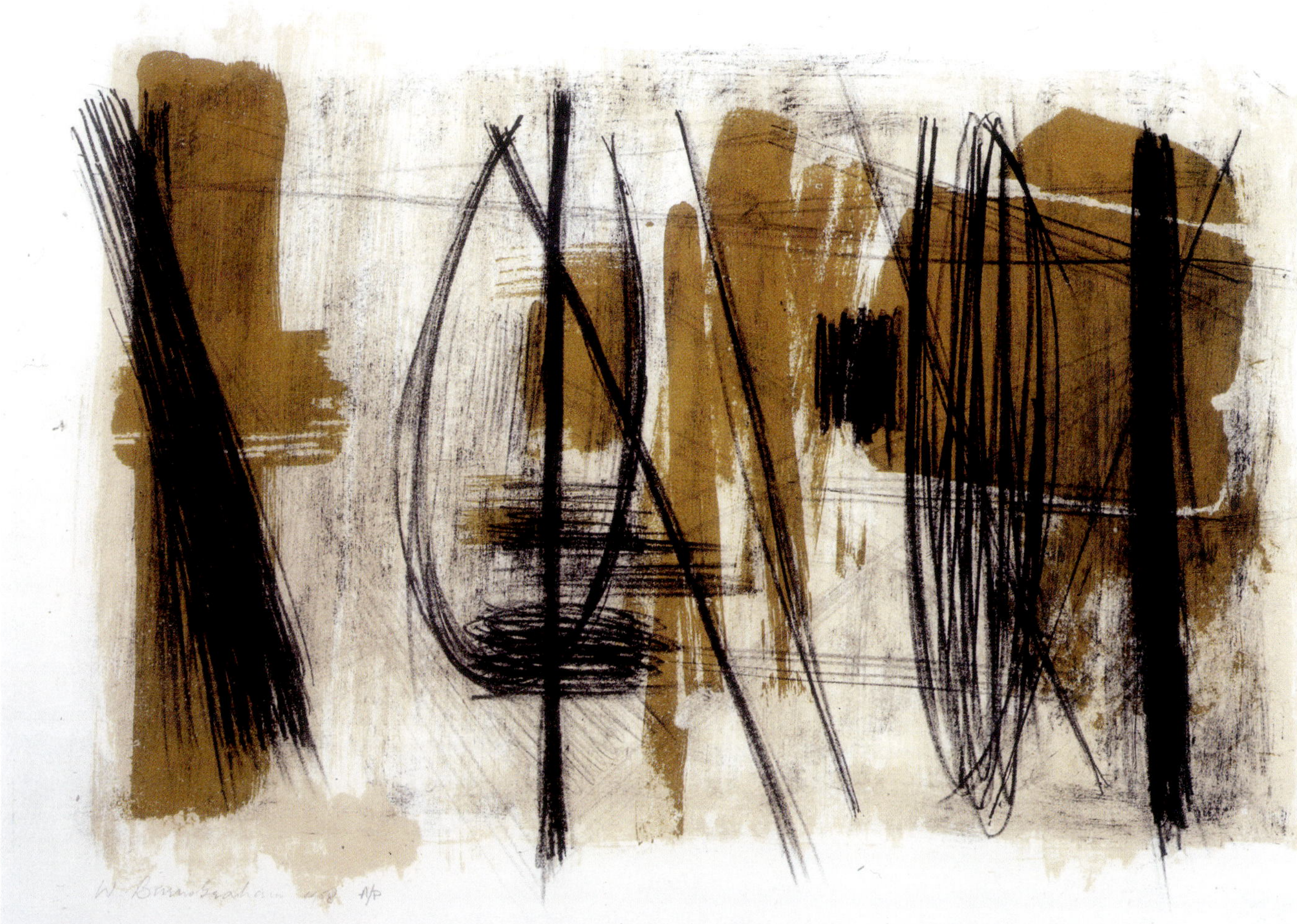

LITHOGRAPHS

Cat.22

***Linear Abstract*, 1958**

Lithograph

51.5 x 63.5 (paper size)

Signed and dated, lower left: *W Barns Graham 1958*; numbered, lower right

Edition of 30. Stanley Jones, Curwen Press in St Ives 1958

Lit.ref.: Lynne Green, *W. Barns-Graham: A Studio Life* (Lund Humphries, 2001), p.170, fig.92

Note: The title *Linear Abstract* seems to have been given by the Tate Gallery when the museum bought a copy in 1992. In Lynne Green's *W. Barns-Graham: A Studio Life* it is called *Untitled*; in the Government Art Collection it is *Brown and Yellow*; and in Rowan James's inventory it is *Brown and Tan*.

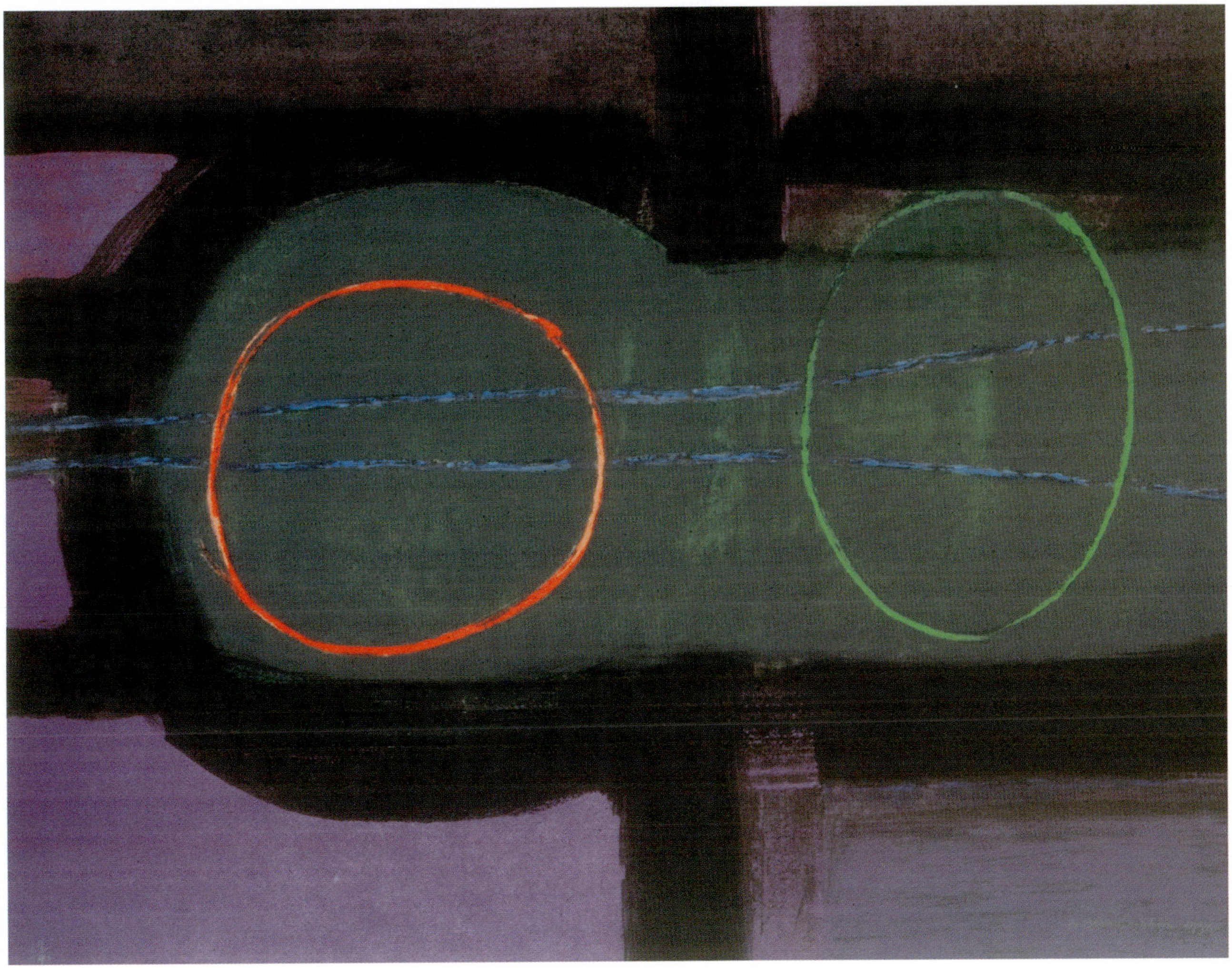

Cat.23

Two Circles on Purple, 1992

Lithograph, eight colours

60.0 x 75.2

Somerset Textured White 300gsm

Signed and dated, lower right: *W Barns-Graham 1992*; numbered, lower left

Edition of 70. Stanley Jones and Serena Castle, Curwen Studio, Curwen Chilford Prints Ltd

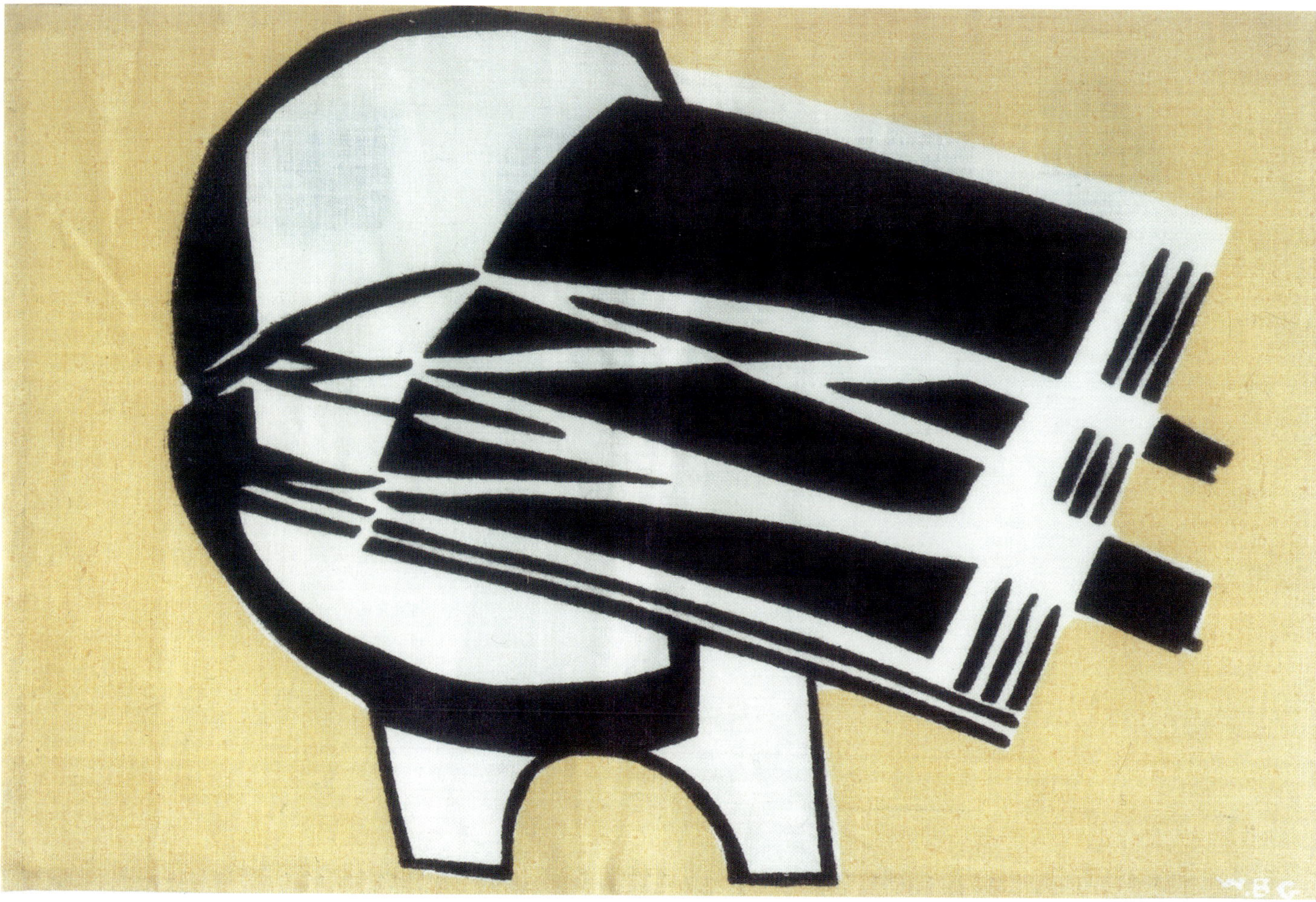

SCREENPRINTS

Cat.24

Table Mat, 1955

Screenprint, two colours

29.0 x 42.0

On linen

Initialled in the design, lower right: *WBG*

Printed on Denis Mitchell's press for Porthia Prints

Cat.25

Vermilion Discs onto Turquoise Square, 1972

Screenprint, two colours

35.7 x 36.0 (image)

59.5 x 84.0 (paper size)

One copy in the archive is signed and dated on mount, lower right *W Barns Graham 1972*; numbered lower left. Some unmounted copies are numbered

Edition of 12. Jim Whitlock, Penwith Print Workshop

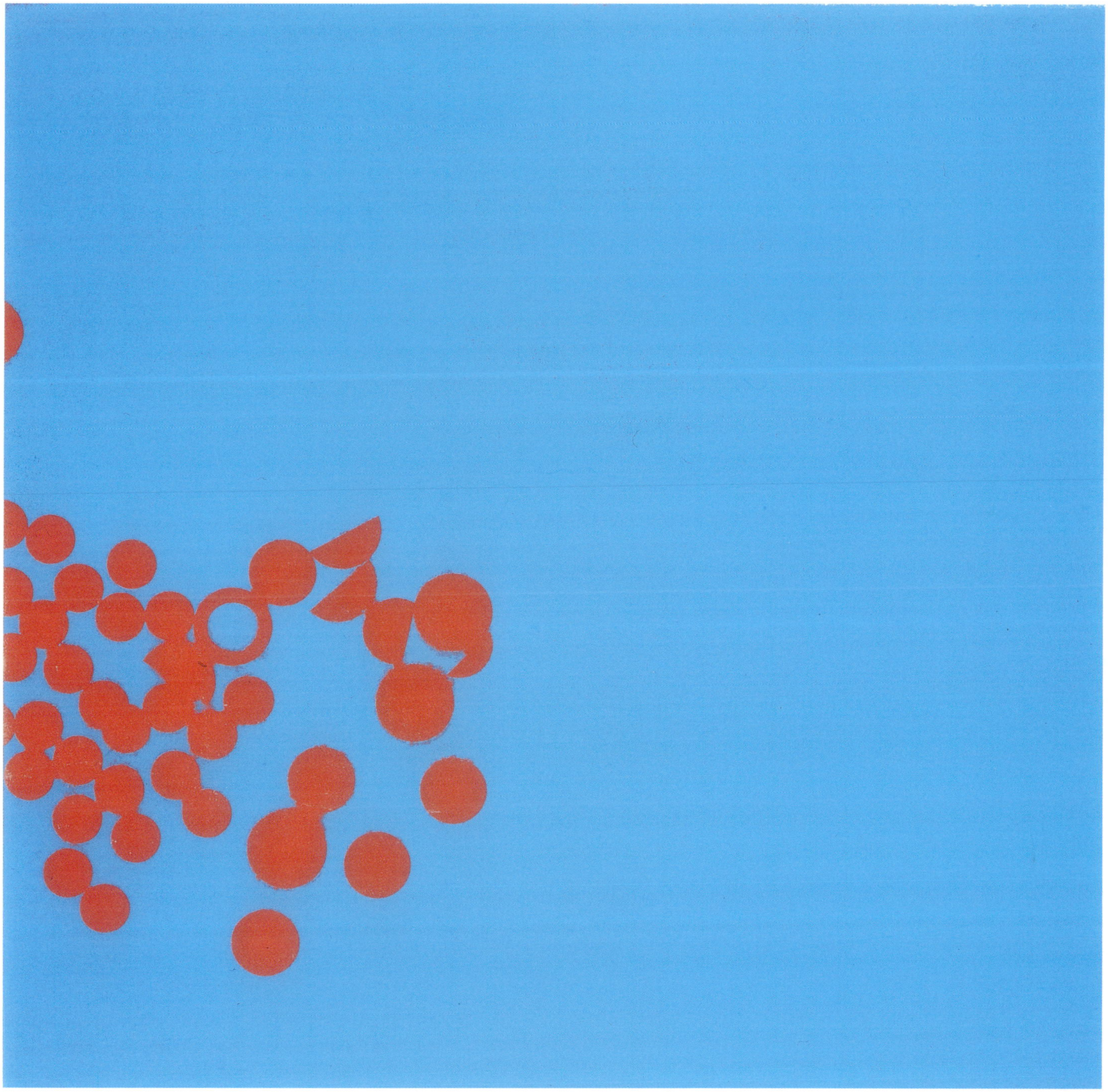

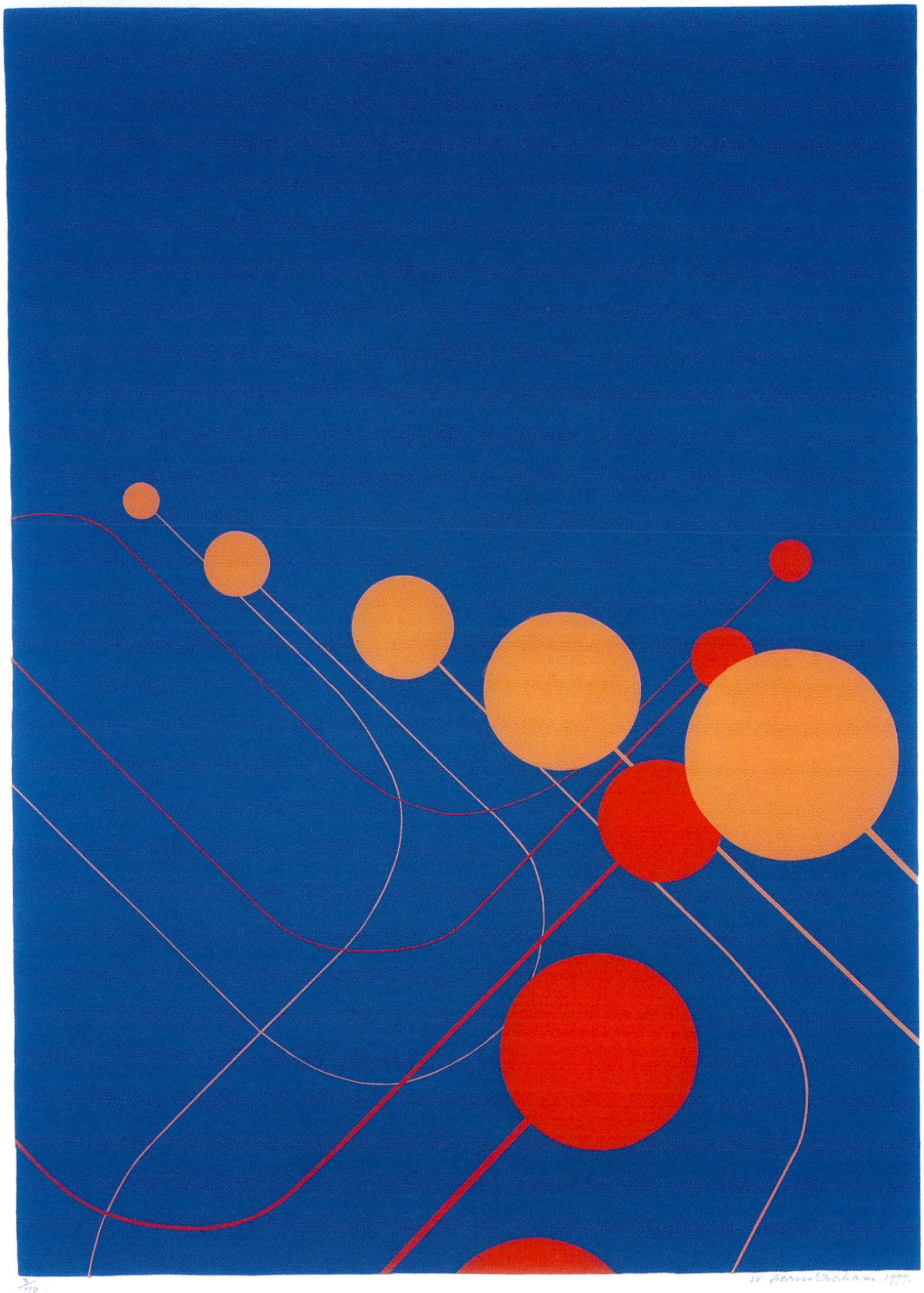

Cat.26

Orange and Red on Blue, 1977–8

Screenprint, Marlercolour oil-based inks, three colours

68.5 x 49.0 (image)

90.0 x 64.0 (paper size)

Signed and dated lower right: *W Barns Graham 1977–8*; numbered lower left: 4/75

Edition of 75. Ivan Polley, Edinburgh Printmakers

Note: The printing was completed in 1978. Very few prints were signed and dated.

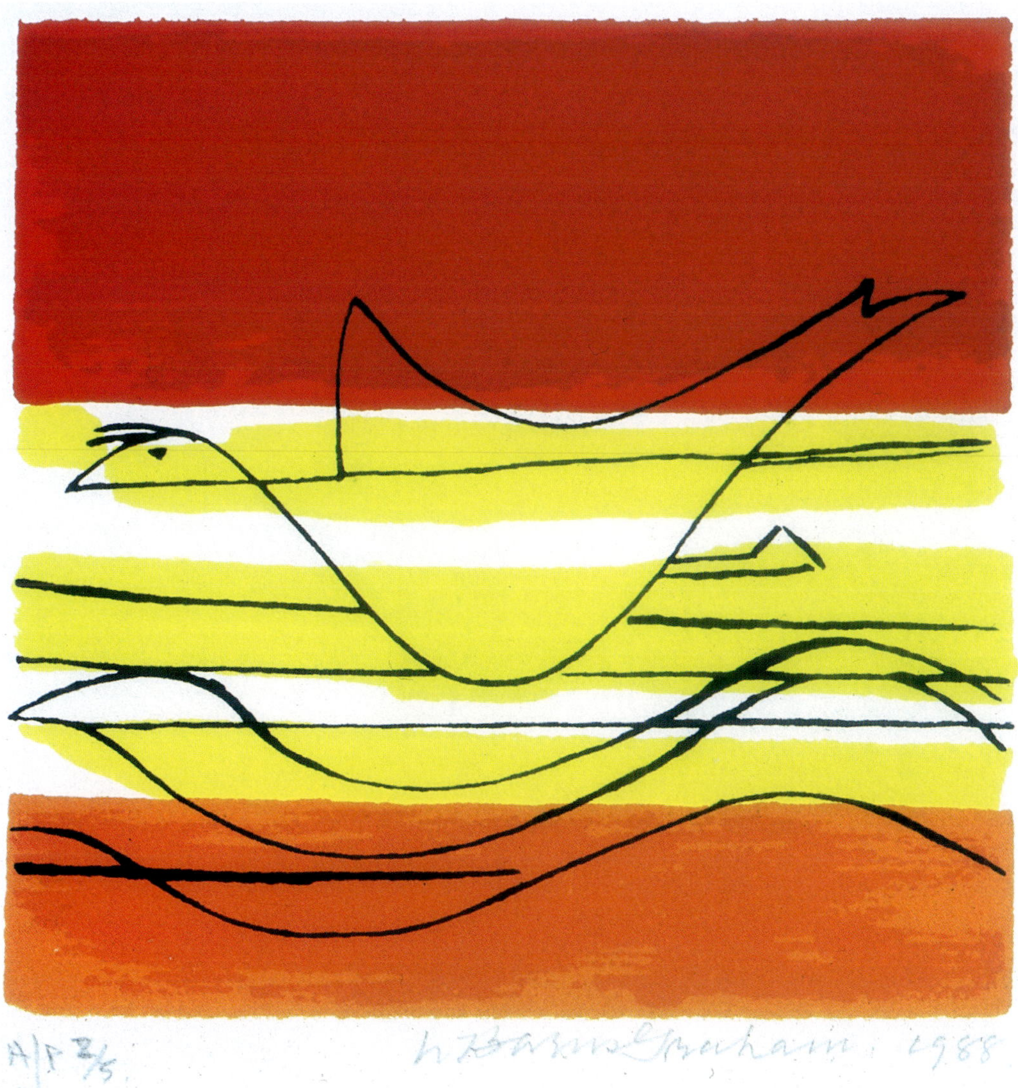

Cat.27

Peace Bird, 1988

Screenprint, four colours

10.3 x 10.2 (image size)

23.0 x 20.5 (paper size)

Signed and dated, lower right: *W Barns Graham 1988*; numbered, lower left.

Edition of 75. Fergus McLachlan, Dundee Printmakers Workshop

Lit.ref.: Sheila Oliner, 'It's a beginning', *Printmaking Today*, vol.3, no.4 (Winter 1994), pp 8–9

Note: Commissioned by the Scottish Arts Council, for a boxed set of twelve miniature prints by twelve artists, entitled *With an Eye to the East.*

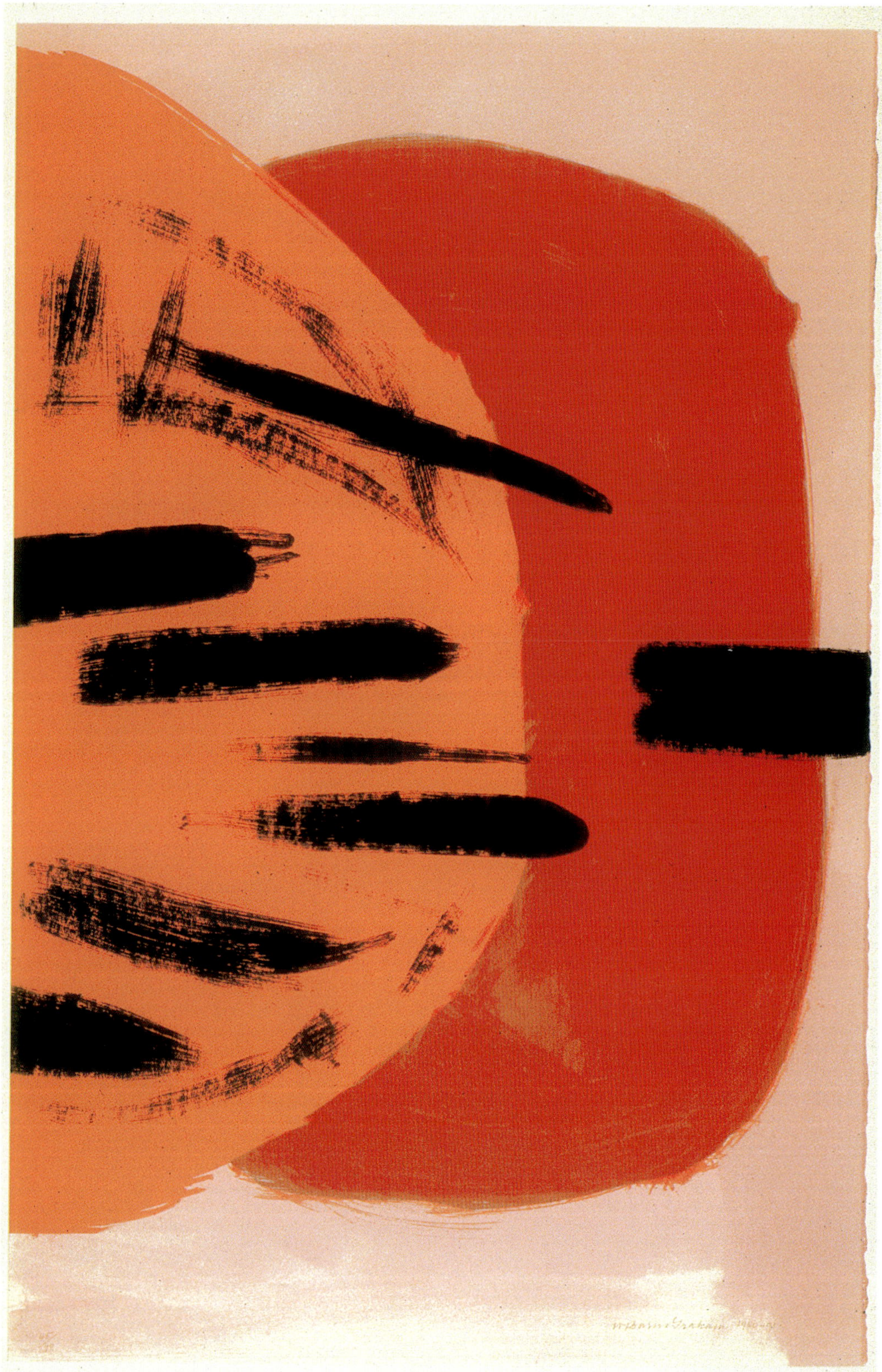

Cat.28

Orange and Red on Pink, 1991

Screenprint, six colours

48.8 x 76.3 (image and paper size)

Somerset Textured White 300gsm

Signed and dated, lower right: *W Barns Graham 1960–1991*; numbered, lower left: 1960–1991

Edition of 70. Kip Gresham and Andrea Bowden, Curwen Studio, Curwen Chilford Prints Ltd

Lit.ref.: Sheila Oliner, 'It's a beginning', *Printmaking Today*, vol.3, no.4 (Winter 1994), pp 8–9, illustrated p.8; Lynne Green, *W. Barns-Graham: A Studio Life* (Lund Humphries, 2001), p.173, fig.95

Note: Based on an original gouache from 1960. The artist included this date in the dating of the print. The print is smaller than the original painting which measures 91.5 x 58.5.

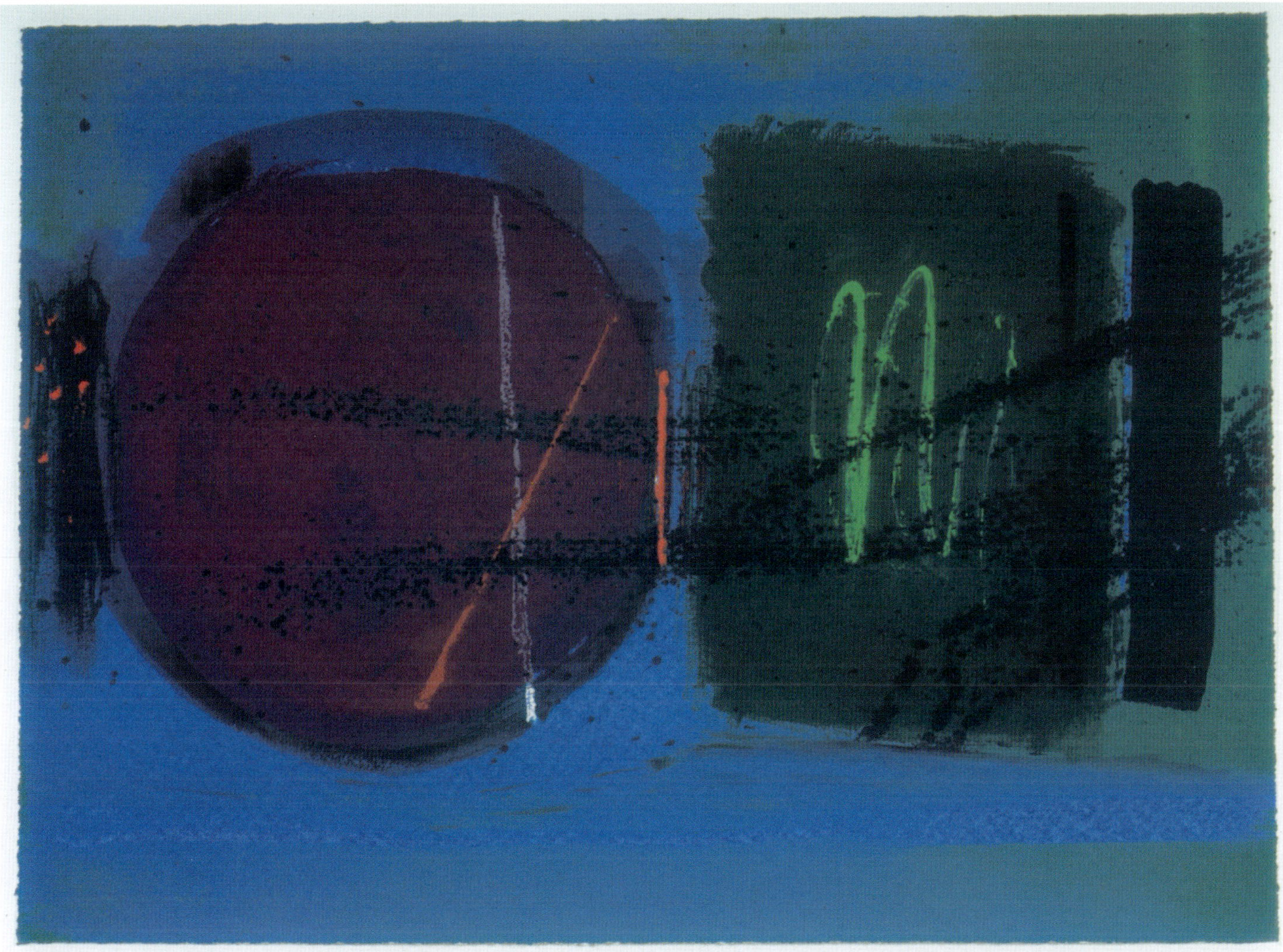

Cat.29

Untitled, April 1991, 1991

Screenprint, thirteen colours

56.8 x 76.0 (image and paper size)

Moulin du Gué 300gsm

Signed and dated, lower right: *W Barns Graham April 1991*; numbered, lower left

Edition of 70. Kip Gresham and Andrea Bowden, Curwen Studio, Curwen Chilford Prints Ltd

Lit.ref.: Sheila Oliner, 'It's a beginning', *Printmaking Today*, vol.3, no.4 (Winter 1994), pp 8–9, illustrated p.8

Note: Signed with date of original painting. The print was made in October 1991.

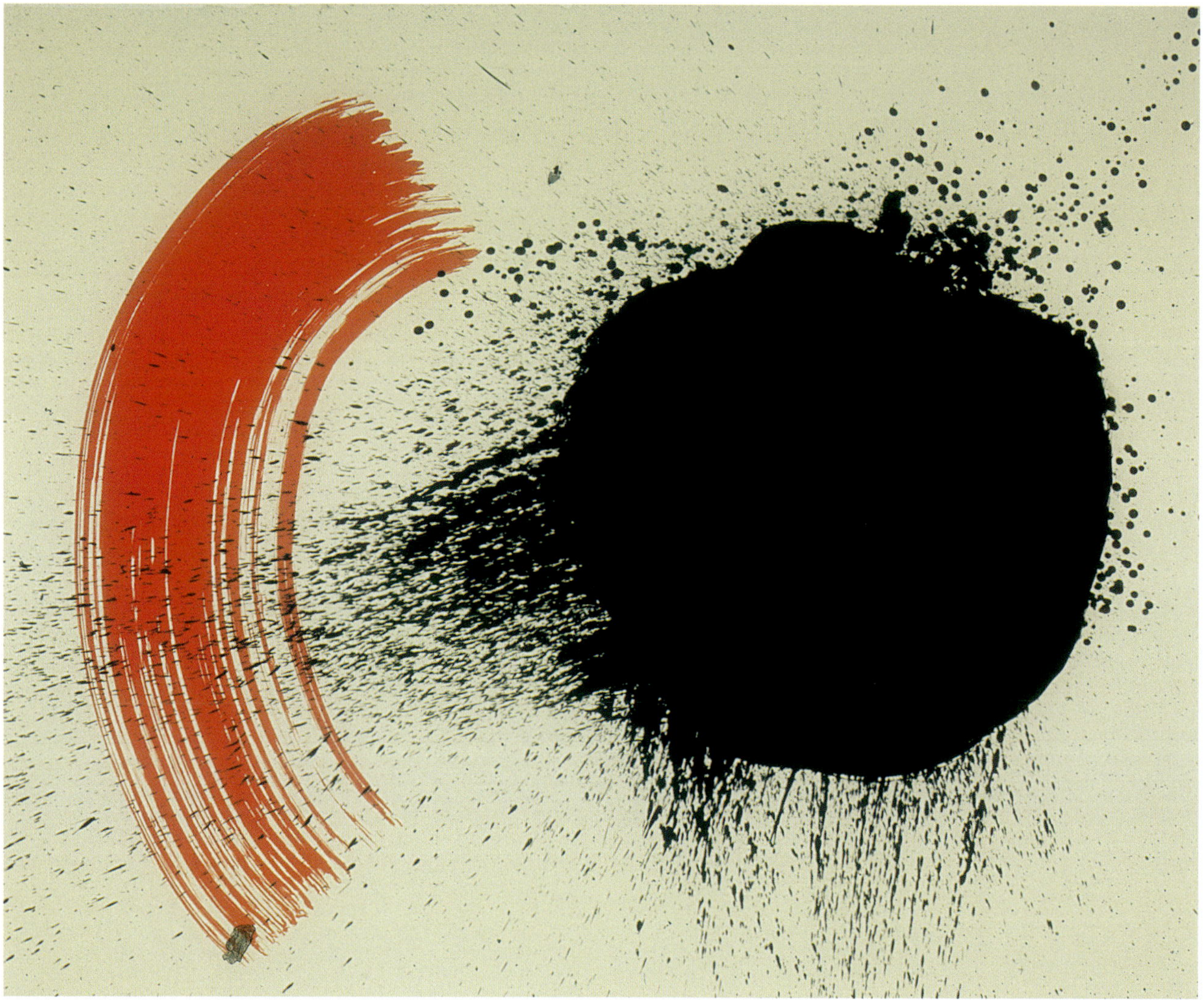

Cat.30

November I, 1991

Screenprint, two colours

55.2 x 64.7 (image and paper size)

Barcham Green Penshurst

Signed and dated, lower left: *W Barns Graham '91*; numbered, lower right

Edition of 20. Kip Gresham, Curwen Studio, Curwen Chilford Prints Ltd

Note: One of seven prints produced during a six-day experimental printing and editioning visit to the Curwen Studio between 28 November and 5 December 1991. Versions of this exist as mixed-media works with added gouache or acrylic, some entitled *Happening III* etc.

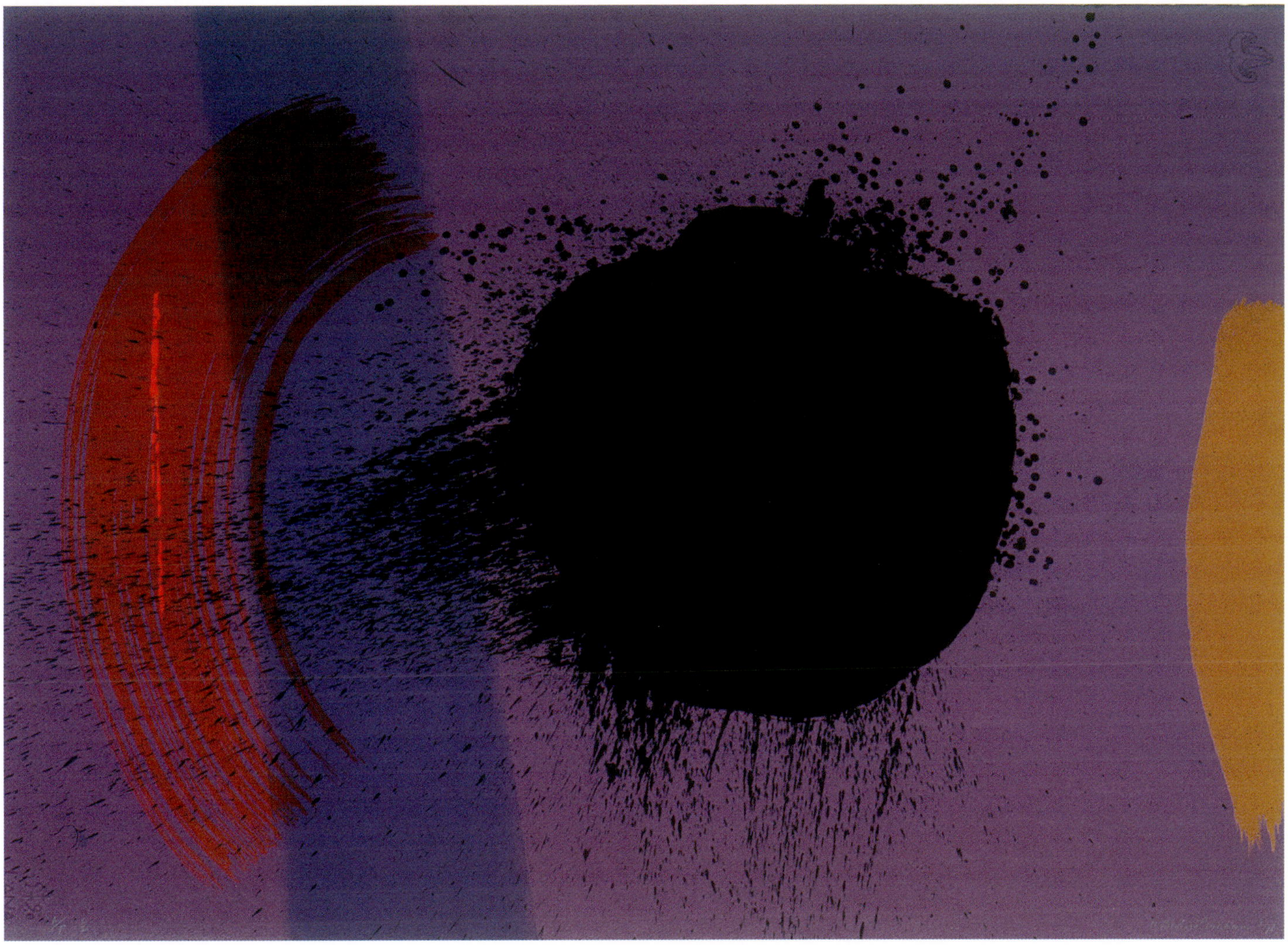

Cat.31

November II, 1991

Screenprint, five colours

55.5 x 75.5 (image and paper size)

Lana 1590

Signed and dated, lower left: *W Barns Graham '91*; numbered, lower right

Edition of 20. Kip Gresham, Curwen Studio, Curwen Chilford Prints Ltd.

Note: Versions of this exist as mixed-media works with added gouache or acrylic.

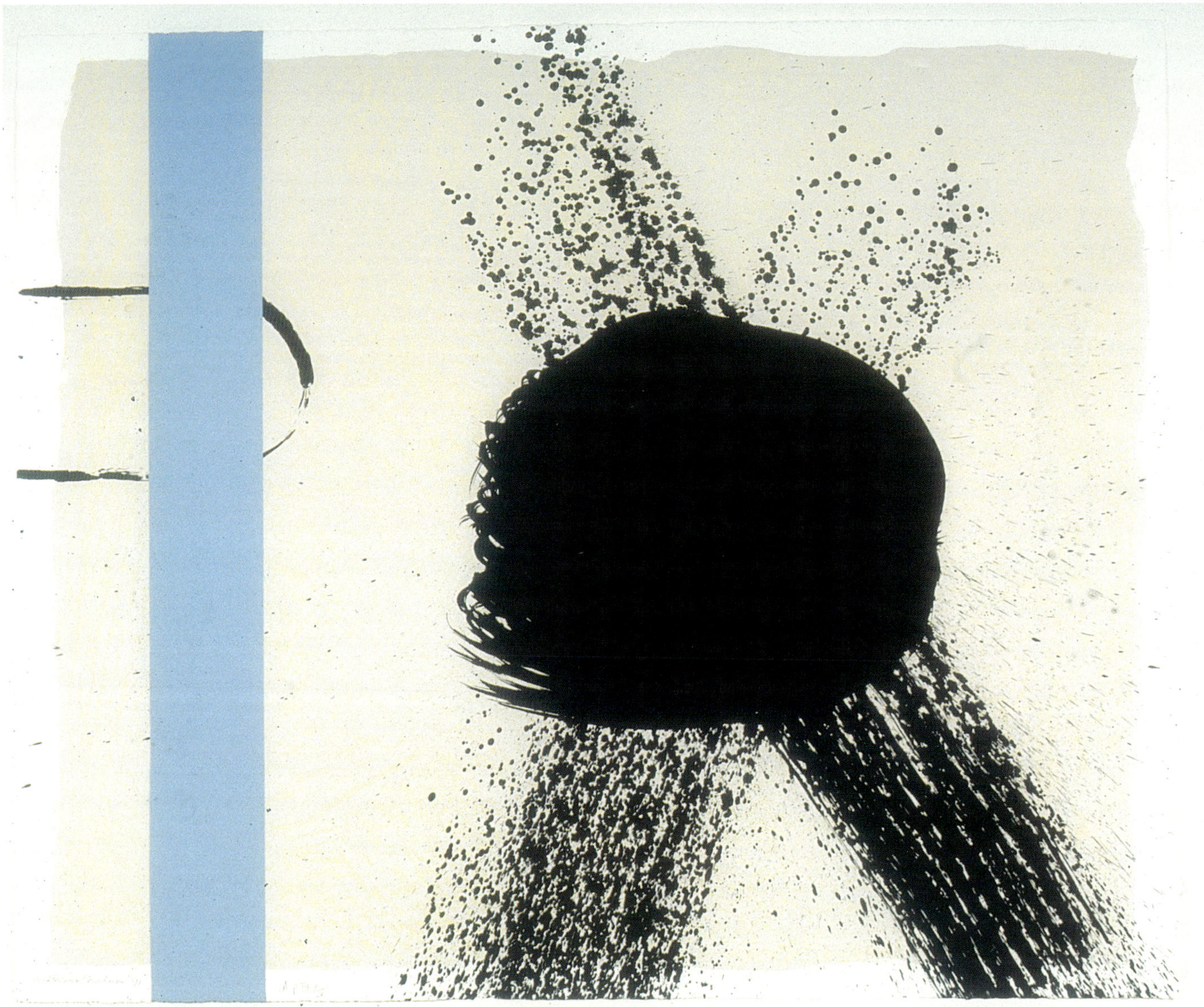

Cat.32

November III (St Andrews), 1991

Screenprint, four colours

64.7 x 76.0 (image and paper size)

Zerkall

Signed and dated, lower left: *W Barns Graham '91*; numbered, lower left

Edition of 20. Kip Gresham, Curwen Studio, Curwen Chilford Prints Ltd

Note: The ground texture was made from a rubbing from the concrete studio floor and was used again in *November IV*. Versions of this exist as mixed-media works with added gouache or acrylic. One is inscribed, verso: *Cross II W Barns Graham 1995*

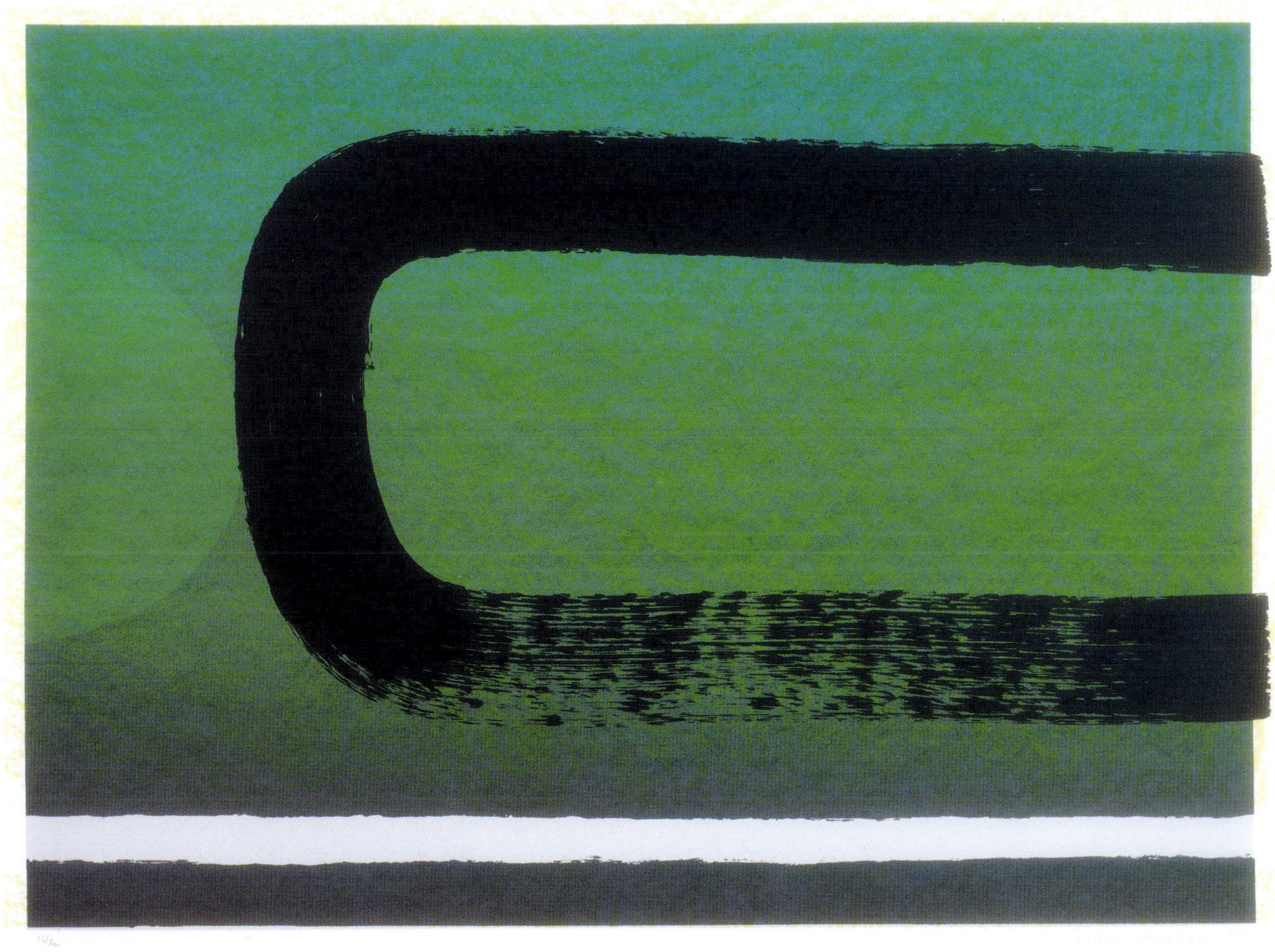

Cat.33

November IV, 1991

Screenprint, six colours including green

56.0 x 75.5 (image and paper size)

Fabriano Tiepolo

Signed and dated, lower right: *W Barns Graham '91*; numbered, lower left

Edition of 20. Kip Gresham, Curwen Studio, Curwen Chilford Prints Ltd

Note: Based on the 'Green Field – To Margaret' series of paintings in memory of Barns-Graham's friend Margaret Christie who died in 1988. The ground texture was the same as that used for *November III* and was made from a rubbing from the studio floor.

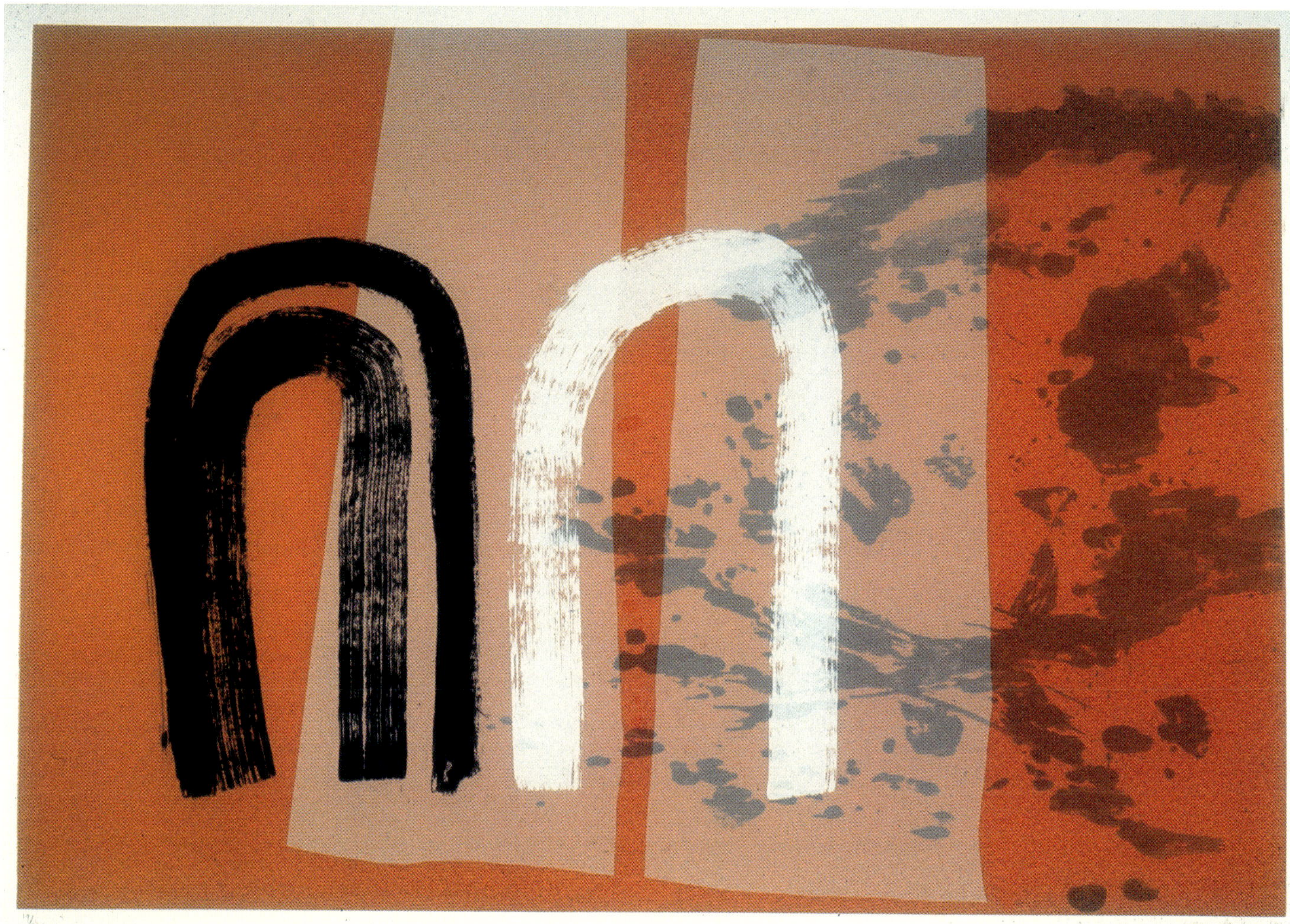

Cat.34

November V, 1991

Screenprint, five colours including orange

89.5 x 118.5 (image and paper size)

Arches Moulin du Gué

Signed and dated, lower right: *W Barns Graham '91*; numbered, lower left.

Edition of 20. Kip Gresham, Curwen Studio, Curwen Chilford Prints Ltd

Cat.35

November VI, 1991

Screenprint, four colours

89.5 x 118.5 (image and paper size)

Arches Moulin du Gué

Edition of 20. Kip Gresham, Curwen Studio, Curwen Chilford Prints Ltd

Note: Withdrawn from the series by Barns-Graham. No copies of this print exist in the Barns-Graham archive.

Cat.36 (unillustrated)

November VII, 1991

Screenprint, four colours

Size unknown

Arches Moulin du Gué

Edition of 5. Kip Gresham, Curwen Studio, Curwen Chilford Prints Ltd

Note: No copies of this print exist in the Barns-Graham archive. A print of this name was sold by the Art Business Gallery in 1995 with the edition number 1/3.

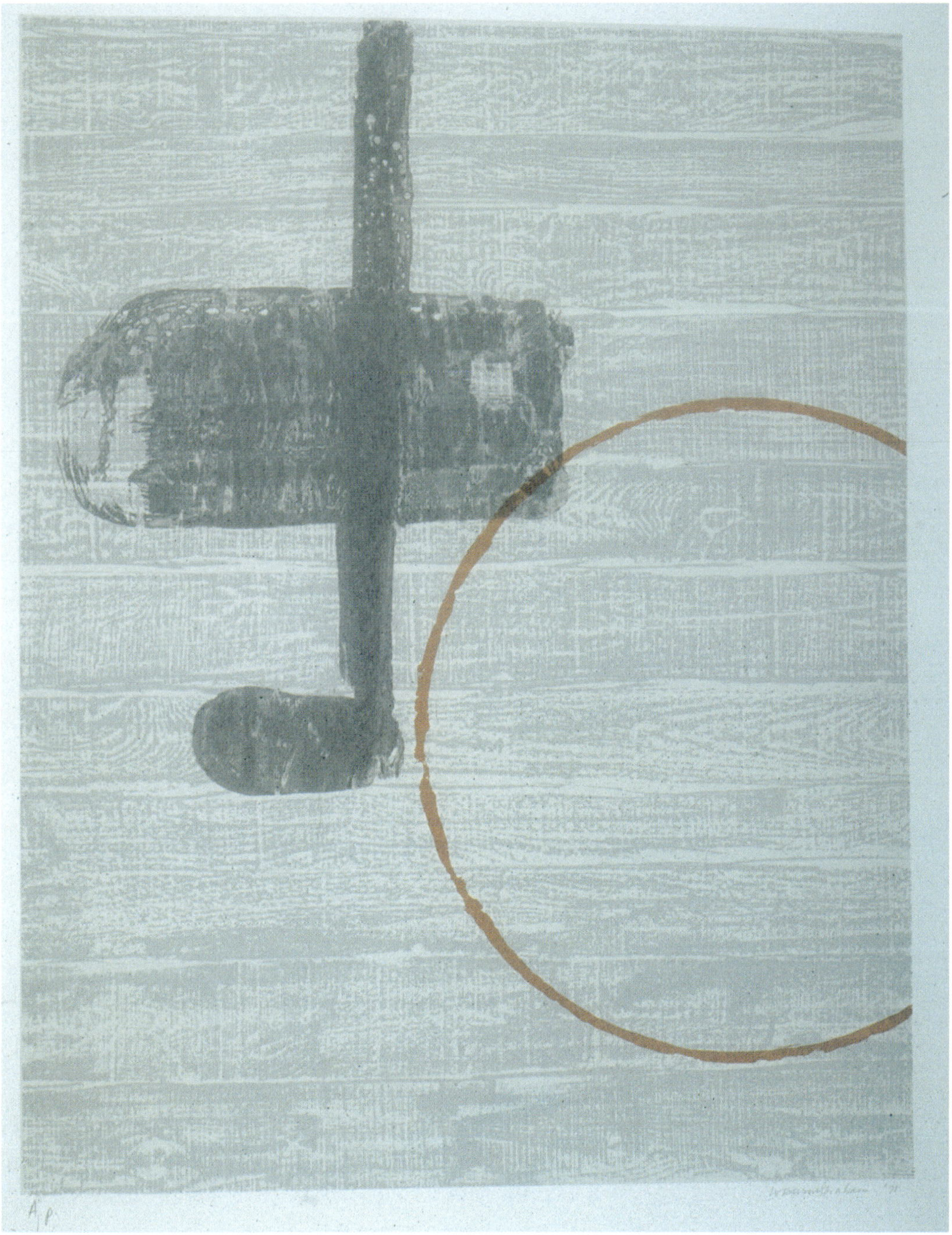

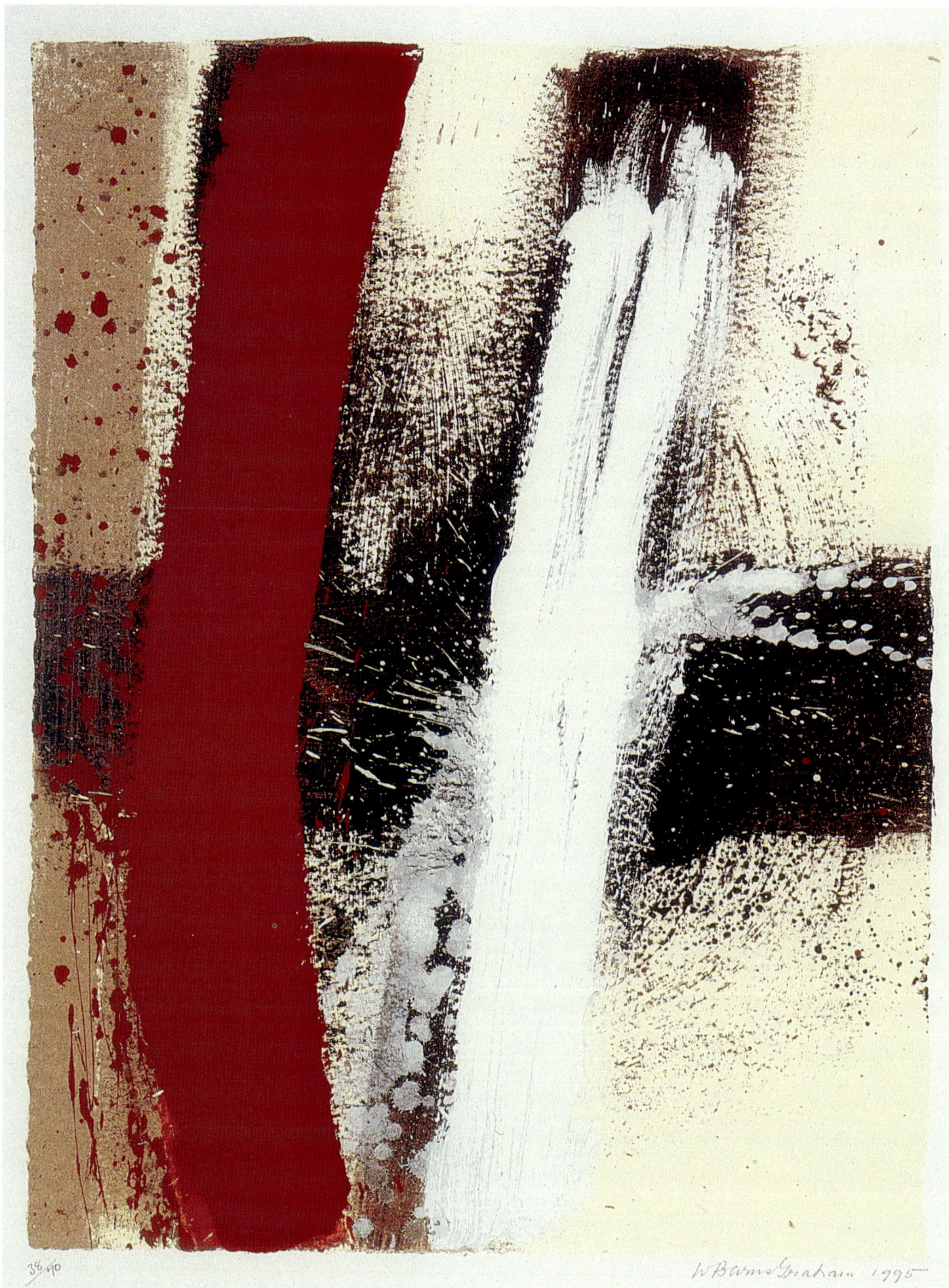

Cat.37

Venetian Red, 1995

Screenprint, twenty colours

45.2 x 33.8 (image)

74.0 x 57.5 (paper size)

Moulin du Gué 300gsm

Edition of 70. Kip Gresham, Ian Wilkinson, Samantha Johnson, Gresham Studio Ltd

Signed and dated, lower right: *W Barns Graham 1995*; numbered, lower left; blindstamp of Gresham Studio (Gamma) and Ian Wilkinson (IW)

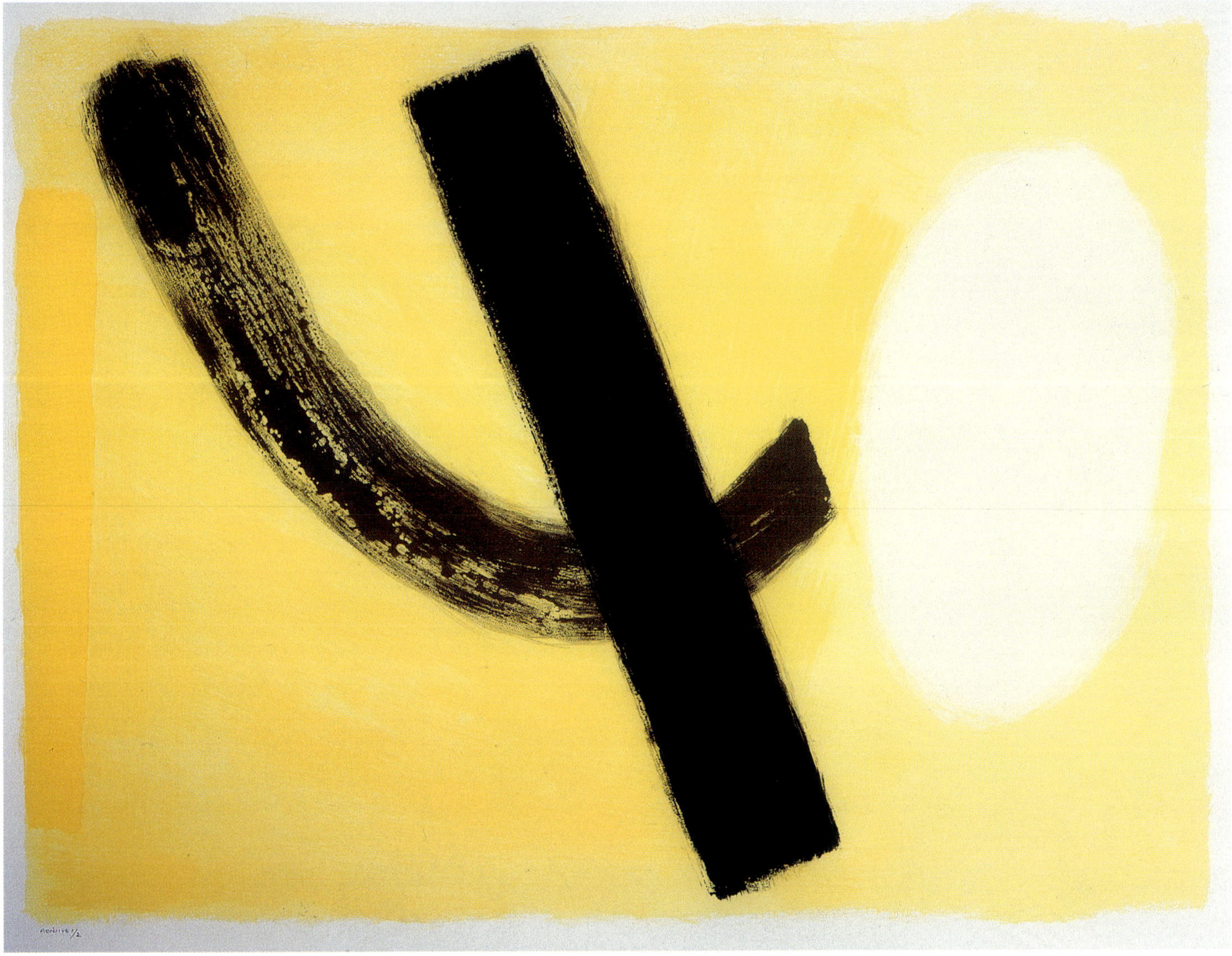

Cat.38

Spring, 1998

Screenprint

66.0 x 85.0 (paper size)

Fabriano 50% cotton

Edition of 30. Alasdair Currie, Dundee Printmakers Workshop

Signed and dated, lower right: *W Barns Graham 1998*

Note: Several unsigned prints remain in the Barns-Graham archive. This print and cat.39 were not signed in a batch but as needed.

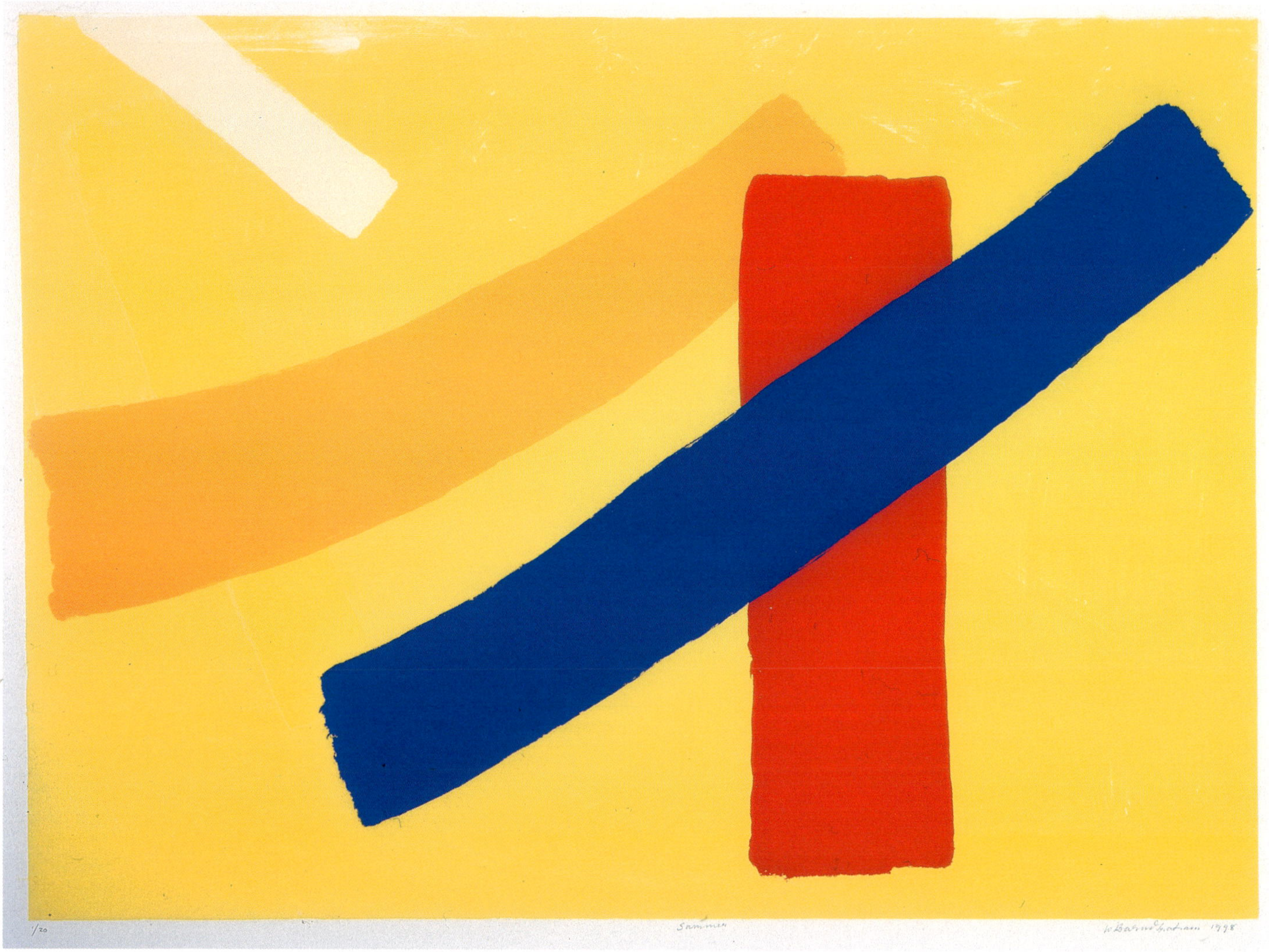

Cat.39
Summer, 1998
Screenprint
56.0 x 76.0 (image)
66.0 x 85.0 (paper size)
Fabriano 50% cotton
Edition of 20. Alasdair Currie, Dundee Printmakers Workshop
Note: Several unsigned prints remain in the Barns-Graham archive. This print and cat.38 were not signed in a batch but as needed.

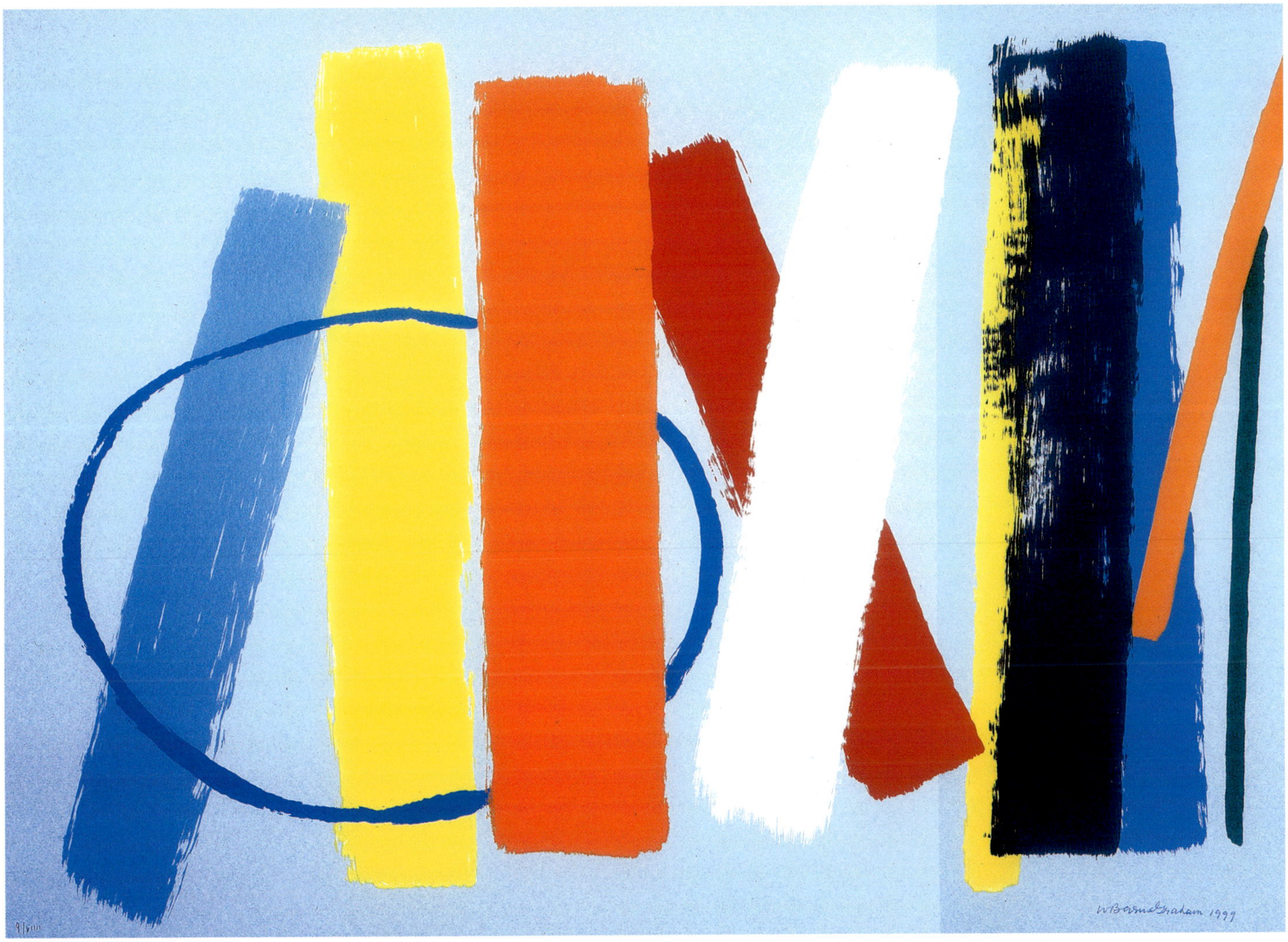

Cat.40

Blue Light, Summer, 1999

Screenprint, fourteen colours

54.7 x 74.0 (image and paper size)

Moulin du Gué 300gsm

Edition of 100. Kip Gresham, Ian Wilkinson and Jimi Kazak, Gresham Studio Ltd

Signed and dated, lower right: *W Barns Graham 1999*; numbered, lower left

Note: Commissioned for *The King's College Portfolio*, a fundraising project for an Arts Centre at King's College, Cambridge. It consisted of ten original prints. The other artists were Peter Blake, Sandra Blow, Stephen Buckley, Alan Davie, Jane Dickson, Anthony Frost, Antony Gormley, Anthony Green and Patrick Procktor. Each artist received a complete portfolio and ten copies of their own print. A/P set at Balmungo numbered v/x. This print is entitled *Blue Light, Summer* on the colophon for the portfolio but has also been sold with the titles *Summer (Blue)* and *Summer, Light Blue*.

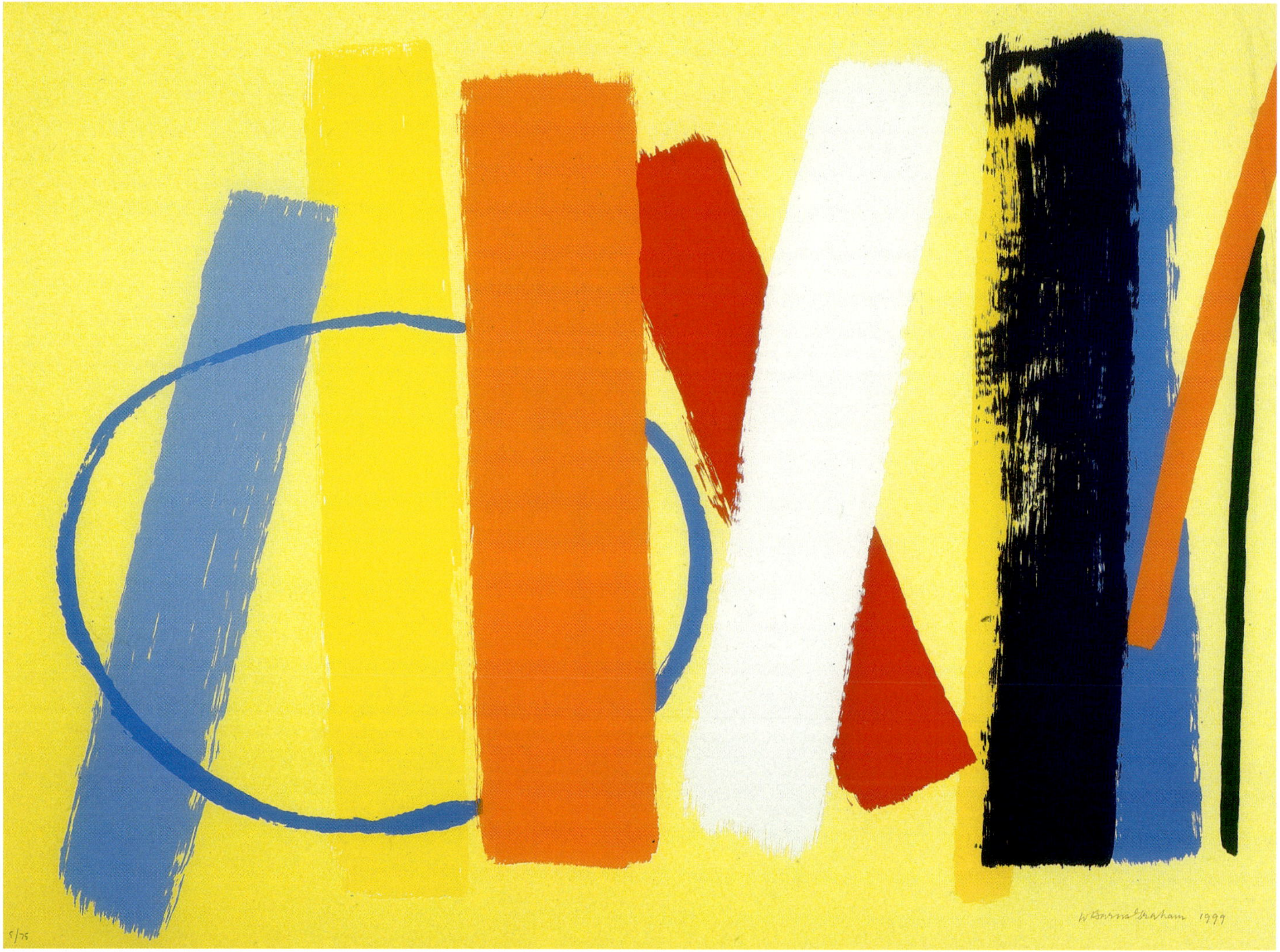

Cat.41

Summer (Yellow), 1999

Screenprint, fourteen colours

54.7 x 74.0 (image and paper size)

Moulin du Gué 300gsm

Edition of 100. Kip Gresham, Ian Wilkinson and Jimi Kazak, Gresham Studio Ltd

Signed and dated, lower right: *W Barns Graham* 1999; numbered, lower left

Note: A version of *Blue Light, Summer* from *The King's College Portfolio*, with a yellow ground.

SCREENPRINTS MADE WITH GRAAL PRESS

Except where noted on individual entries, these images were all painted with Lascaux Tusches and Golden and Lascaux acrylic paints on clear and frosted sheets to create paintings. Some marks were drawn with waterproof pen, typing correction pen or conté crayon. These were used as positives, and the resulting screens were screenprinted by hand. Lascaux gouache, Lascaux Resonance® Gouache, Lascaux acrylic paints, Kremer pigments and a variety of Lascaux painting aids were used to create a range of opaque and translucent printing mixtures. The paper used was either Moulin du Gué or Arches Velin Blanc. All prints carry the Graal Press chop mark lower right (except cats 59 and 60, *Earth Series IV* and *Earth Series V*). Prints that were editioned posthumously are numbered, lower left, and stamped with a statement of authentication on the reverse.

The prints are arranged here by series alphabetically, with single images listed alphabetically first. The prints are not arranged chronologically because editions were often printed a year or more after the proof had been approved. The artist dated prints using the date of editionin, therefore some series are spread over a number of years. Some images were approved but not printed at the time of Barns-Graham's death. These were printed posthumously in 2006 and 2007.

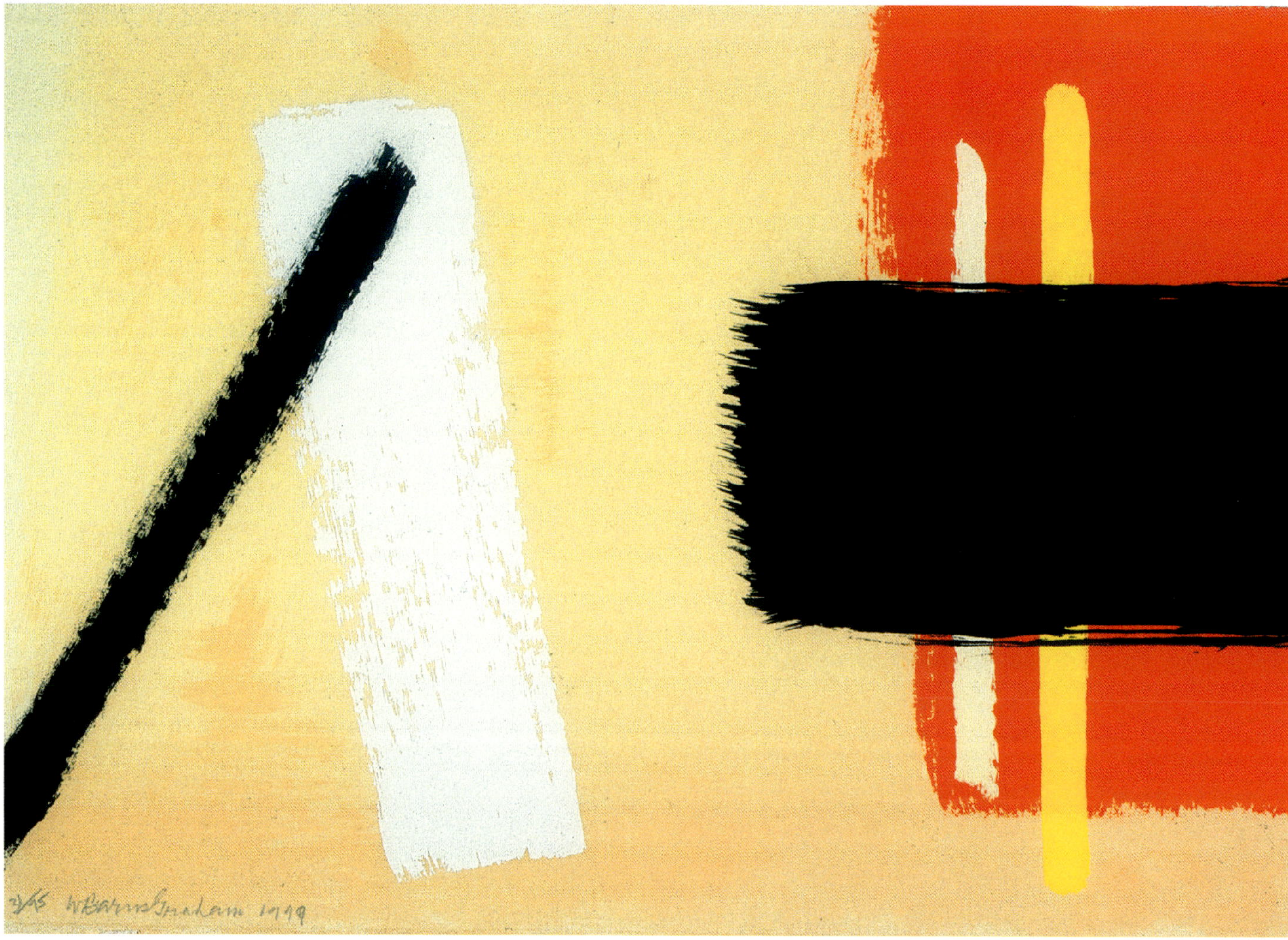

Cat.42

Beach, 1999

Screenprint, ten colours

29.0 x 40.0 (image and paper size)

Moulin du Gué 300gsm

Edition of 75. Carol Robertson, Graal Press

Signed, dated and numbered, lower left: *W Barns Graham 1999*

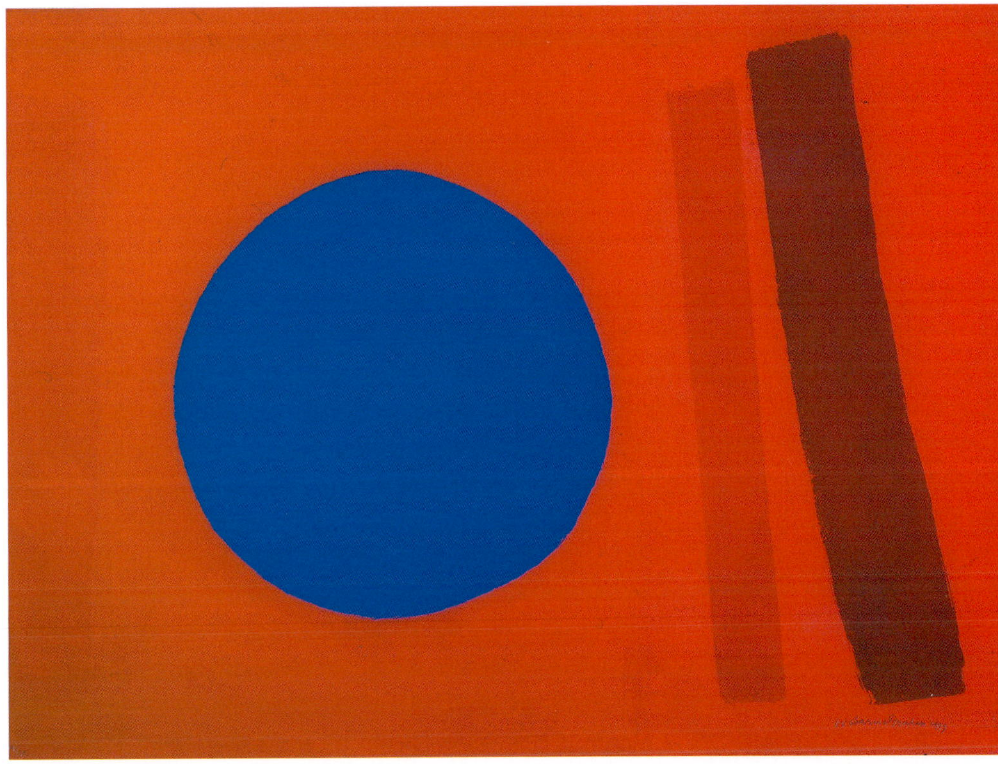

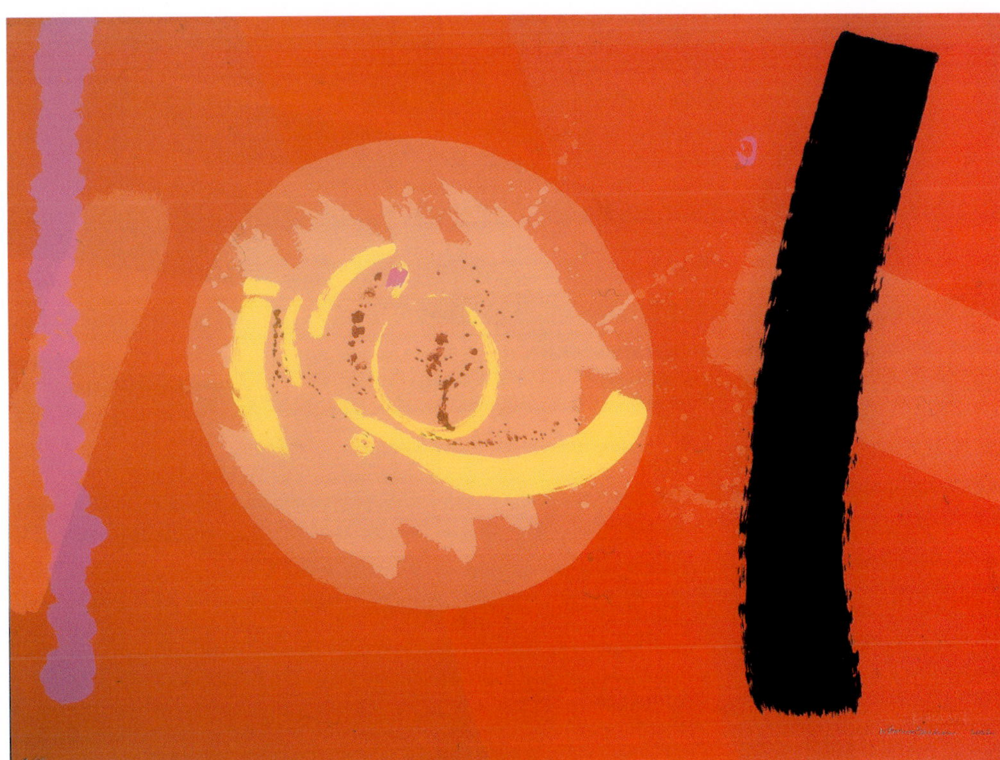

Cat.43

Cardinal, 1999

Screenprint, eight colours

58.0 x 76.8 (image and paper size)

Arches Velin Blanc 400gsm

Edition of 70. Carol Robertson, Graal Press

Signed and dated, lower right: *W Barns Graham 1999*; numbered, lower left

Cat.44

Celebration at 90, 2002

Screenprint, twelve colours

57.3 x 76.6 (image and paper size)

Arches Velin Blanc 400gsm

Edition of 70. Carol Robertson, Graal Press

Signed and dated, lower right: *W Barns Graham 2002*; numbered, lower left

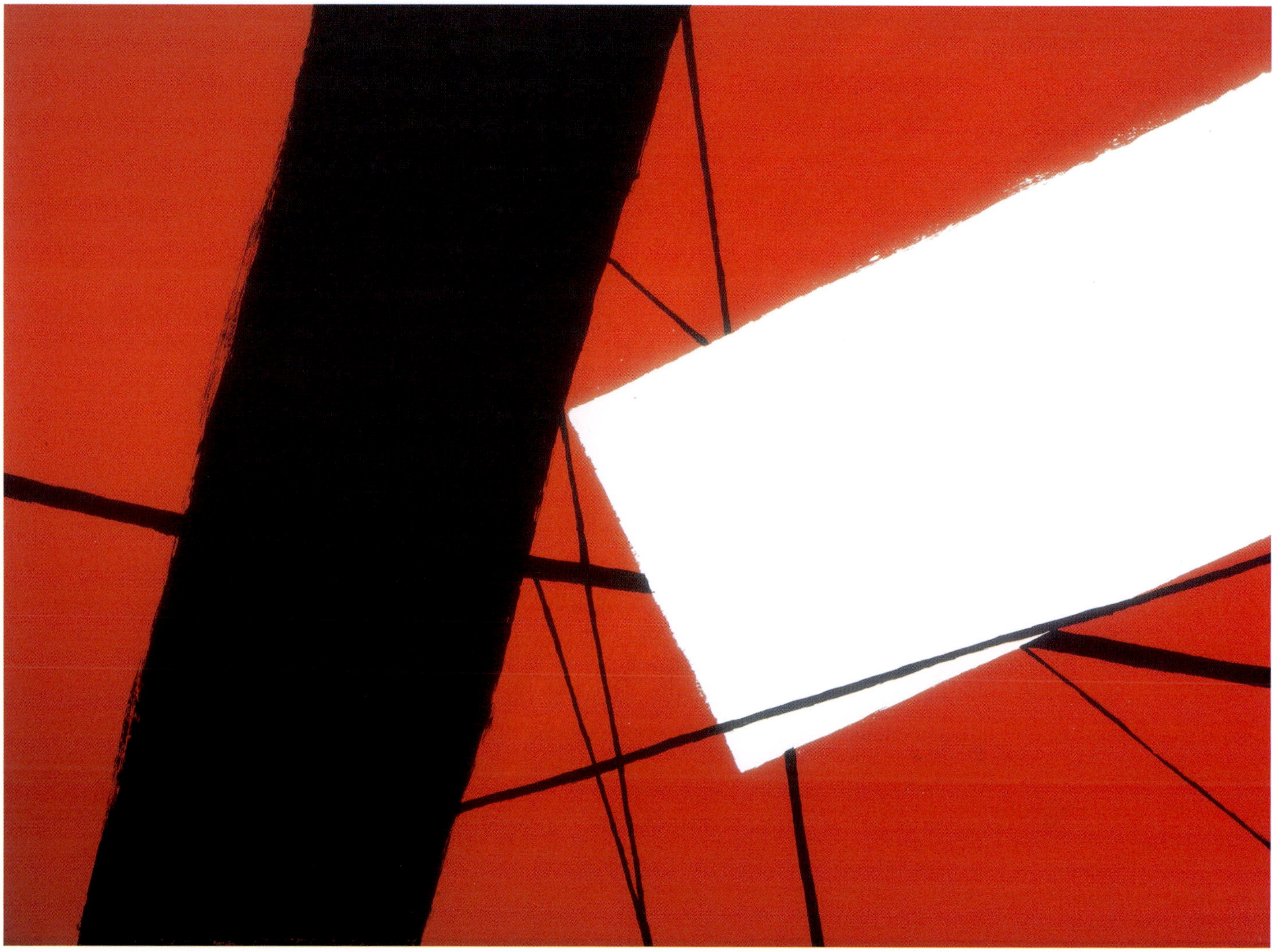

Cat.45

Construction Series I (editioned posthumously, 2006)

Screenprint, nine colours

56.0 x 76.0 (image and paper size)

Arches Velin Blanc 400gsm

Edition of 70. Carol Robertson, Graal Press

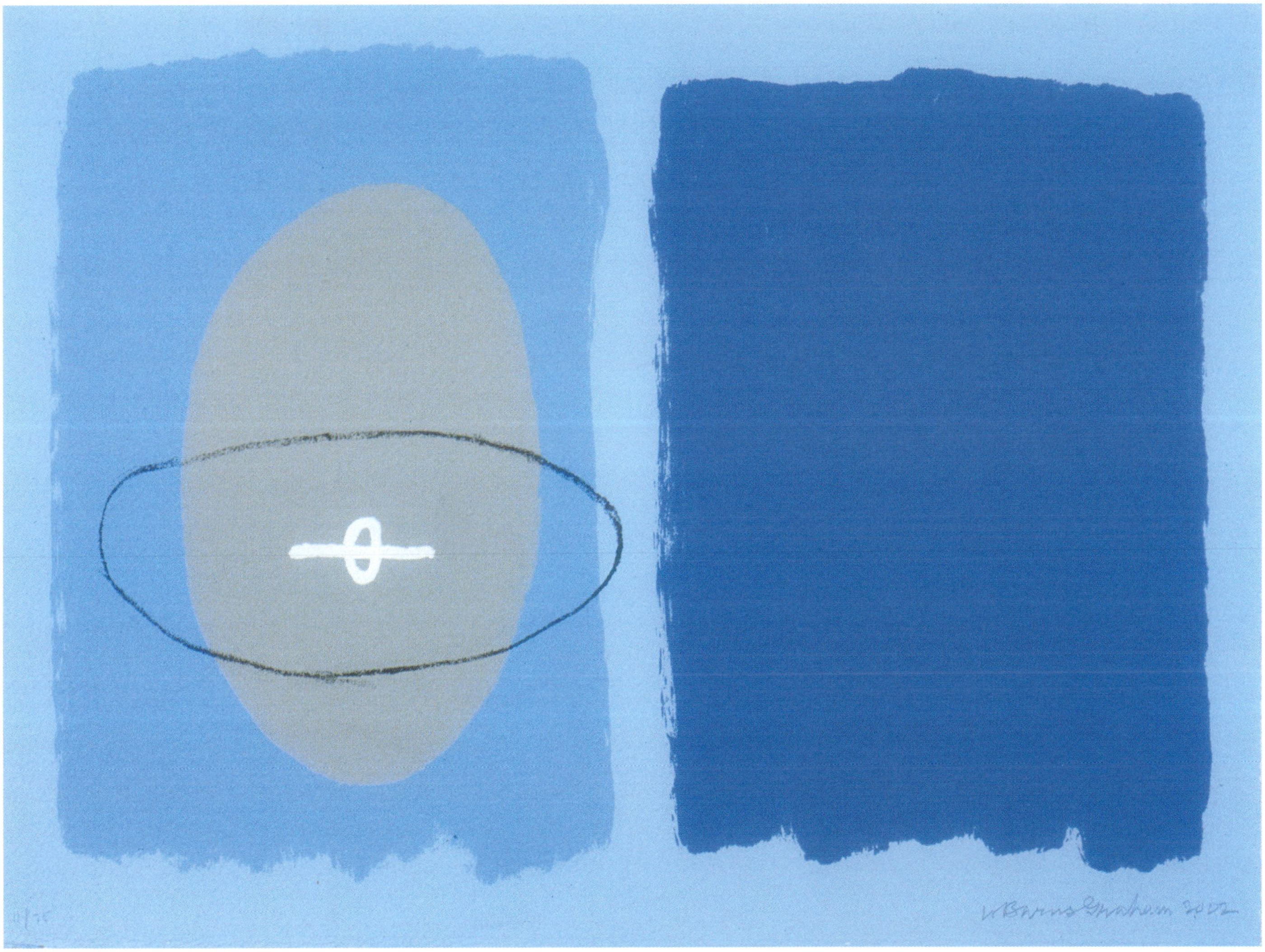

Cat.46

Homage to Johnny, 2002

Screenprint, ten colours

26.5 x 35.0 (image and paper size)

Arches Velin Blanc 400gsm

Edition of 75. Carol Robertson, Graal Press

Signed and dated, lower right: *W Barns Graham 2002*; numbered, lower left

Note: Related to three paintings entitled *Goodbye to Johnny*, made after the death of the artist John Wells in 2000 (see fig 25).

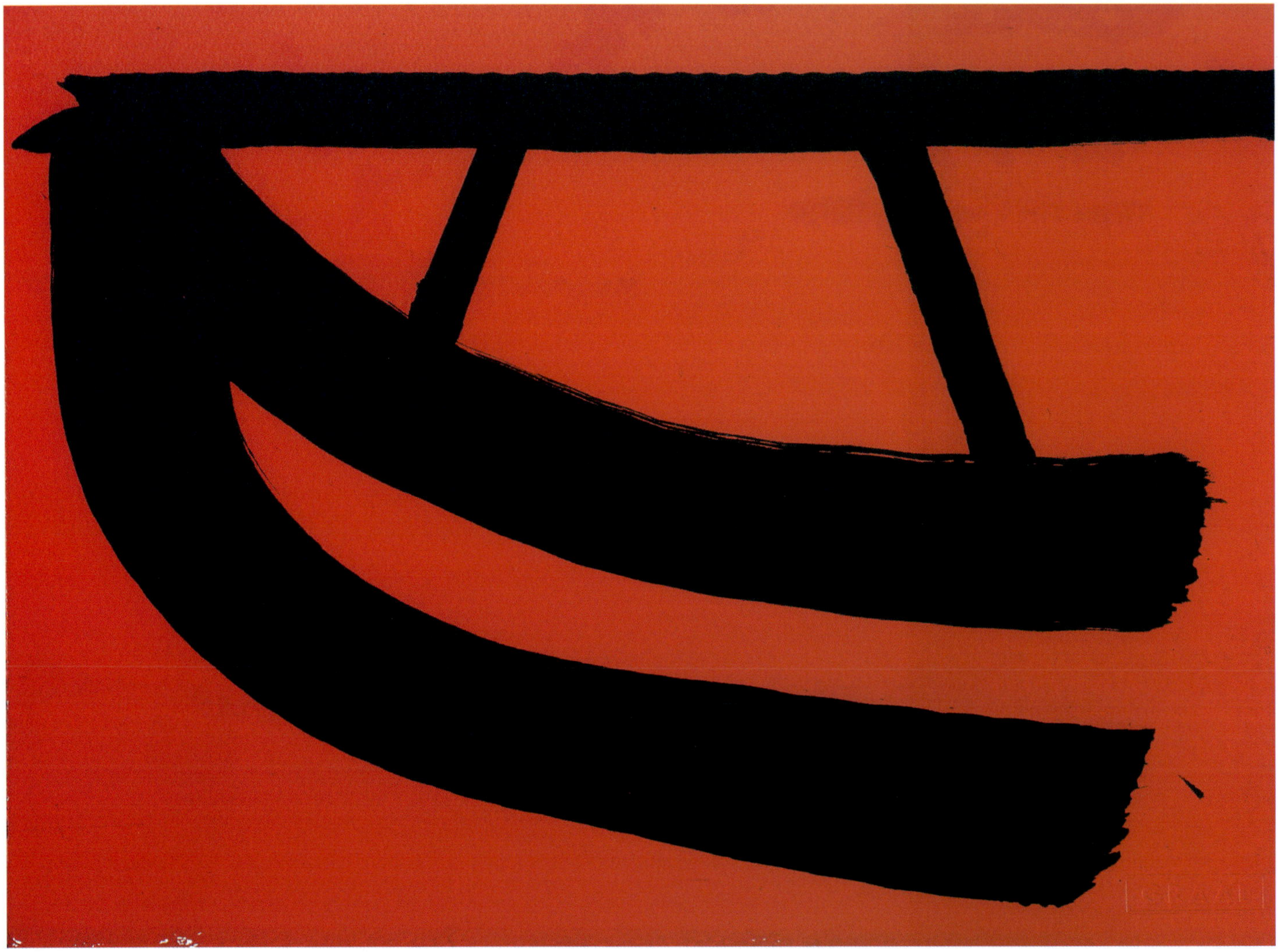

Cat.47

June (editioned posthumously, 2006)

Screenprint, three colours

27.0 x 36.2 (image and paper size)

Arches Velin Blanc 400gsm

Edition of 25. Carol Robertson, Graal Press

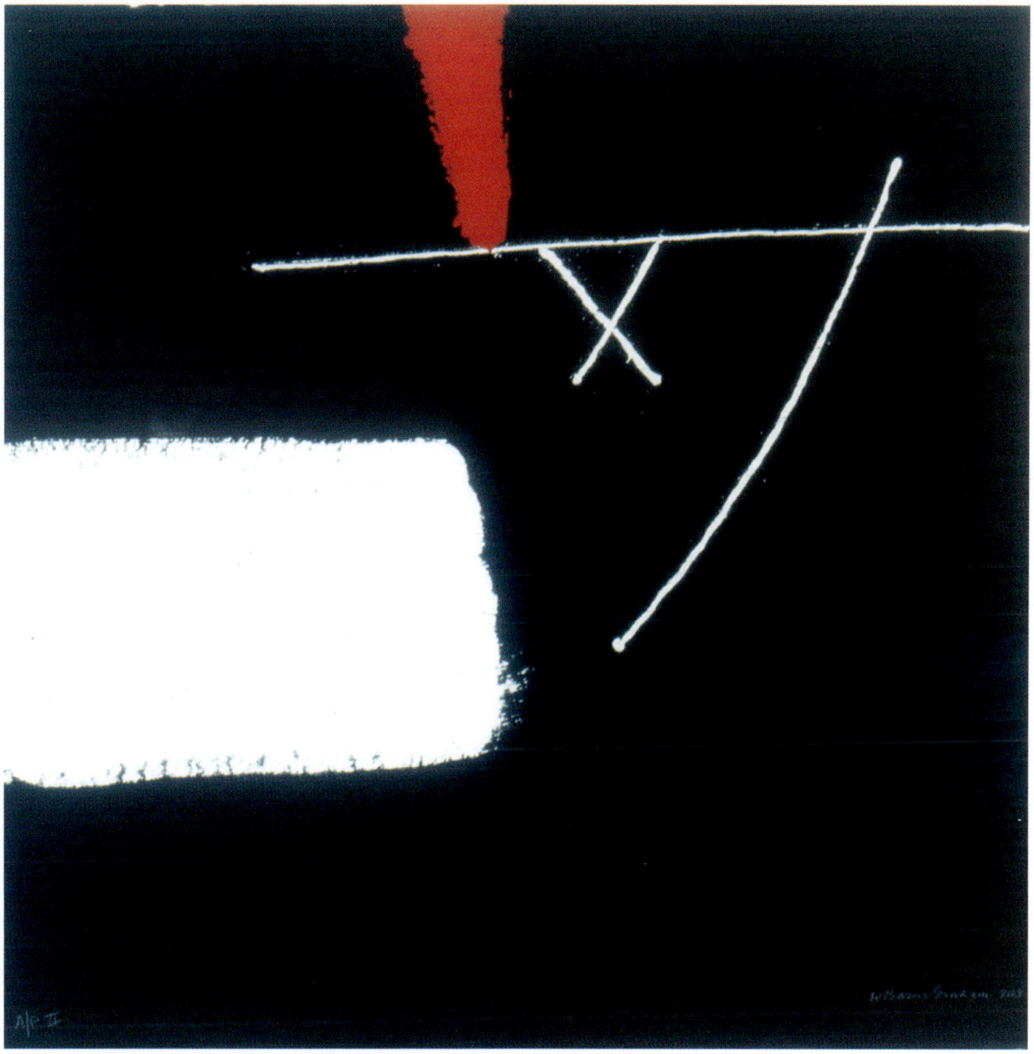

Cat.48

Tango, 2003

Screenprint, four colours

58.0 x 58.0 (image and paper size)

Arches Velin Blanc 400gsm

Edition of 70. Carol Robertson, Graal Press

Signed and dated, lower right: *W Barns Graham 2003*; numbered, lower left

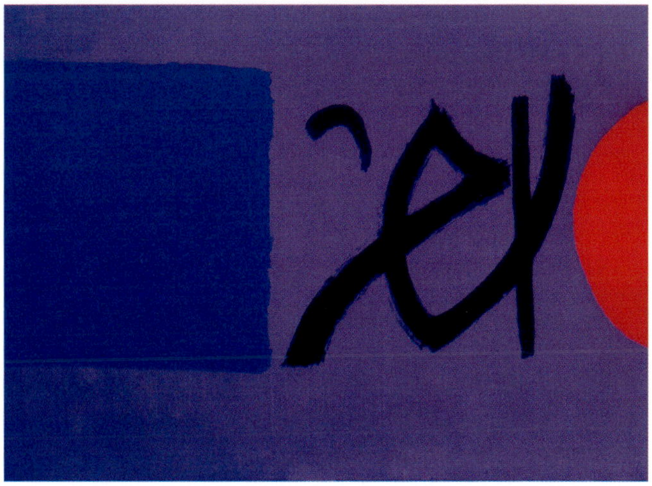

Cat.49

Three Elements (editioned posthumously, 2006)

Screenprint, seven colours

58.0 x 76.0 (image and paper size)

Arches Velin Blanc 400gsm

Edition of 25. Carol Robertson, Graal Press

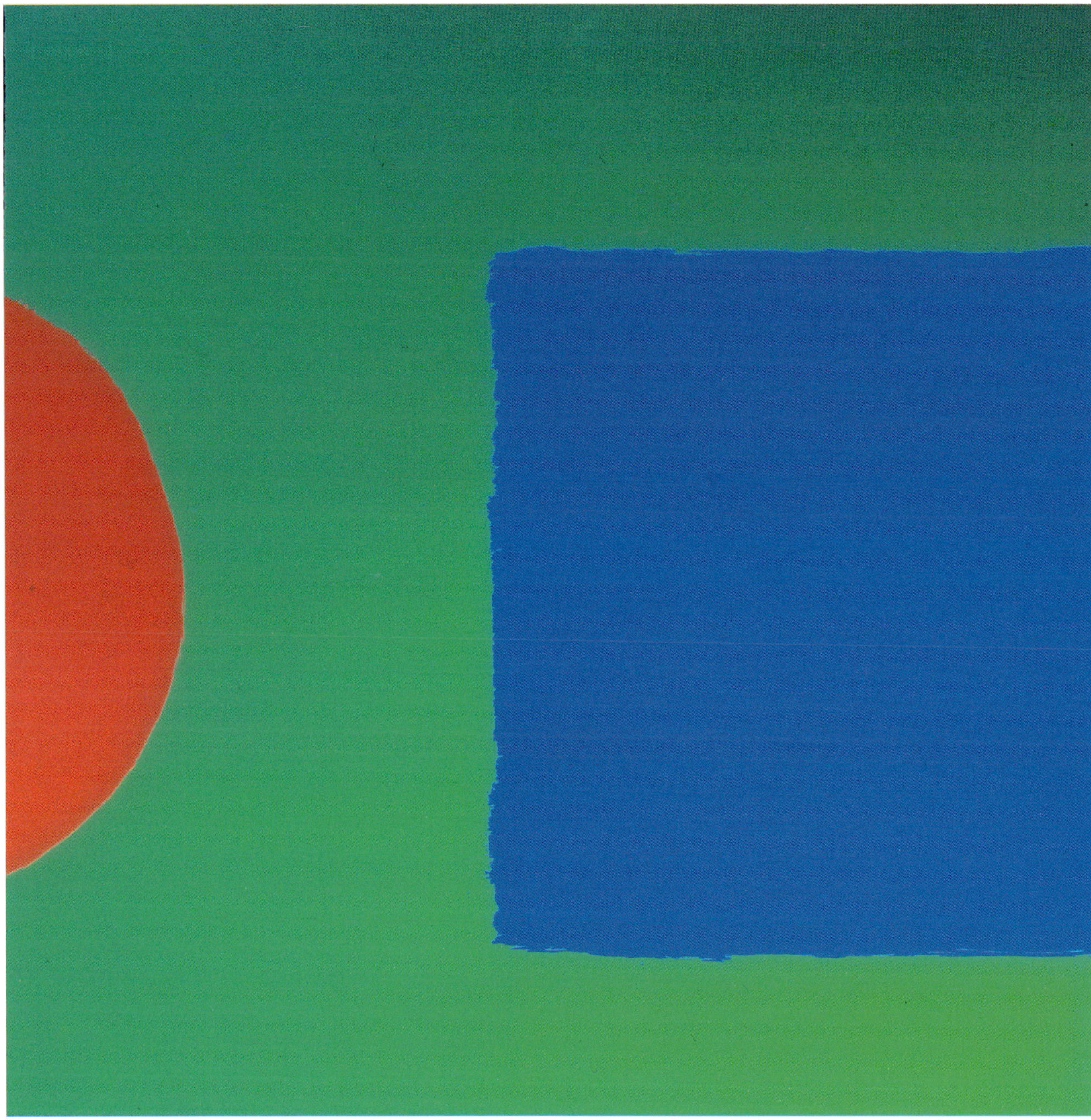

Cat.50

Two Elements (editioned posthumously, 2006)

Screenprint, four colours

57.3 x 56.0 (image and paper size)

Arches Velin Blanc 400gsm

Edition of 25. Carol Robertson, Graal Press

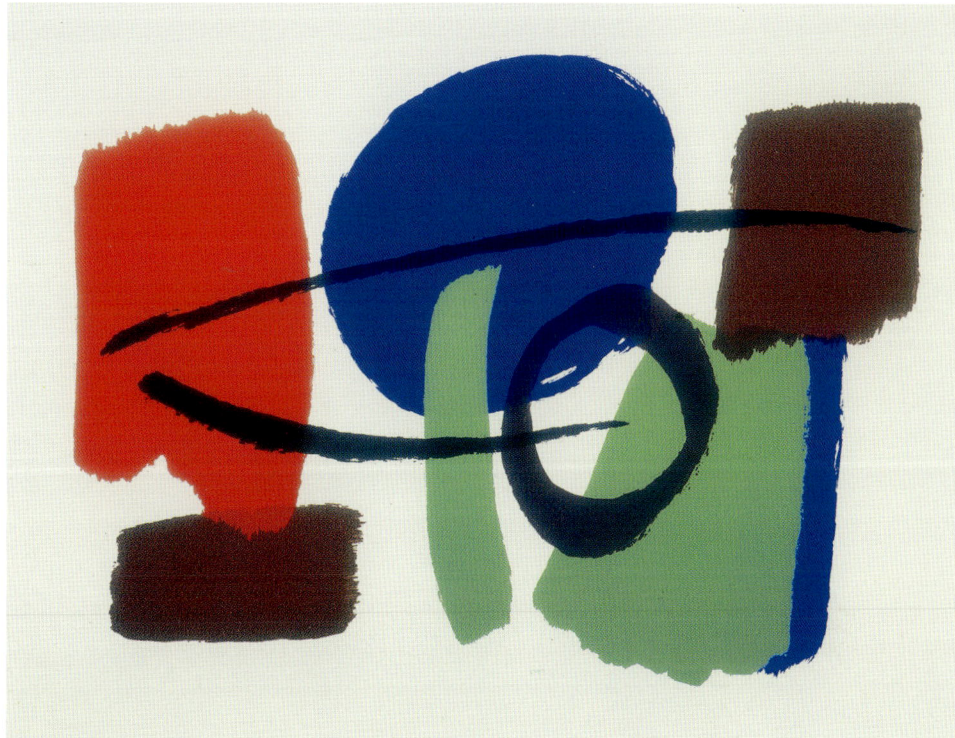

Cat.51

Untitled, Composition (editioned posthumously, 2006)

Screenprint, seven colours

29.0 x 36.0 (image and paper size)

Arches Velin Blanc 400gsm

Edition of 25. Carol Robertson, Graal Press

Note: The separations for this print were made before the collaboration with Graal Press began. It is not known if they were made for a project with the Curwen Studio, with Kip Gresham or with Dundee Printmakers Workshop. Rowan James asked Carol Robertson to edition the print after the death of Barns-Graham.

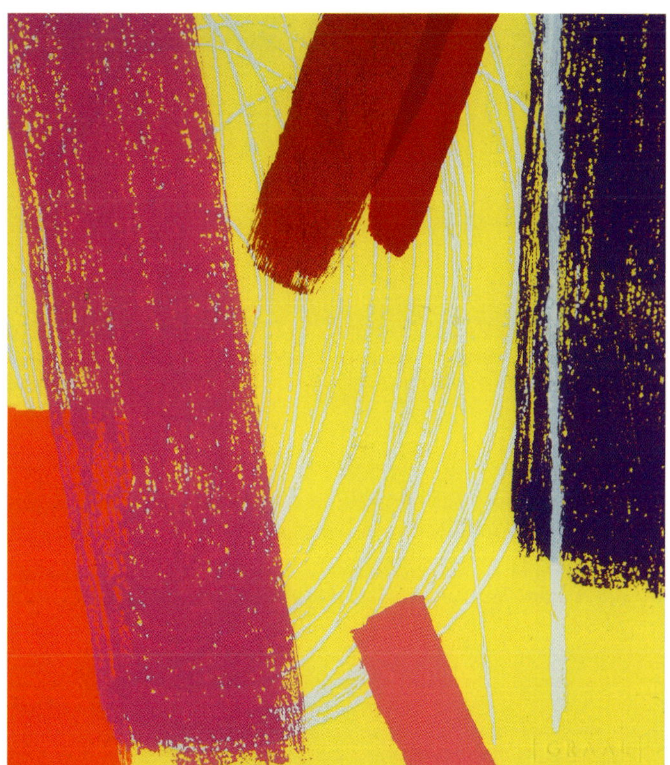

Cat.52

Untitled (editioned posthumously, 2007)

Screen print, ten colours

29.0 x 24.0 (image and paper size)

Arches Velin Blanc 400gsm

Edition of 25. Carol Robertson, Graal Press

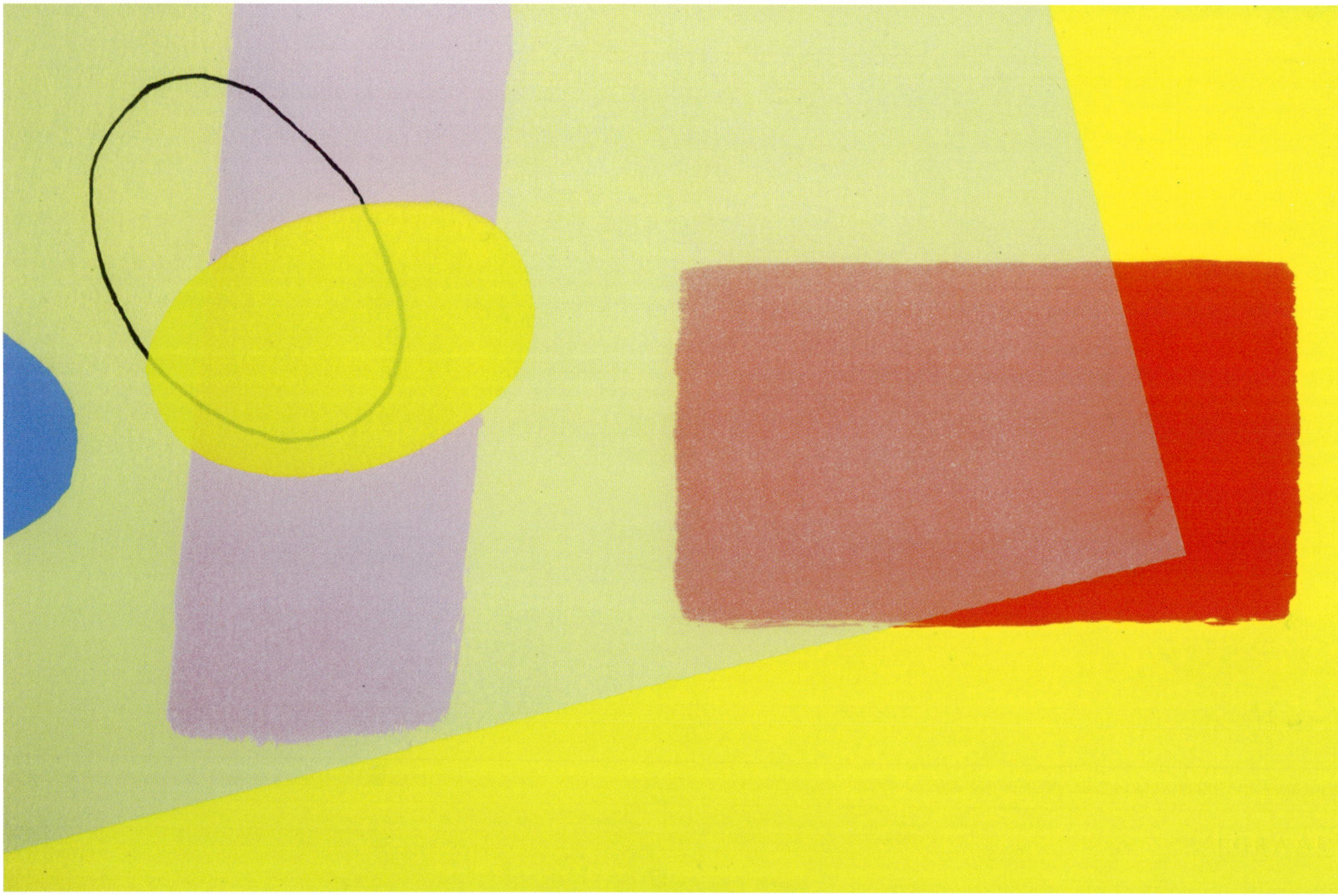

THE SERIES

(i) Cobalt Playing Games Series

Cat.53

Cobalt Playing Games (editioned posthumously, 2006)

Screenprint, eight colours

29.5 x 40.0 (image and paper size)

Arches Velin Blanc paper 400gsm

Edition of 25. Carol Robertson, Graal Press

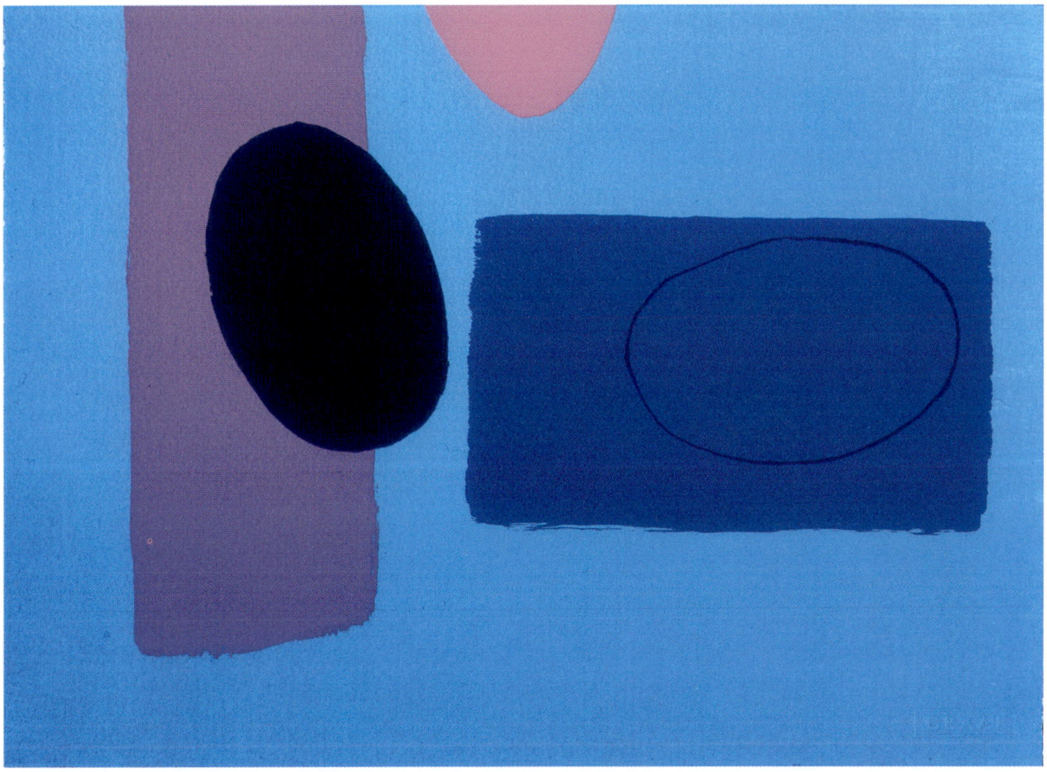

CAT.54

Cobalt and Pink Playing Games
(editioned posthumously, 2006)

Screenprint, nine colours

29.5 x 40.0 (image and paper size)

Arches Velin Blanc 400gsm

Edition of 25. Carol Robertson, Graal Press

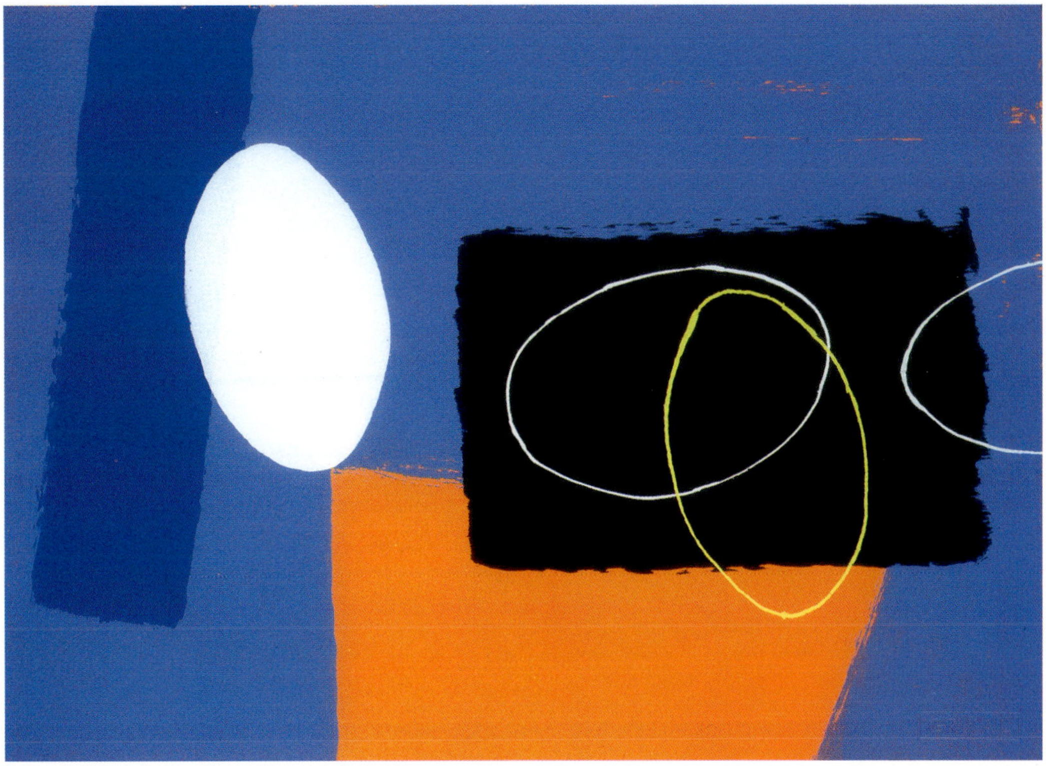

CAT.55

Cobalt and Orange Playing Games
(editioned posthumously, 2007)

Screenprint, nine colours

29.5 x 40.0 (image and paper size)

Arches Velin Blanc 400gsm

Edition of 25. Carol Robertson, Graal Press

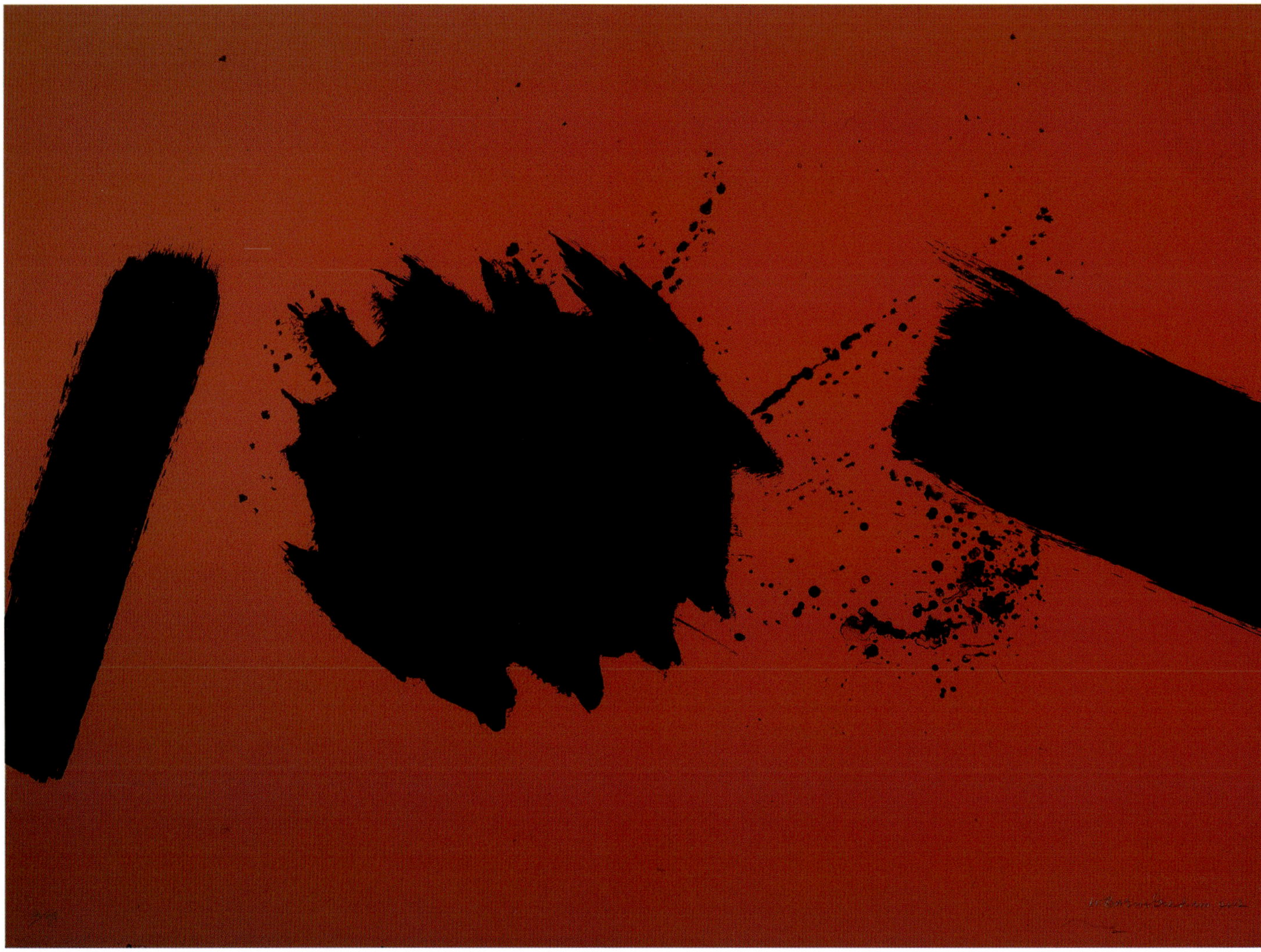

(ii) Earth Series

CAT.56

Earth Series I, 2002

Screenprint, five colours from three separations

58.2 x 76.3

Arches Velin Blanc 400gsm

Edition of 70. Carol Robertson, Graal Press

Signed and dated, lower right: *W Barns Graham 2002*; numbered, lower left

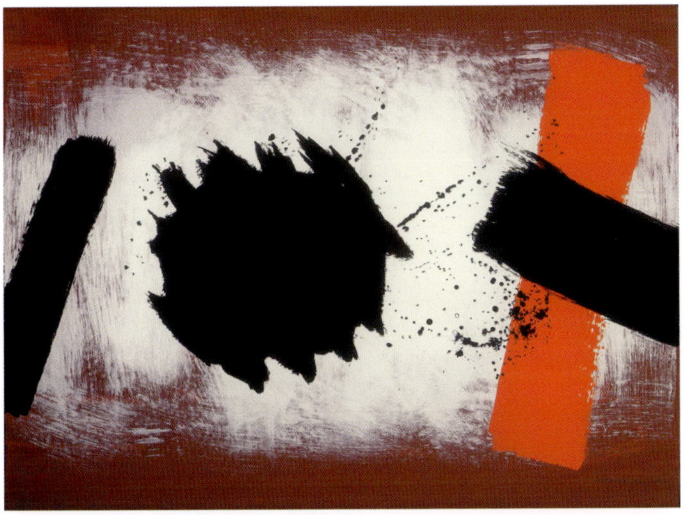

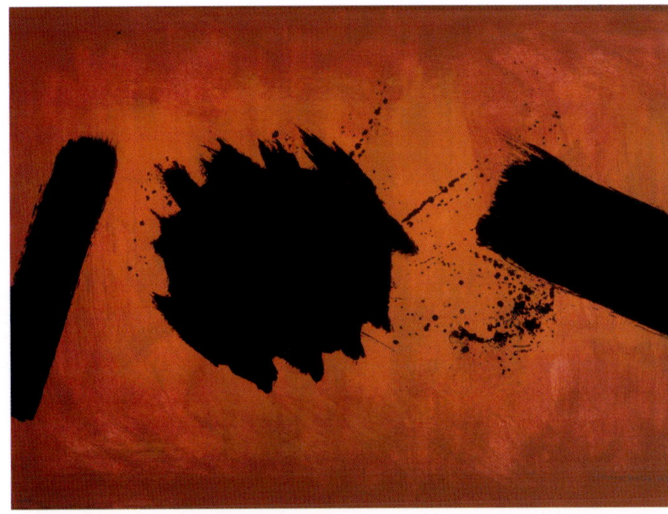

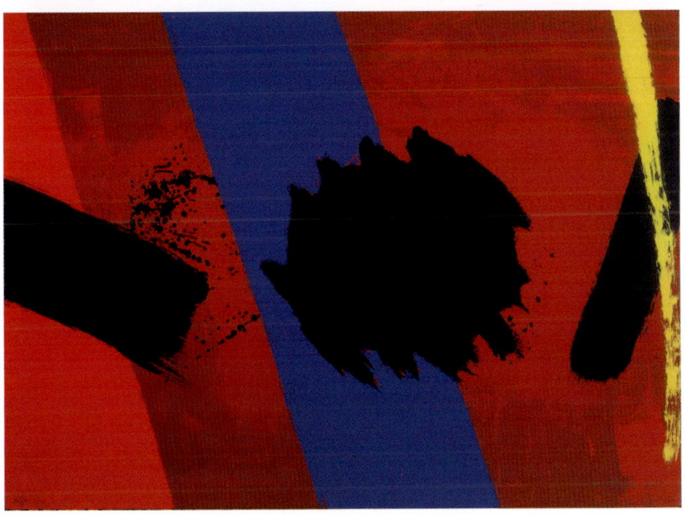

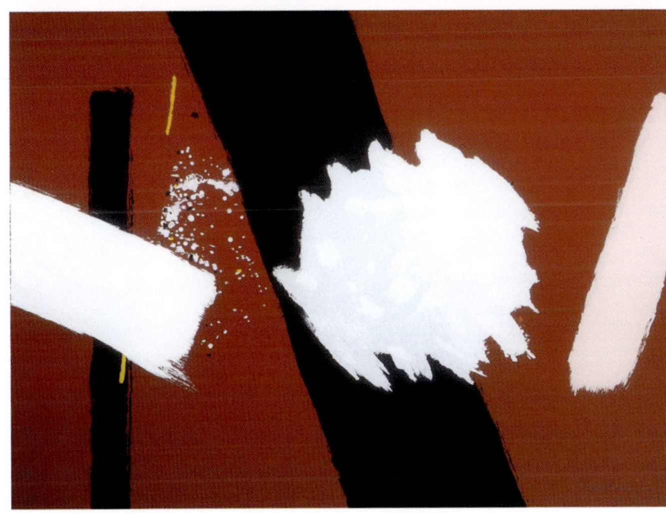

Cat. 57

***Earth Series II*, 2002**

Screenprint, eight colours from seven separations

58.0 x 76.0 (image and paper size)

Arches Velin Blanc 400gsm

Edition of 70. Carol Robertson, Graal Press

Signed and dated, lower right: *W Barns Graham 2002*; numbered, lower left

Cat.58

***Earth Series III*, 2002**

Screenprint, five colours

58.5 x 76.2 (image and paper size)

Arches Velin Blanc 400gsm

Edition of 70. Carol Robertson, Graal Press

Signed and dated, lower right: *W Barns Graham 2002*; numbered, lower left

Cat.59

***Earth Series IV*, 2002**

Screenprint, eleven colours

58.0 x 76.0 (image and paper size)

Arches Velin Blanc 400gsm

Edition of 70. Carol Robertson, Graal Press

Signed and dated, lower right: *W Barns Graham 2002*; numbered, lower left

Note: Graal blind stamp top left corner upside down.

Cat.60

***Earth Series V*, 2002**

Screenprint, five colours

58.0 x 76.0 (image and paper size)

Arches Velin Blanc 400gsm

Edition of 65. Carol Robertson, Graal Press

Signed and dated, lower right: *W Barns Graham 2002*; numbered, lower left

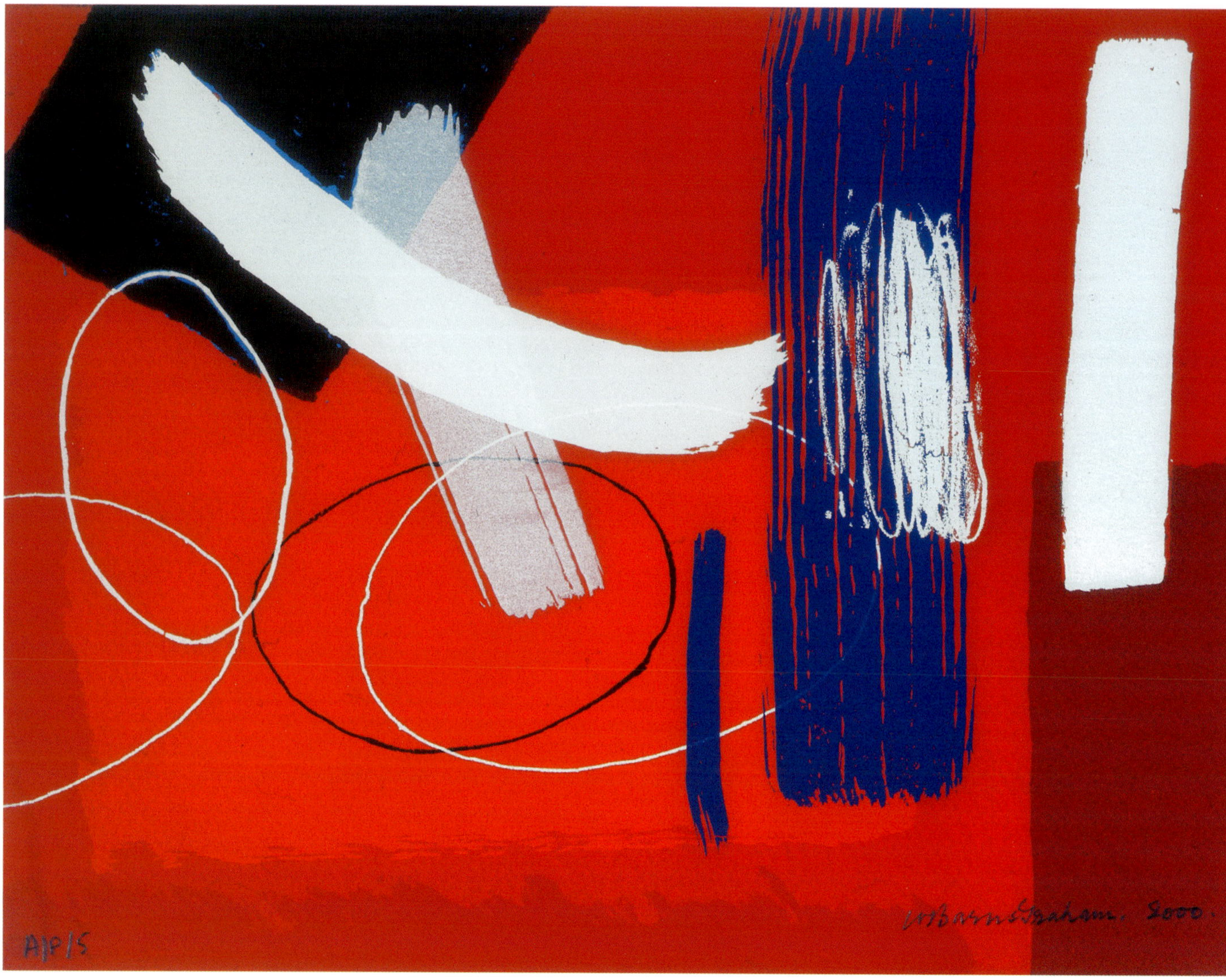

(iii) Millennium Series

CAT.61

***Millennium Series Red*, 2000**

Screenprint, fourteen colours

22.0 x 28.0 (image and paper size)

Arches Velin Blanc 400gsm

Edition of 140. Carol Robertson, Graal Press, Edinburgh

Signed and dated, lower right: *W Barns Graham 2000*; numbered, lower left.

Illustrated: Lynne Green, *W. Barns-Graham: A Studio Life* (Lund Humphries, 2001), p.270, fig.193

Note: Produced for limited edition of Lynne Green, *W. Barns-Graham: A Studio Life*; smaller than the other *Millennium Series* prints.

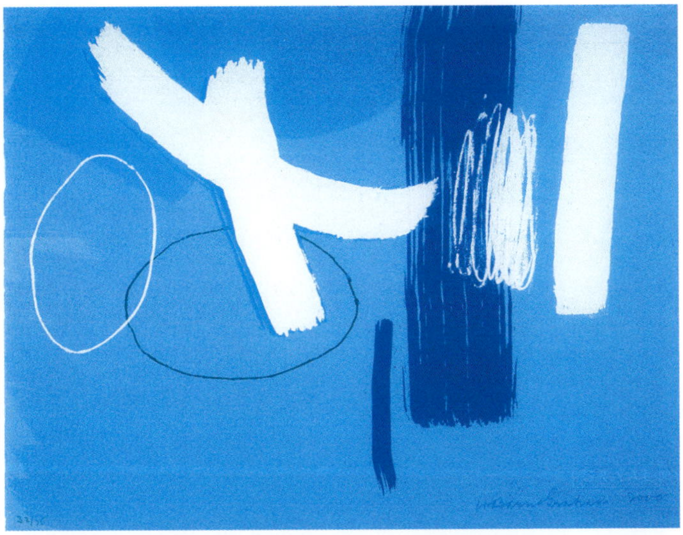

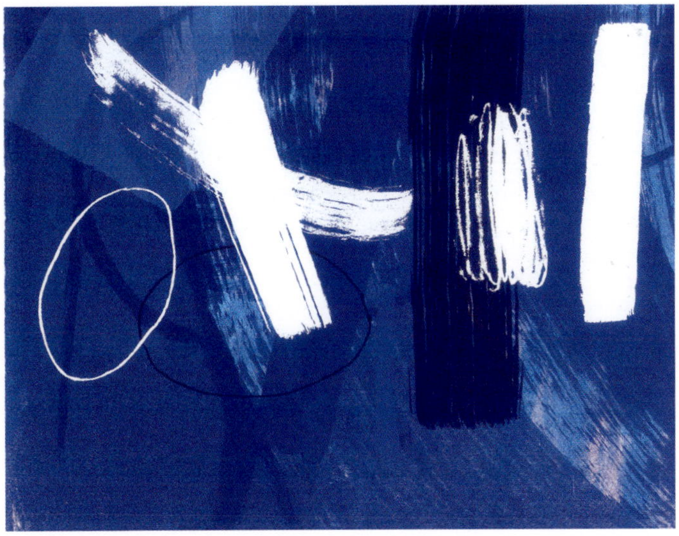

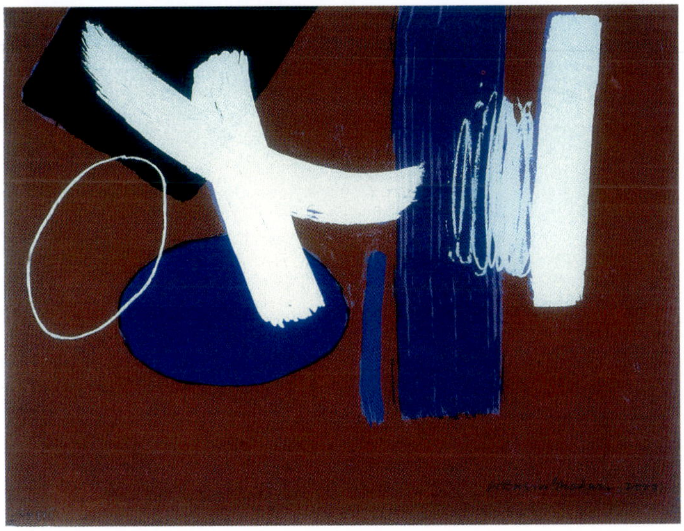

Cat.62

Millennium Series Blue I, 2000

Screenprint, thirteen colours

24.0 x 30.5 (image and paper size)

Arches Velin Blanc 400gsm

Edition of 75. Carol Robertson, Graal Press

Signed and dated, lower right: *W Barns Graham 1999*; numbered, lower left

Cat.63

Millennium Series Blue II, 2000

Screenprint, fifteen colours

24.0 x 30.5 (image and paper size)

Arches Velin Blanc 400gsm

Edition of 75. Carol Robertson, Graal Press

Signed and dated, lower right: *W Barns Graham 2000*; numbered, lower left.

Cat. 64

Millennium Series Brown, 2000

Screenprint, fifteen colours

24.0 x 30.5 (image and paper size)

Arches Velin Blanc 400gsm

Edition of 75. Carol Robertson, Graal Press

Signed and dated, lower right: *W Barns Graham 2000*; numbered, lower left

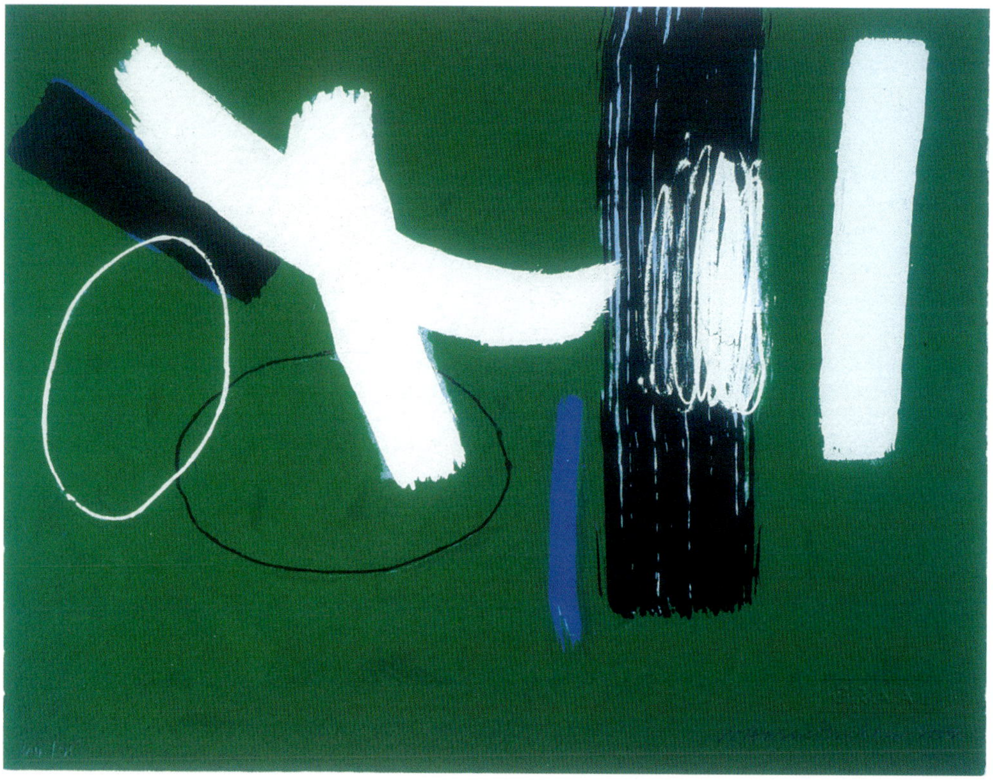

Cat.65

Millennium Series Green, 2000

Screenprint, eleven colours

24.0 x 30.5 (image and paper size)

Arches Velin Blanc 400gsm

Edition of 75. Carol Robertson, Graal Press

Signed and dated, lower right: *W Barns Graham 2000*; numbered, lower left

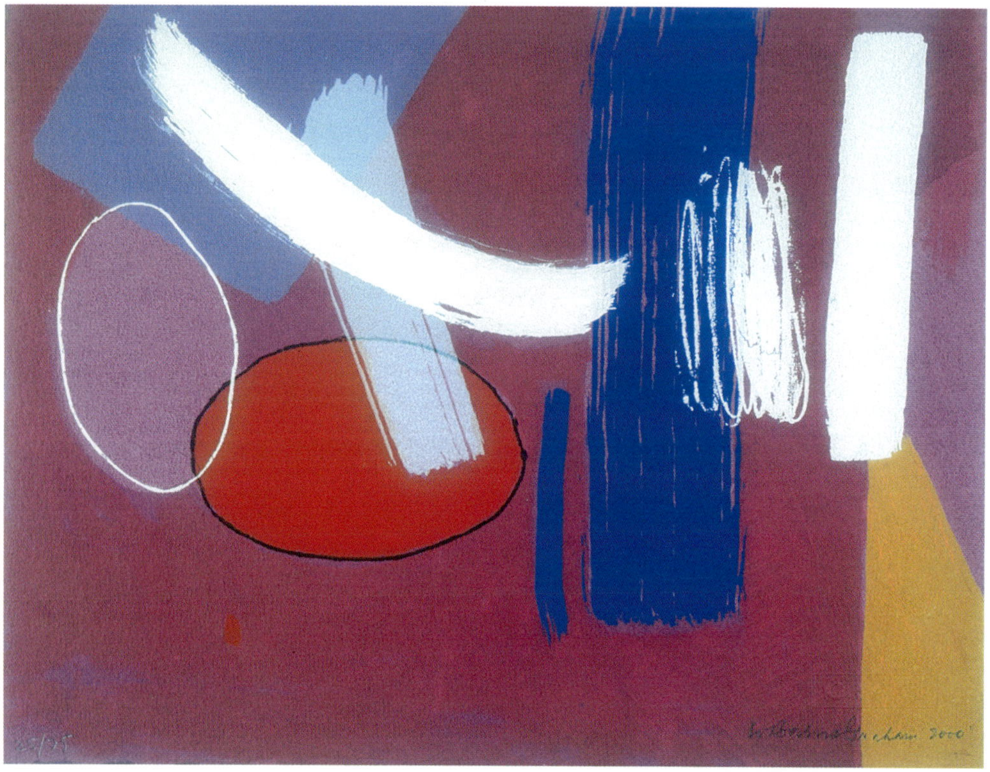

Cat.66

Millennium Series Pink, 2000

Screenprint, fifteen colours

24.0 x 30.5 (image and paper size)

Arches Velin Blanc 400gsm

Edition of 75. Carol Robertson, Graal Press

Signed and dated, lower right: *W Barns Graham 2000*; numbered, lower left

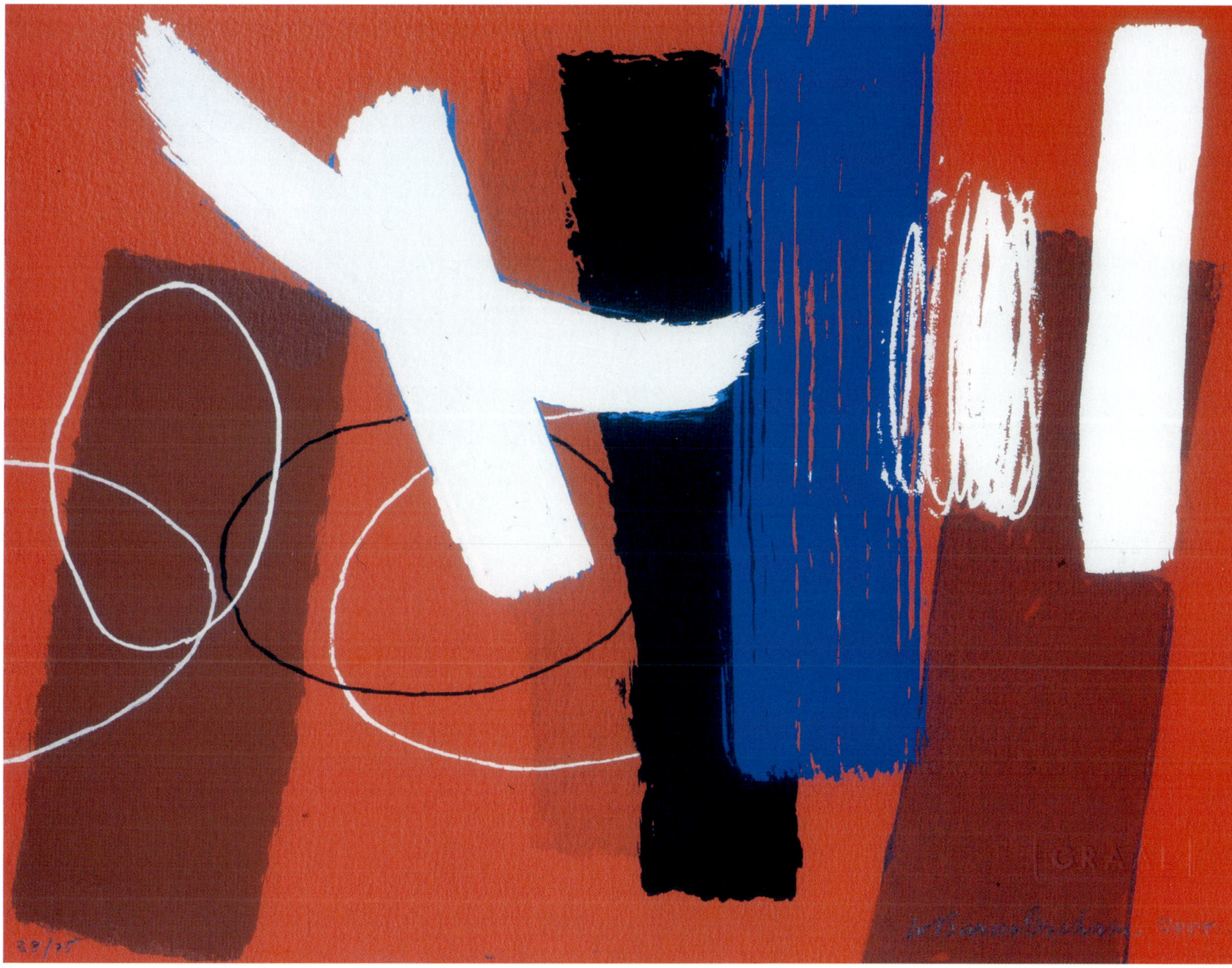

Cat.67

Millennium Series Red, 2000

Screenprint, sixteen colours

24.0 x 30.0 (image and paper size)

Arches Velin Blanc 400gsm

Edition of 75. Carol Robertson, Graal Press

Signed and dated, lower right: *W Barns Graham 2000*; numbered, lower left

Illustrated: Robert Adam and Carol Robertson, *Screenprinting: The Complete Water-based System* (London, 2003), p.156.

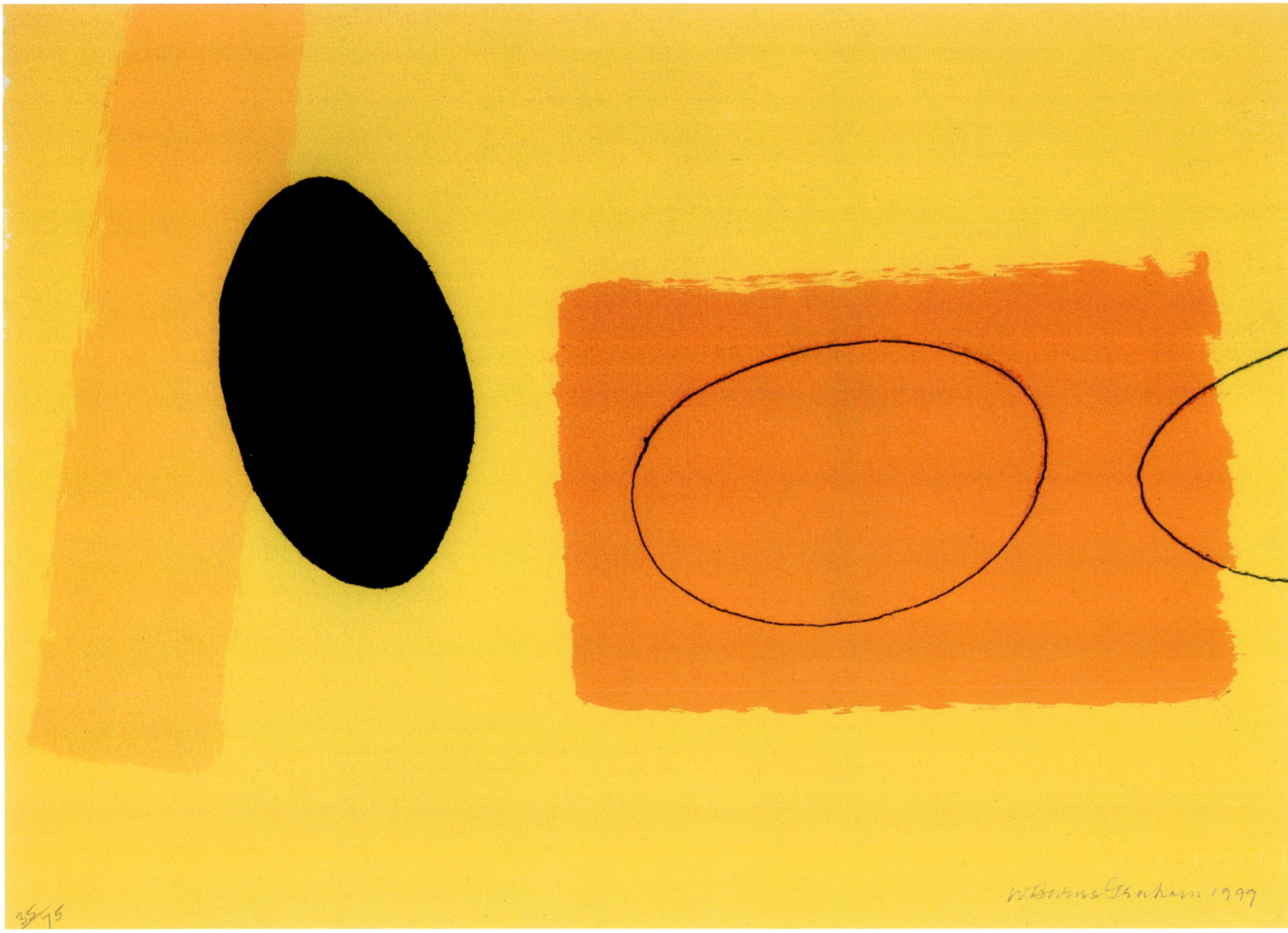

(iv) Orange and Lemon Playing Games Series

CAT.68

Orange and Lemon Playing Games, 1999

Screenprint, eleven colours

29.5 x 40.0 (image and paper size)

Moulin du Gué 300gsm

Edition of 75. Carol Robertson, Graal Press

Signed and dated, lower right: *W Barns Graham 1999*; numbered, lower left

Illustrated: Robert Adam and Carol Robertson, *Screenprinting: The Complete Water-based System* (London, 2003), p. 200.

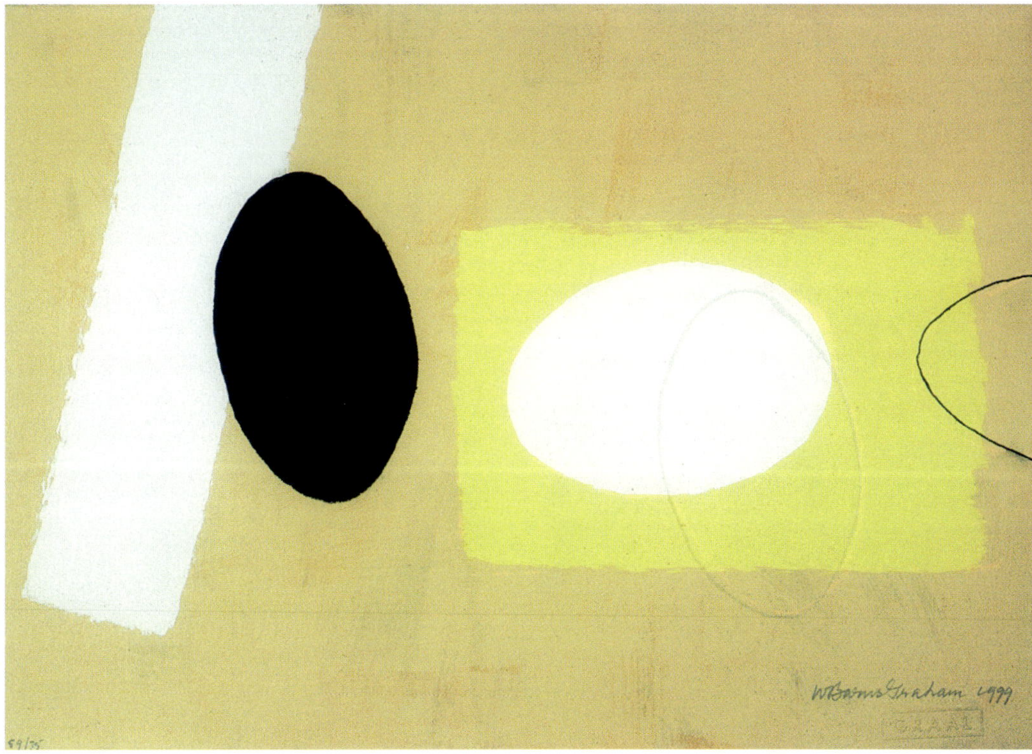

Cat.69

Orange and Lemon Playing Games I, 1999

Screenprint, eleven colours

29.5 x 40.5 (image and paper size)

Arches Velin Blanc 400gsm

Edition of 75. Carol Robertson, Graal Press

Signed and dated, lower right: *W Barns Graham 1999*; numbered, lower left

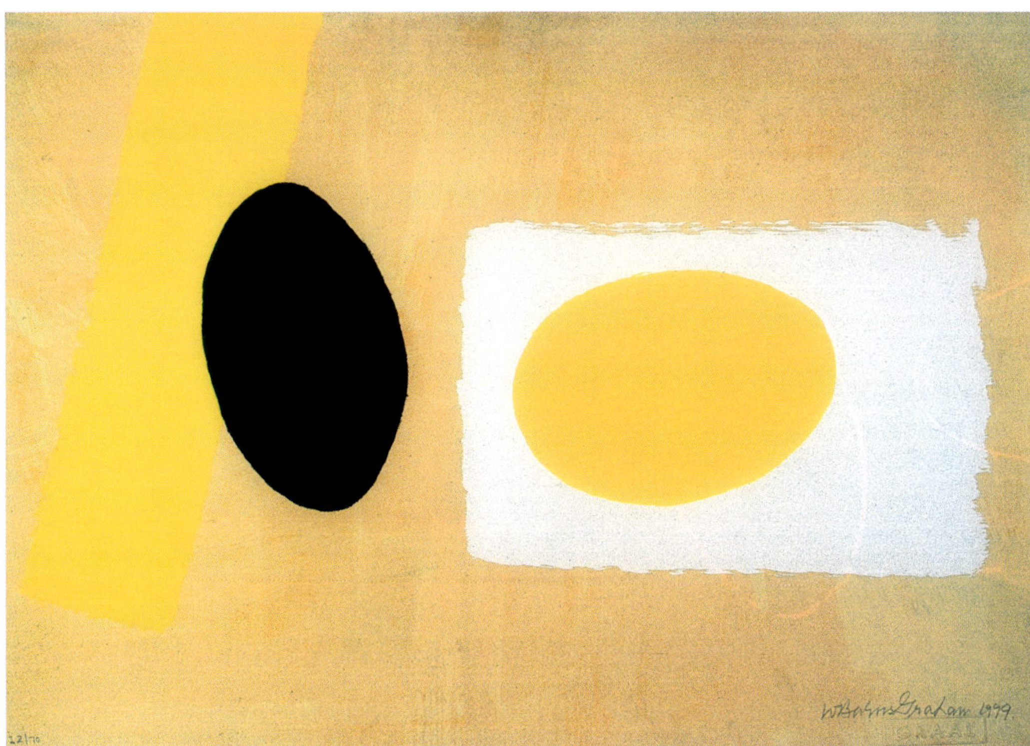

Cat.70

Orange and Lemon Playing Games II, 1999

Screenprint, eight colours

29.3 x 40.5 (image and paper size)

Arches Velin Blanc 400gsm

Edition of 75. Carol Robertson, Graal Press

Signed and dated, lower right: *W Barns Graham 1999*; numbered, lower left

(v) Red Playing Games Series

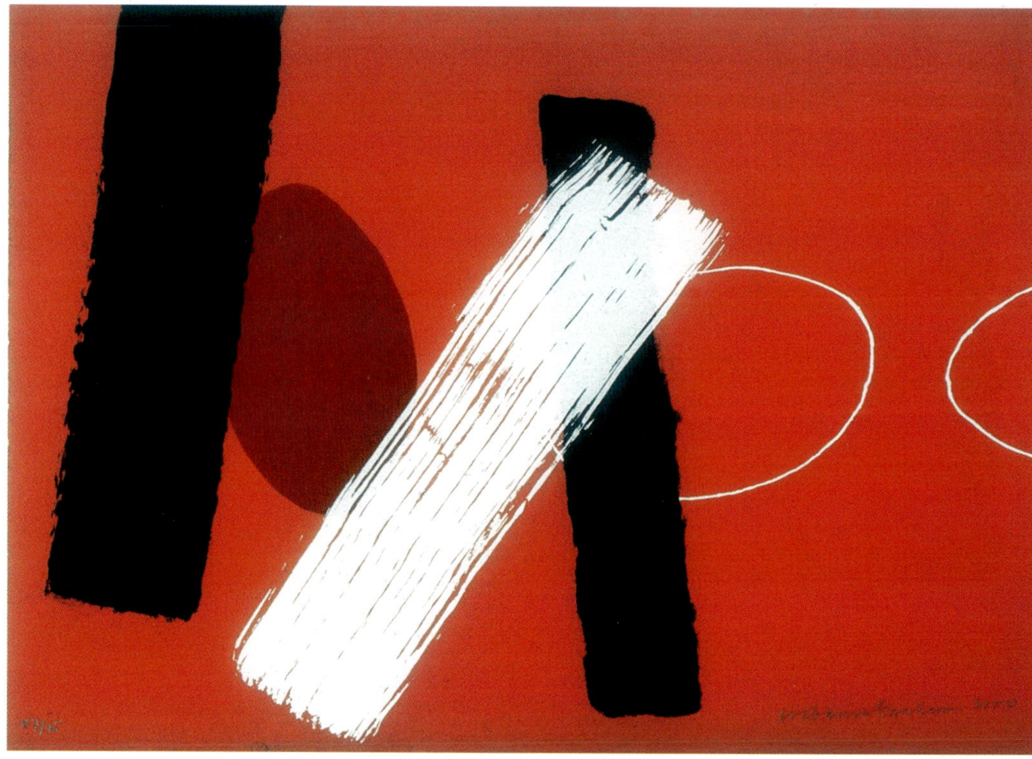

Cat.71

Red Playing Games I, 2000

Screenprint, fifteen colours

29.5 x 40.0 (image and paper size)

Arches Velin Blanc 400gsm

Edition of 75. Carol Robertson, Graal Press

Signed and dated, lower right: *W Barns Graham 2000*; numbered, lower left

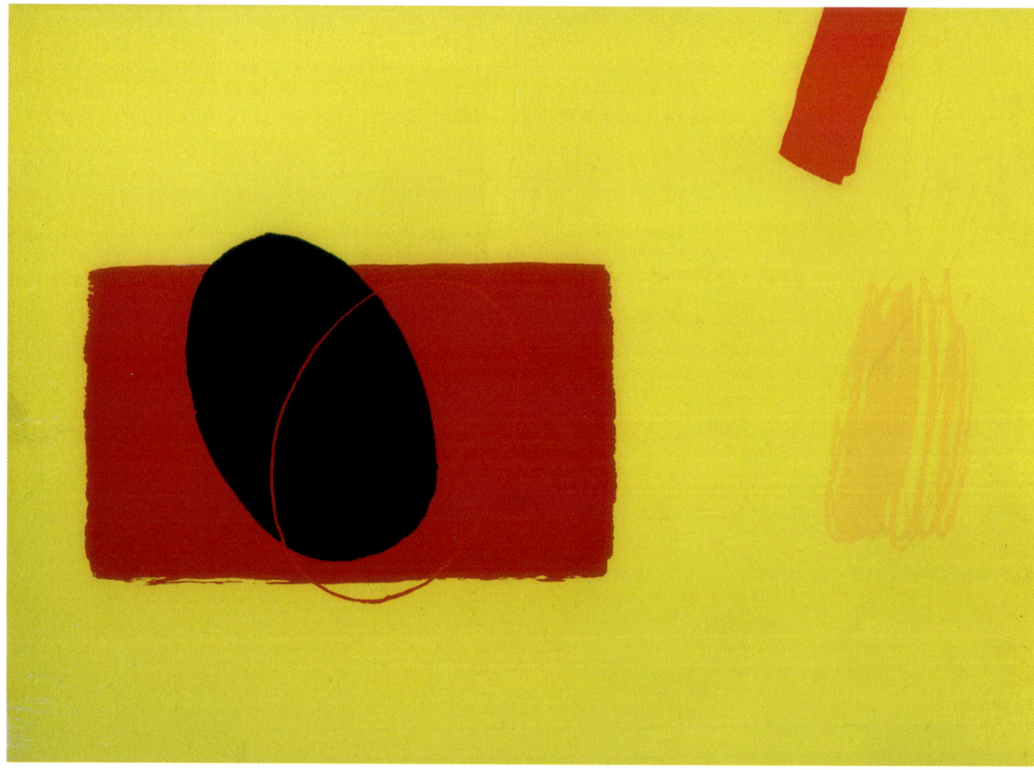

Cat.72

Red Playing Games II (editioned posthumously, 2006)

Screenprint, seven colours

29.0 x 40.0 (image and paper size)

Arches Velin Blanc 400gsm

Edition of 25. Carol Robertson, Graal Press

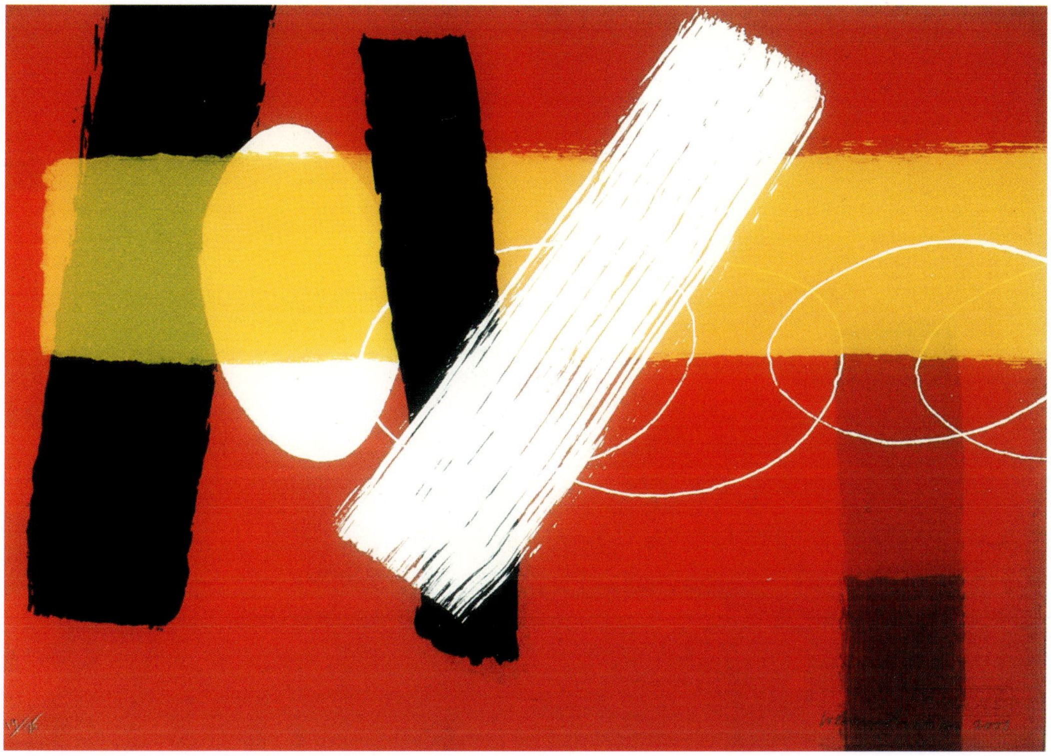

Cat.73

Red Playing Games III, 2001

Screenprint, fifteen colours

29.5 x 40.0 (image and paper size)

Arches Velin Blanc 400gsm

Edition of 75. Carol Robertson, Graal Press

Signed and dated, lower right: *W Barns Graham 2001*; numbered, lower left

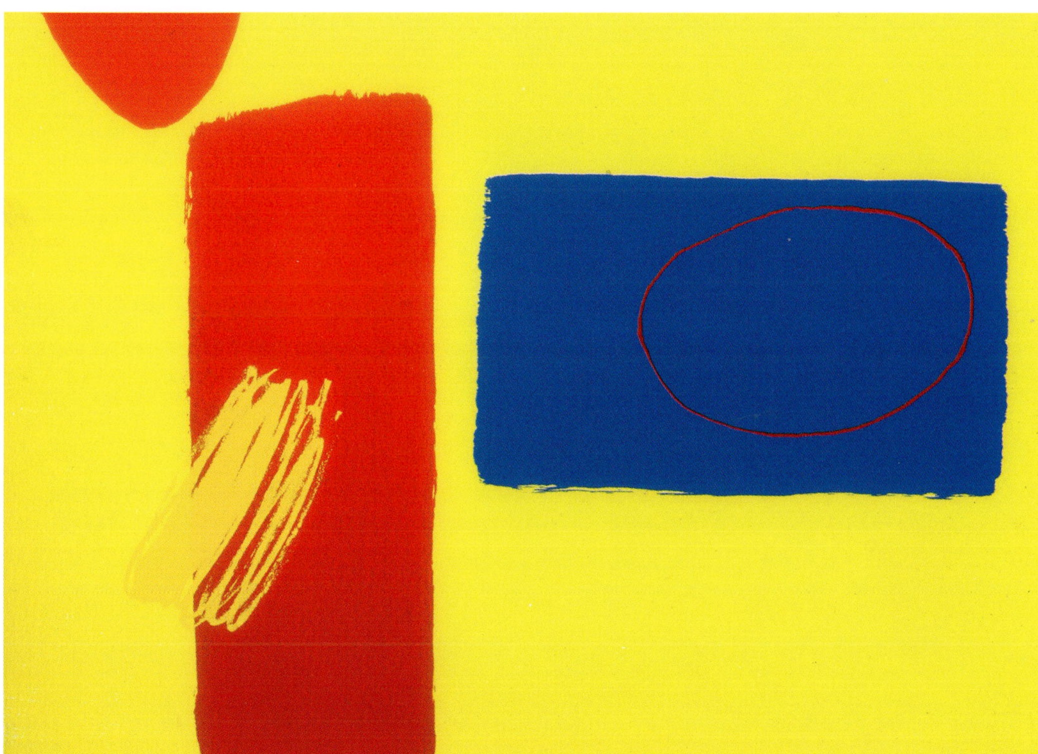

Cat.74

Red Playing Games IV (editioned posthumously, 2006)

Screenprint, seven colours

29.7 x 40.0 (image and paper size)

Arches Velin Blanc 400gsm

Edition of 25. Carol Robertson, Graal Press

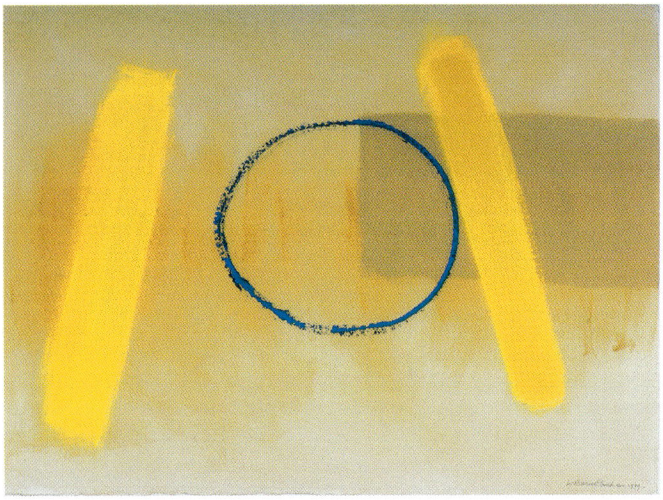

(vi) Sunghrie Series

Cat.75

***Sunghrie I*, 2001**

Screenprint, ten colours

58.0 x 76.0 (image and paper size)

Arches Velin Blanc 400gsm

Edition of 100. Carol Robertson, Graal Press

Signed and dated, lower right: *W Barns Graham* 2001; numbered, lower left

Cat.76

***Sunghrie II*, 2001**

Screenprint, fifteen colours

58.0 x 76.0 (image and paper size)

Arches Velin Blanc 400gsm

Edition of 100. Carol Robertson, Graal Press

Signed and dated, lower right: *W Barns Graham 2001*; numbered, lower left

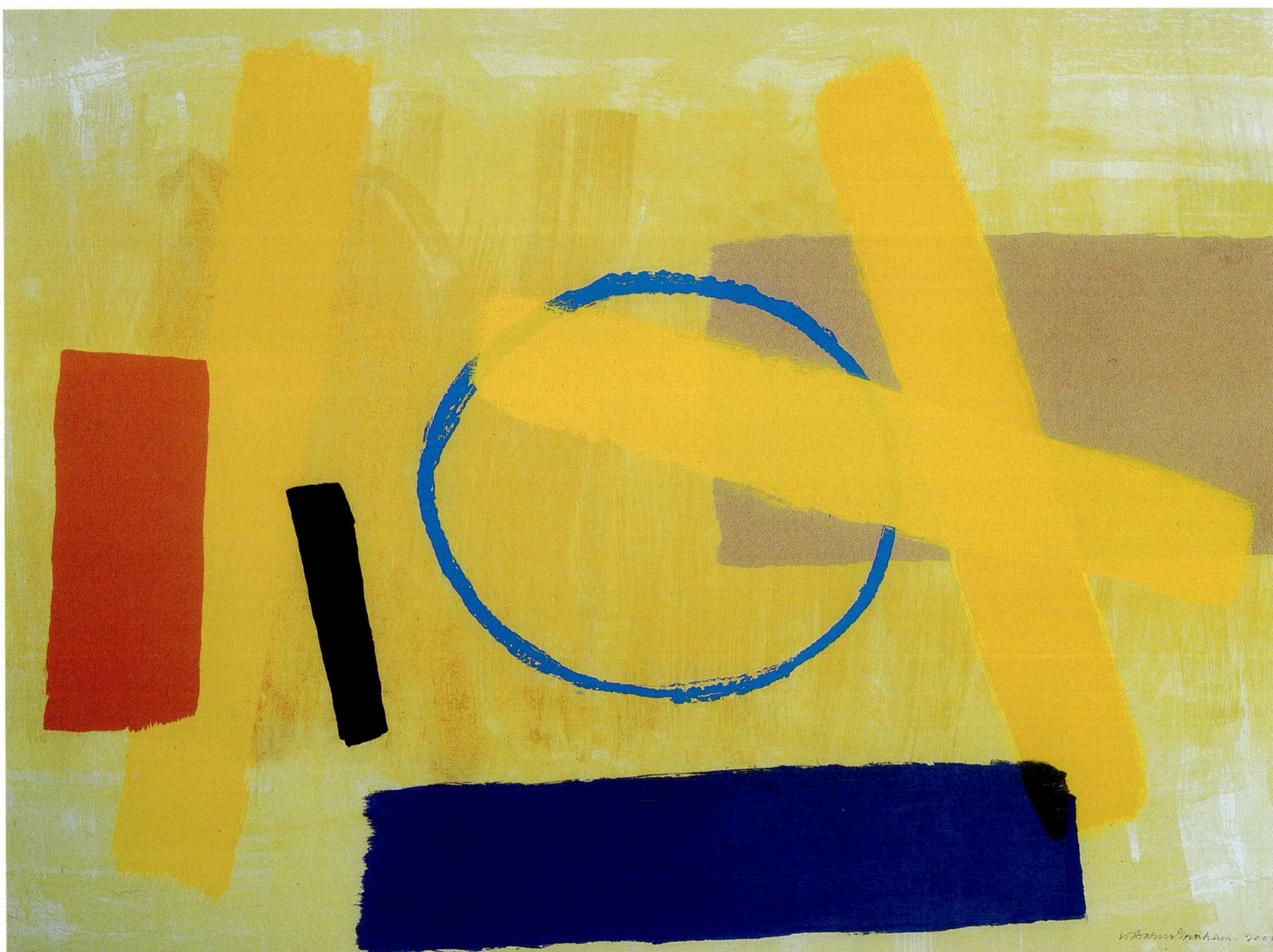

Cat.77

Sunghrie III, 2002

Screenprint, fifteen colours

58.0 x 76.0 (image and paper size)

Arches Velin Blanc 400gsm

Edition of 75. Carol Robertson, Graal Press

Signed and dated, lower right: *W Barns Graham 2002*; numbered, lower left

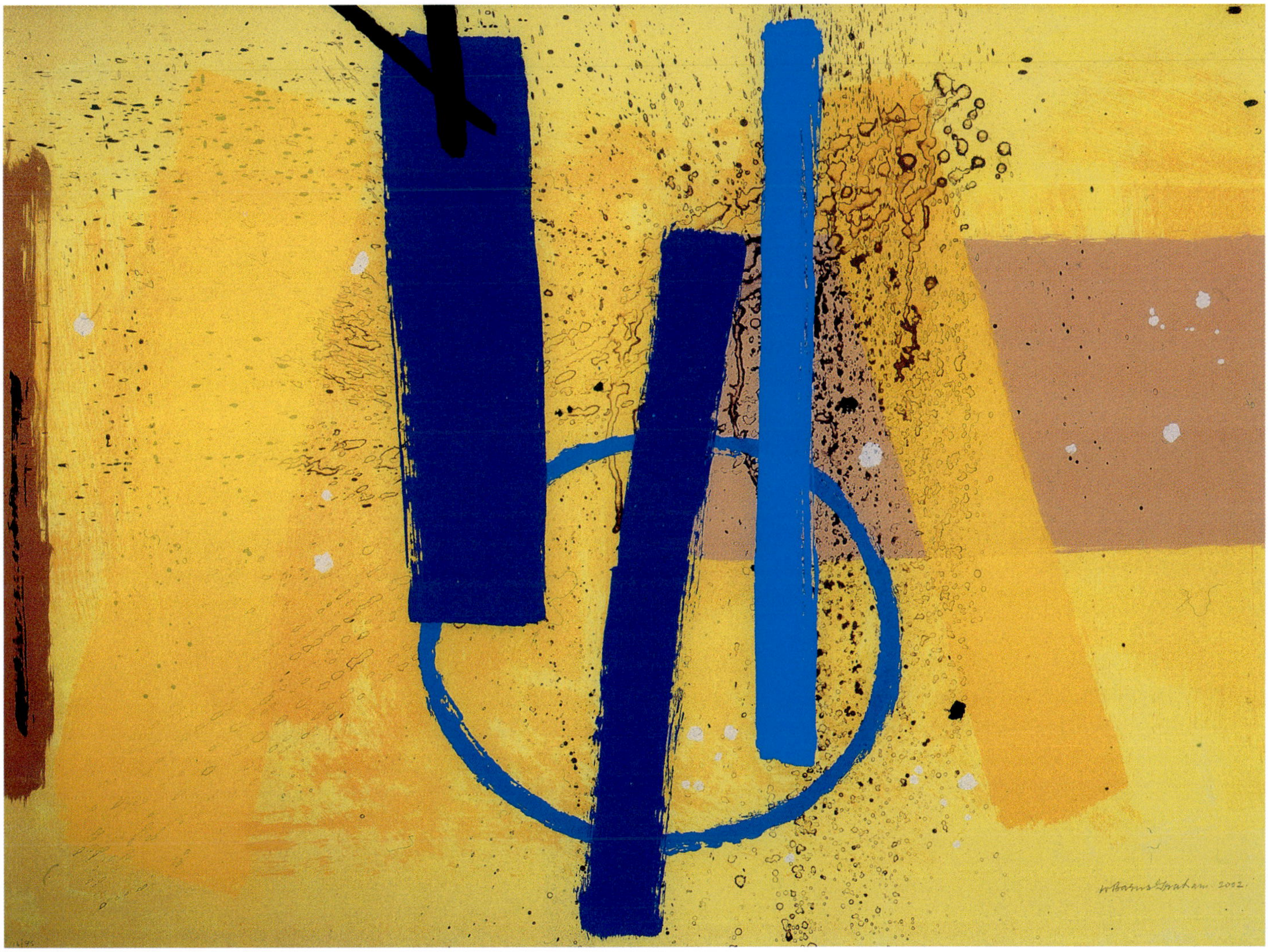

(vii) Time Series

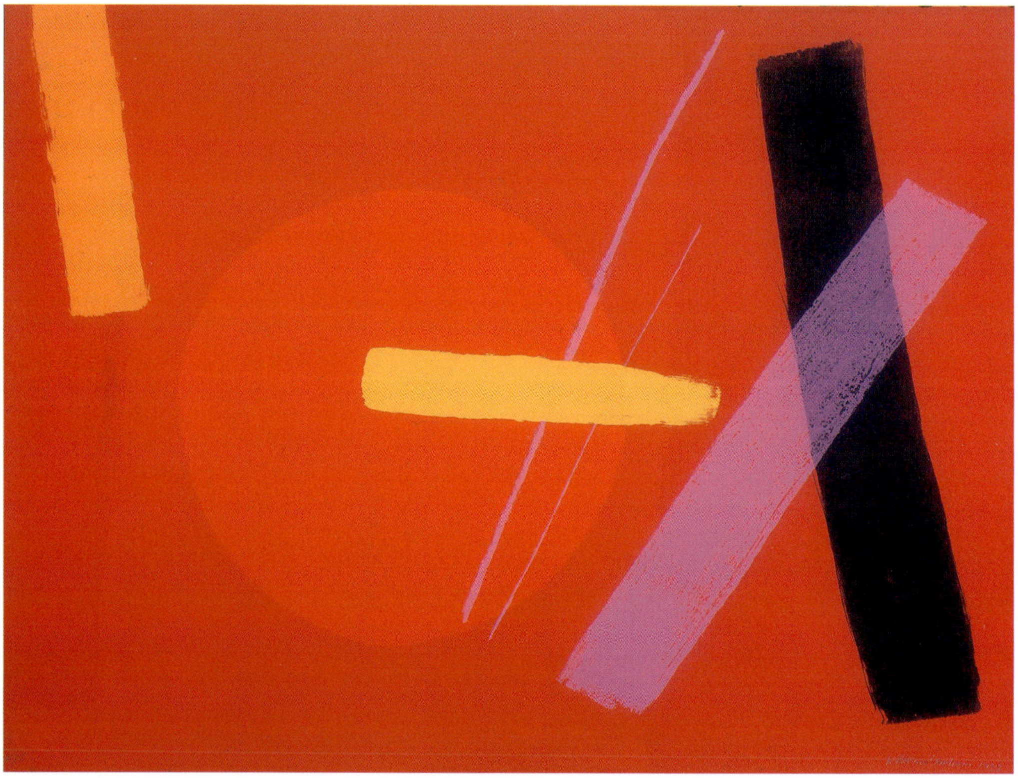

Cat.78

Another Time, 1999

Screenprint, nine colours

58.0 x 76.0 (image and paper size)

Moulin du Gué

Edition of 75. Carol Robertson, Graal Press

Signed and dated, lower right: *W Barns Graham 1999*; numbered, lower left

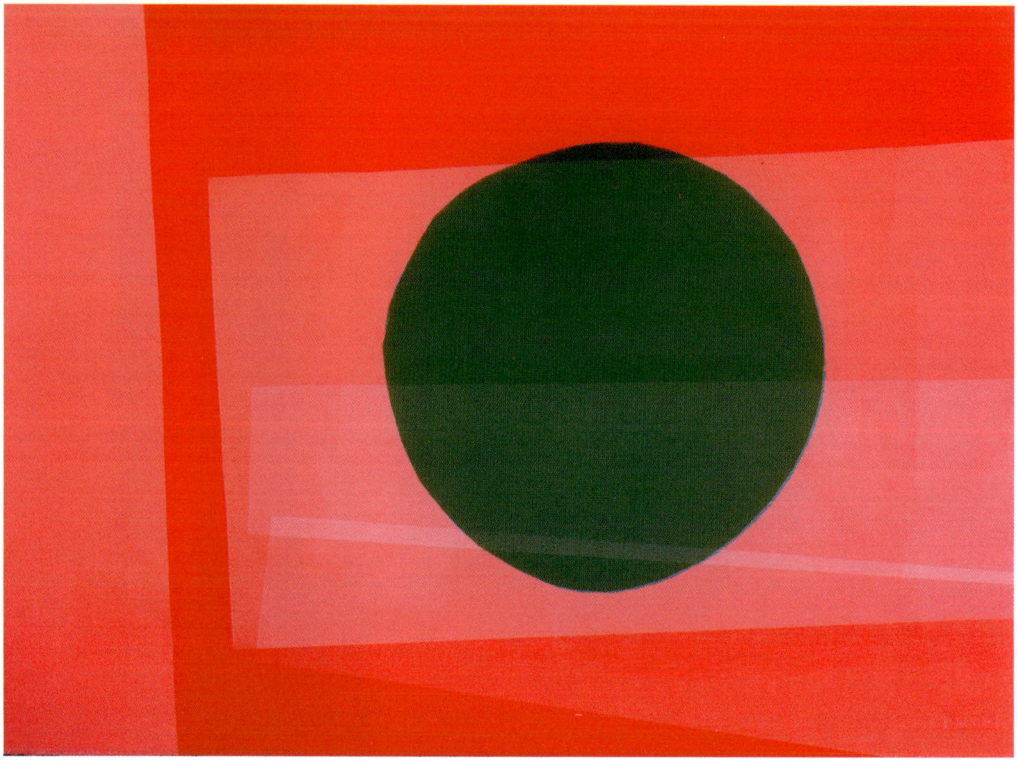

Cat.79

Drifting Time (editioned posthumously, 2006)

Screenprint, seven colours

58.0 x 76.0 (image and paper size)

Arches Velin Blanc 400gsm

Edition of 25. Carol Robertson, Graal Press

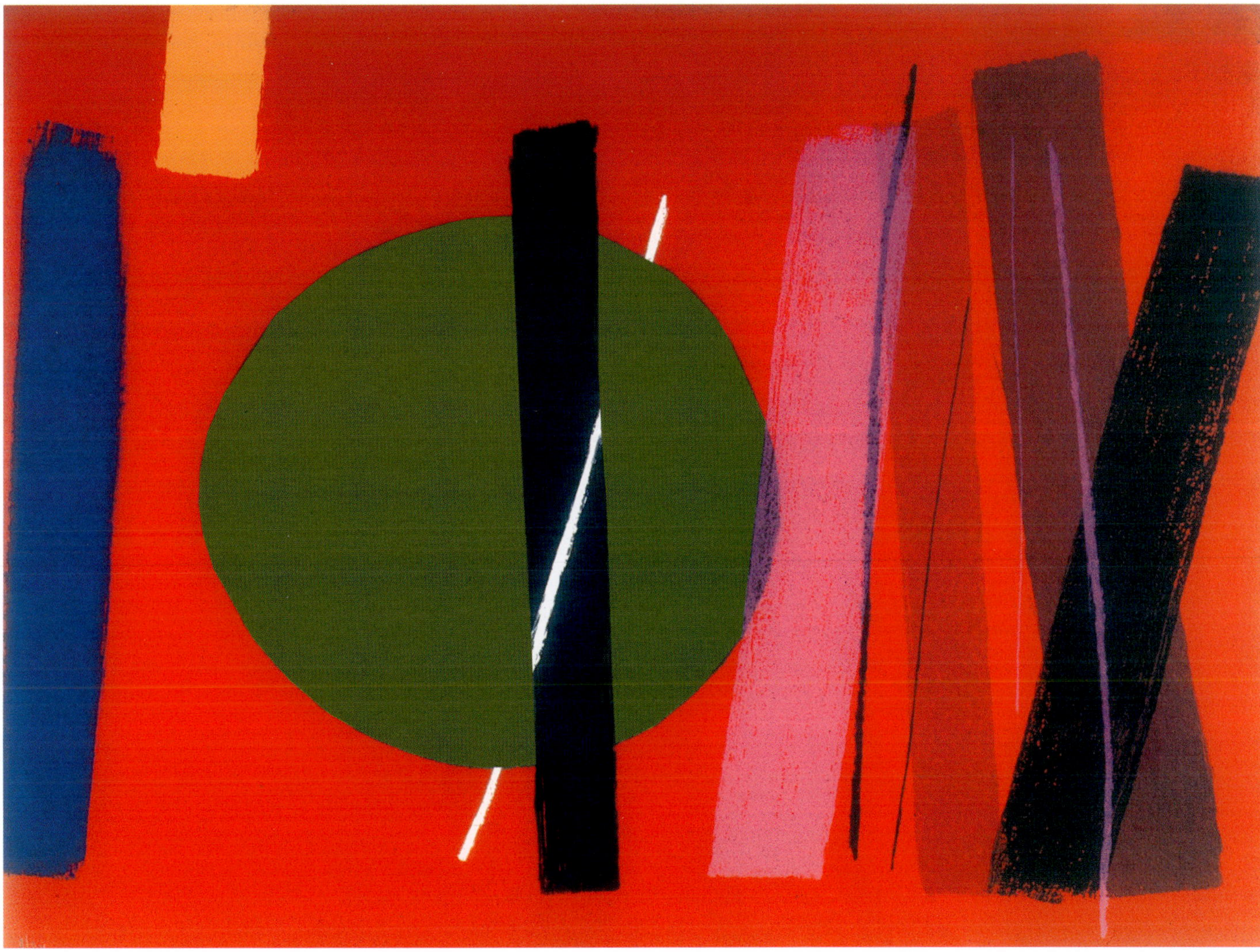

Cat.80

***Just in Time*, 1999**

Screenprint, fourteen colours

58.0 x 76.0 (image and paper size)

Moulin du Gué

Edition of 75. Carol Robertson, Graal Press

Signed and dated, lower right: *W Barns Graham 1999*; numbered, lower left

Lit. ref.: Illustrated in *Printmaking Today* (Winter 2000), p.14, with short note by Robert Adam about developments at Graal Press

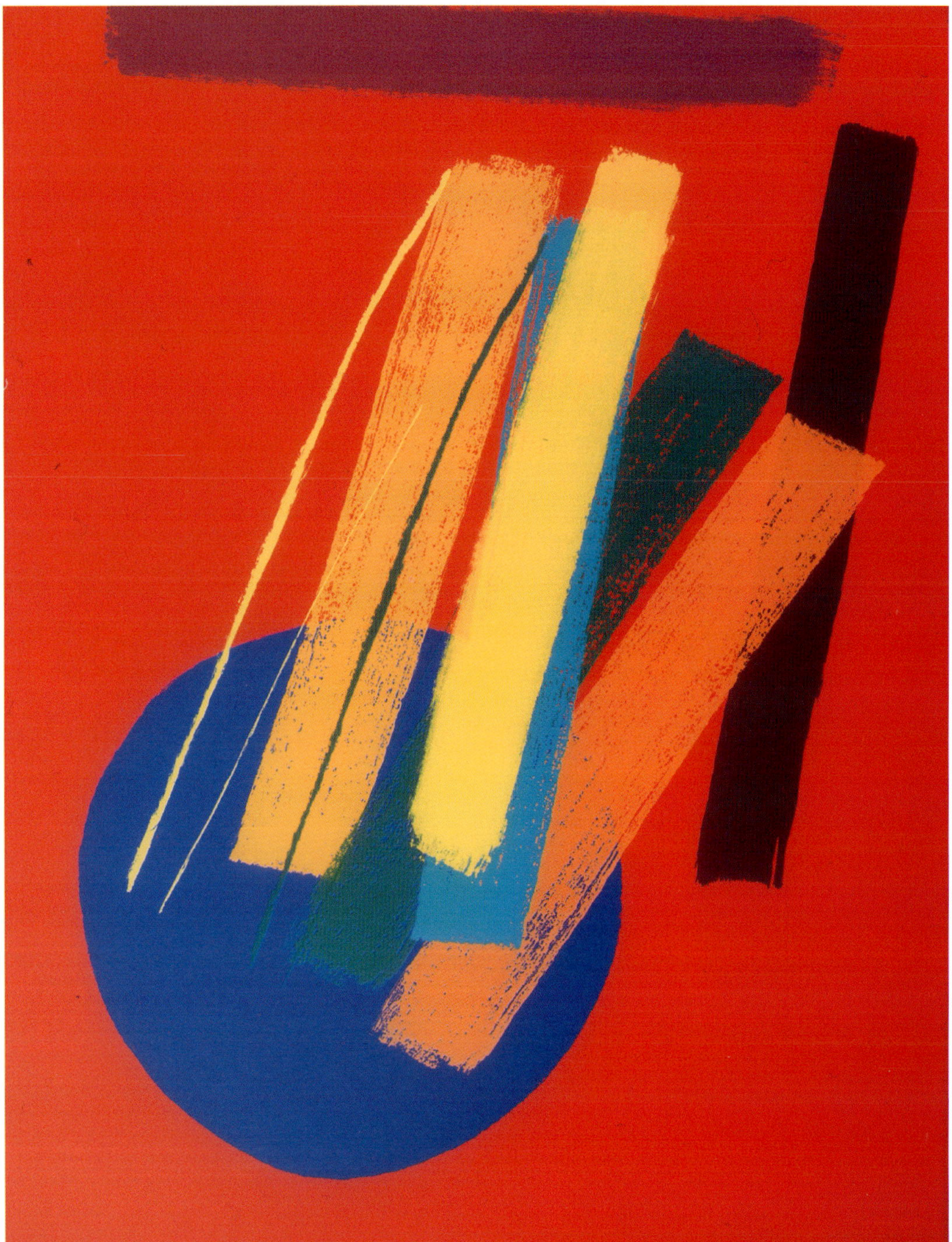

Cat.81

Quick Time (editioned posthumously, 2006)

Screenprint, thirteen colours

58.0 x 76.0 (image and paper size)

Arches Velin Blanc 400gsm

Edition of 25. Carol Robertson, Graal Press

CAT.82

Quiet Time, 1999

Screenprint, eleven colours

56.0 x 77.0 (image and paper size)

Moulin du Gué 275gsm

Edition of 50. Carol Robertson, Graal Press

Signed and dated, lower right: *W Barns Graham 1999*; numbered, lower left

Lit.ref.: Lynne Green, *W. Barns-Graham: A Studio Life* (Lund Humphries, 2001), p.268, illustrated p.269, fig.192; also illustrated in Robert Adam and Carol Robertson, *Screenprinting: The Complete Water-based System* (London, 2003), p.20

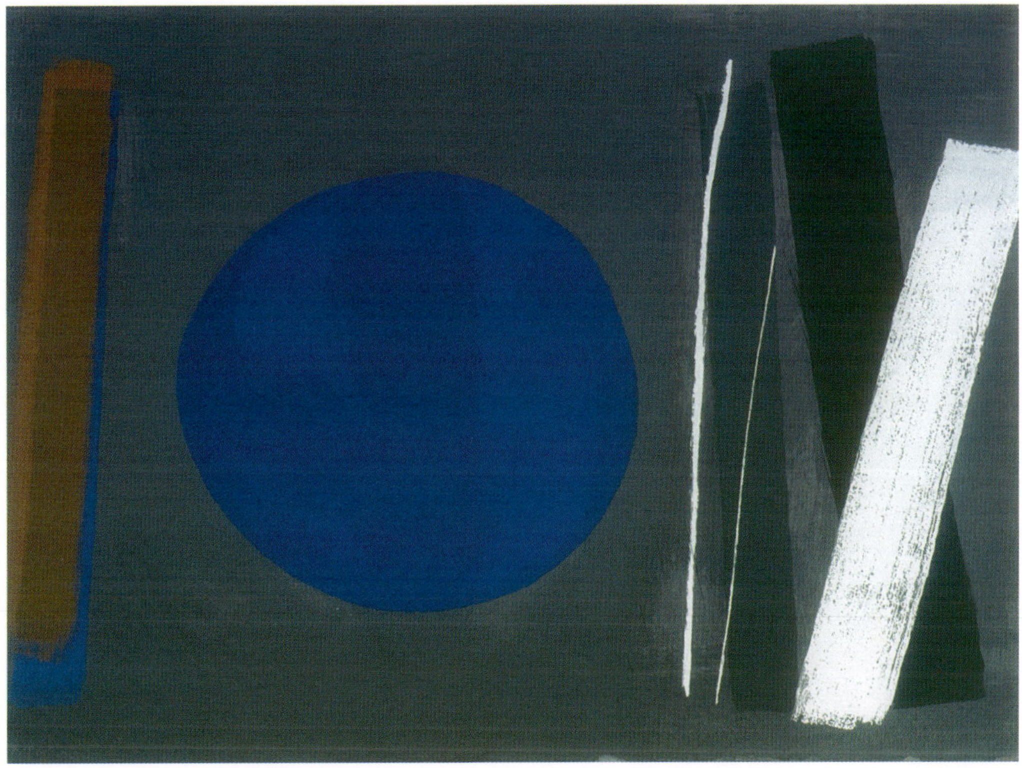

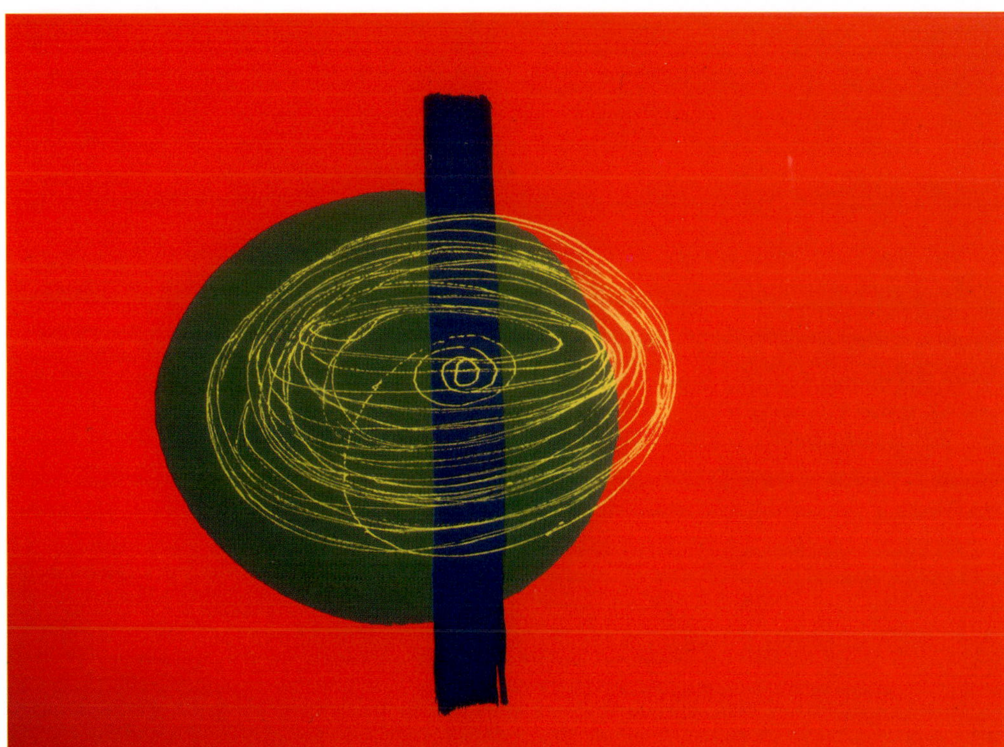

CAT.83

Runabout Time (editioned posthumously, 2006)

Screenprint, six colours

56.0 x 76.0 (image and paper size)

Arches Velin Blanc 400gsm

Edition of 25. Carol Robertson, Graal Press

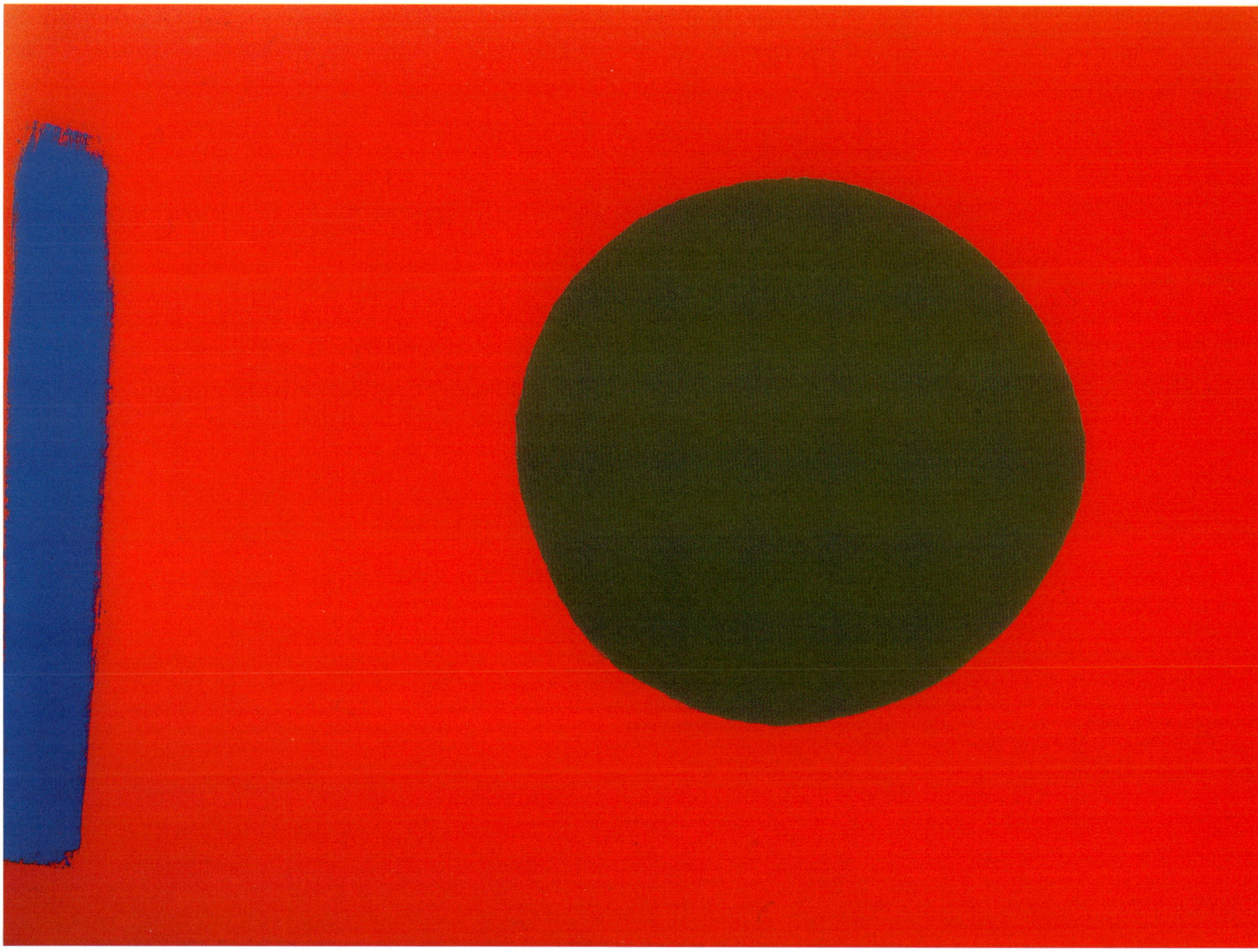

Cat.84

Secret Time (editioned posthumously, 2006)

Screenprint, five colours

58.0 x 76.0 (image and paper size)

Arches Velin Blanc 400gsm

Edition of 25. Carol Robertson, Graal Press

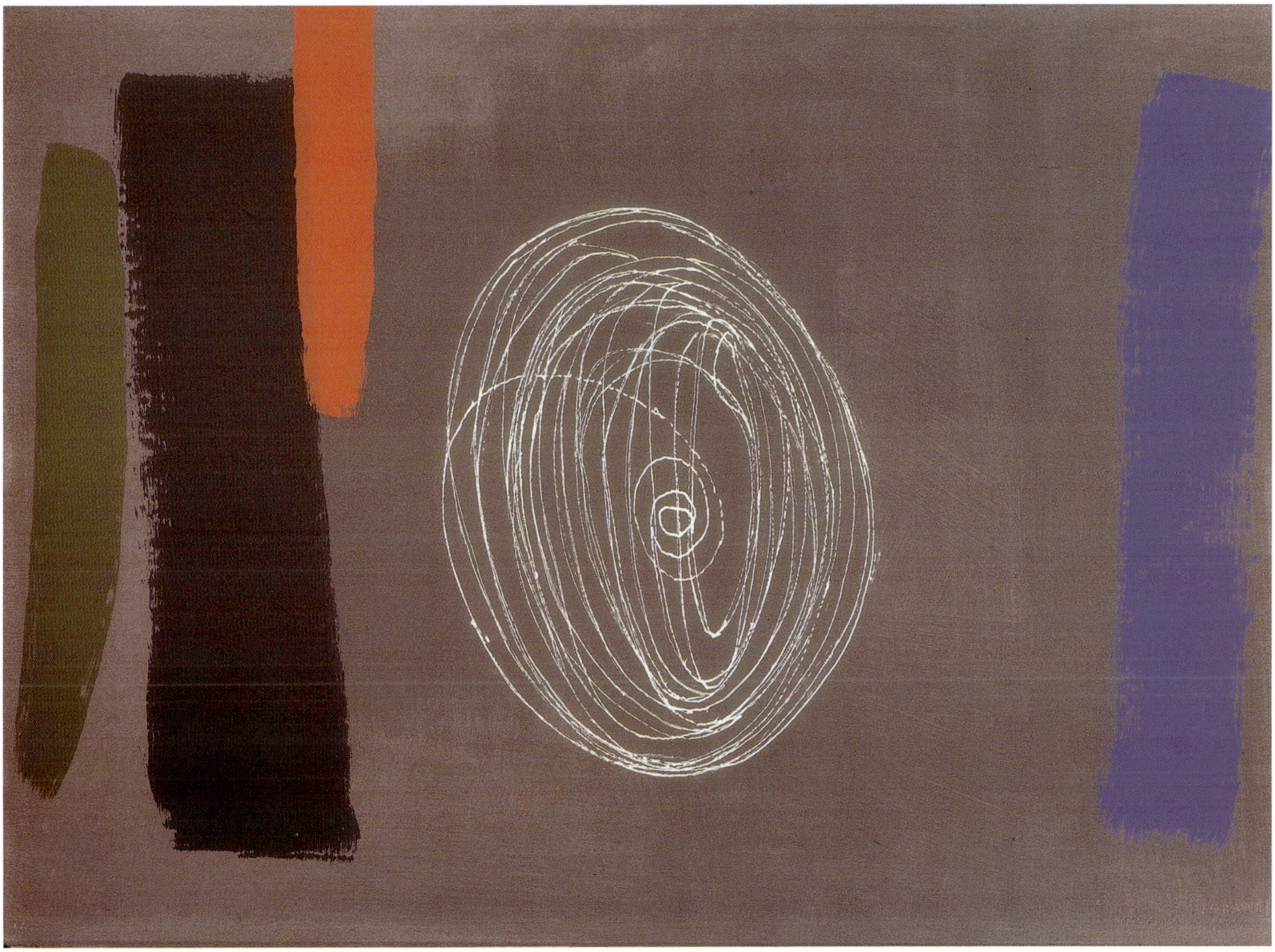

Cat.85

Walkabout Time, 1999

Screenprint, eleven colours

58.0 x 76.0 (image and paper size)

Arches Velin Blanc 400gsm

Edition of 50. Carol Robertson, Graal Press

Signed and dated, lower right: *W Barns Graham 1999*; numbered, lower left

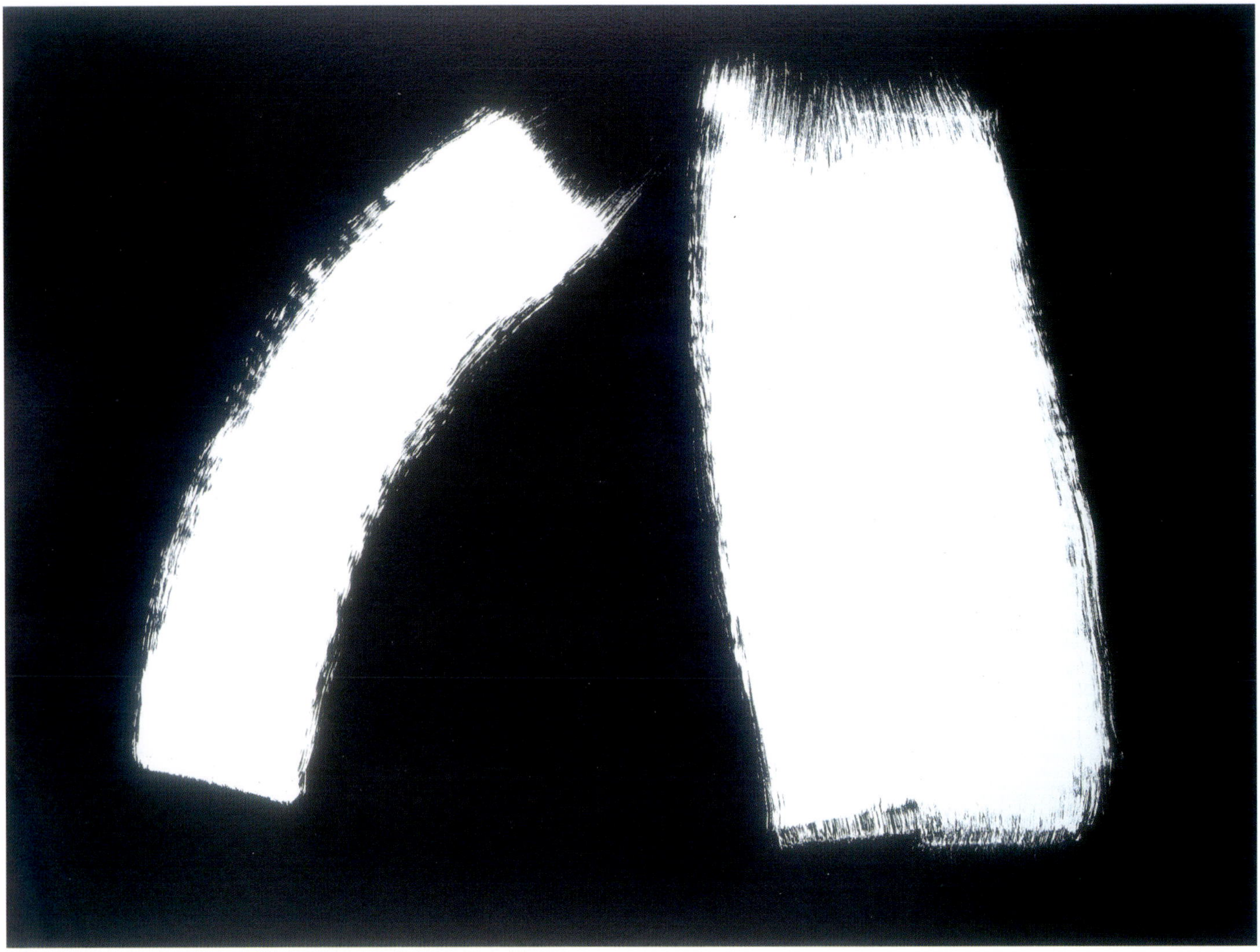

(viii) Two Brushstrokes Series

Cat.86

Two White Brushstrokes
(editioned posthumously, 2007)

Screenprint, five colours

76.0 x 76.0 (image and paper size)

Arches Velin Blanc 400gsm

Edition of 25. Carol Robertson, Graal Press

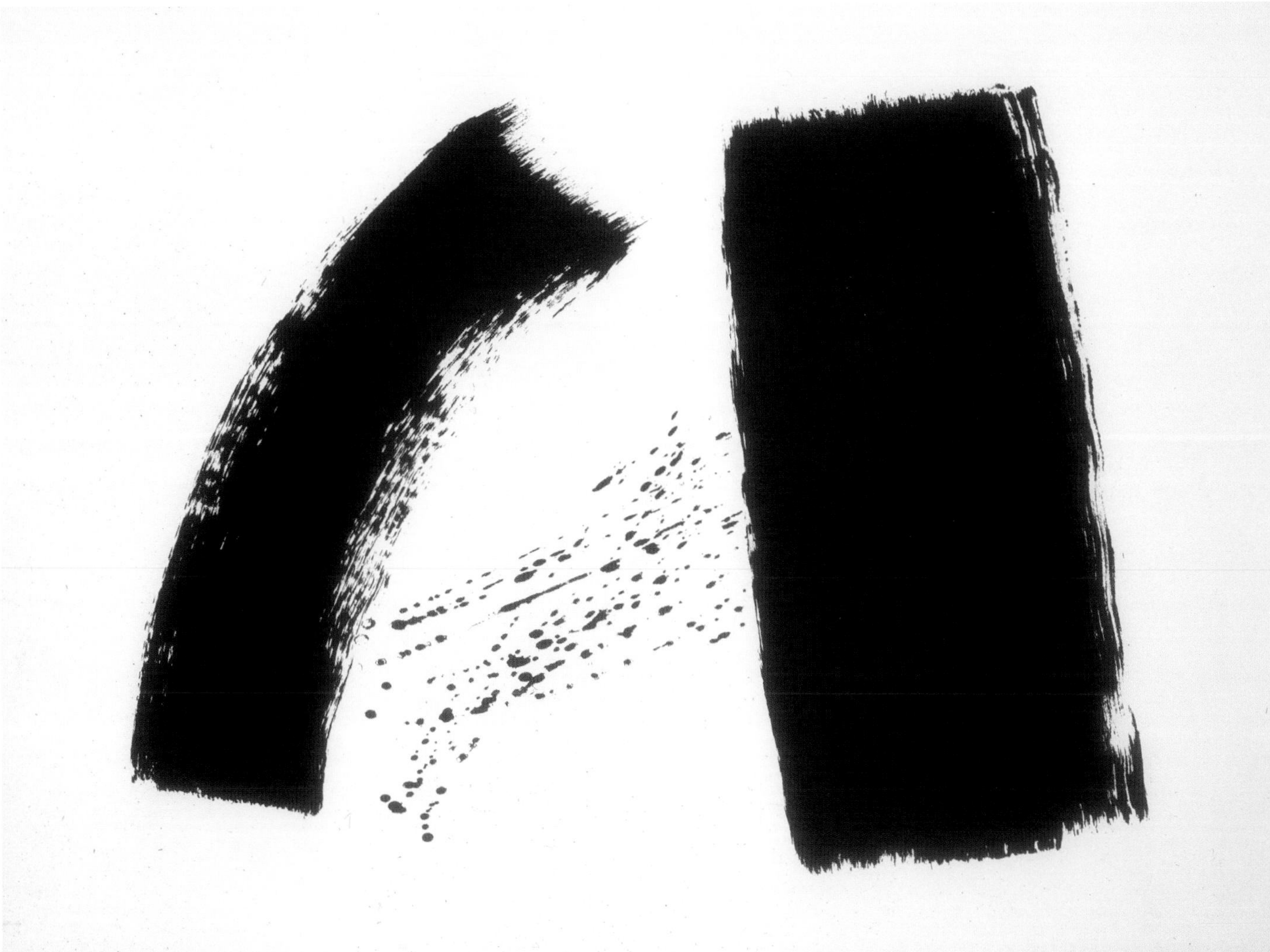

Cat.87

Two Black Brushstrokes
(editioned posthumously, 2007)

Screenprint, three colours

76.0 x 76.0 (image and paper size)

Arches Velin Blanc 400gsm

Edition of 25. Carol Robertson, Graal Press

(ix) Vision in Time Series

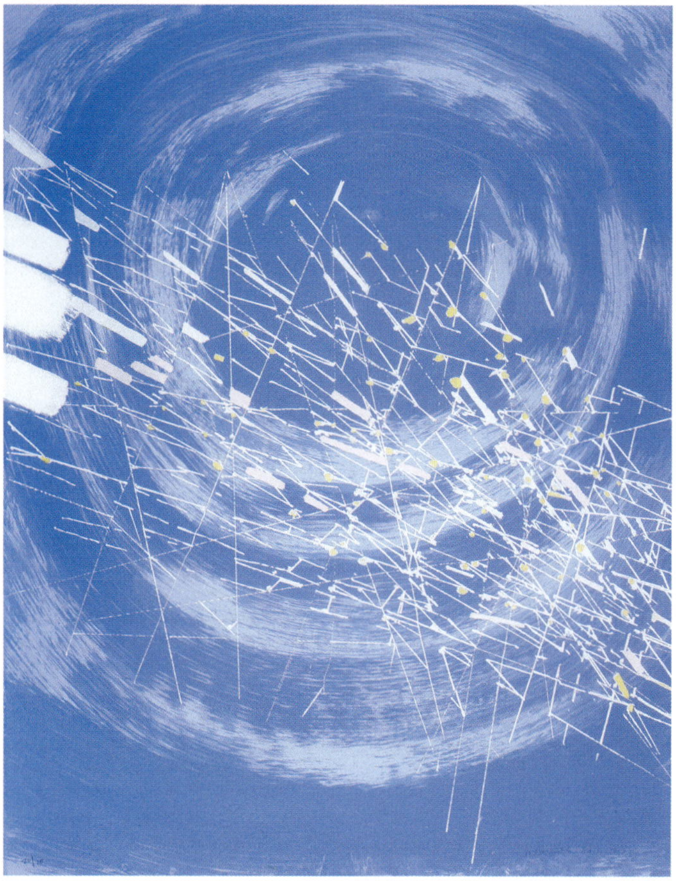

Cat.88

Vision in Time I, 2000

Screenprint, nine colours

76.0 x 58.0 (image and paper size)

Arches Velin Blanc 400gsm

Edition of 50 (but numbered in error up to 50/70). Carol Robertson, Graal Press

Signed and dated, lower right: *W Barns Graham 2000*; numbered, lower left

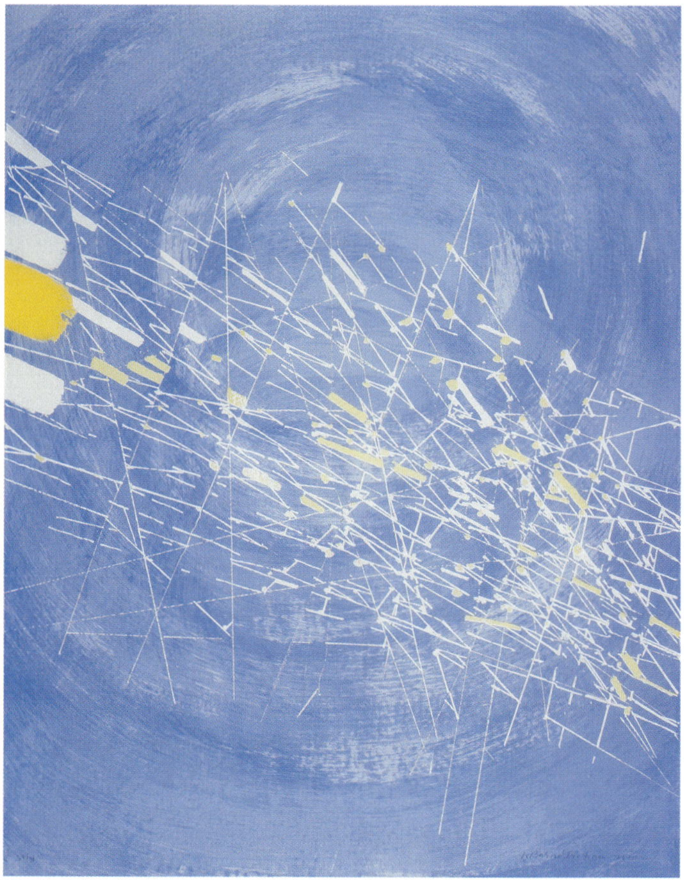

Cat.89

Vision in Time II, 2000

Screenprint, six colours

76.0 x 58.0 (image and paper size)

Arches Velin Blanc 400gsm

Edition of 70. Carol Robertson, Graal Press

Signed and dated, lower right: *W Barns Graham 2000*; numbered, lower left

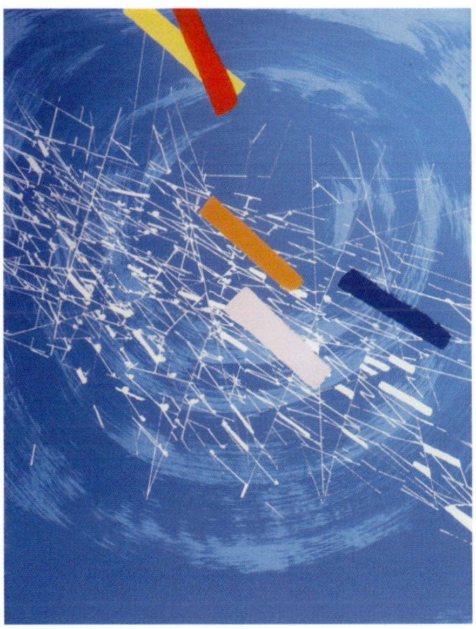

Cat.90

Vision in Time III (editioned posthumously, 2006)

Screenprint, ten colours

76.0 x 58.0 (image and paper size)

Arches Velin Blanc 400gsm

Edition of 25. Carol Robertson, Graal Press

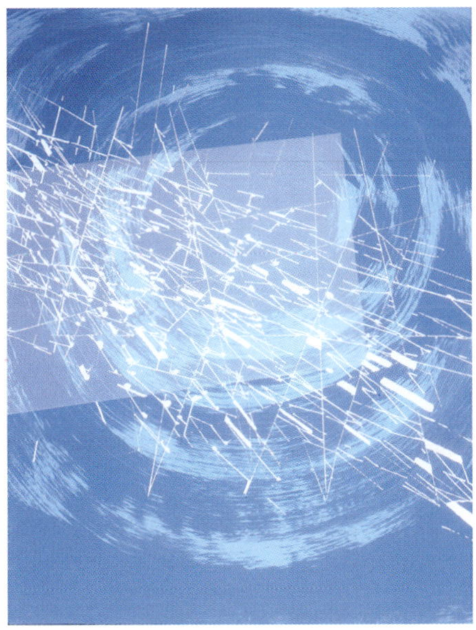

Cat.91

Vision in Time IV (editioned posthumously, 2006)

Screenprint, six colours

76.0 x 58.0 (image and paper size)

Arches Velin Blanc 400gsm

Edition of 25. Carol Robertson, Graal Press

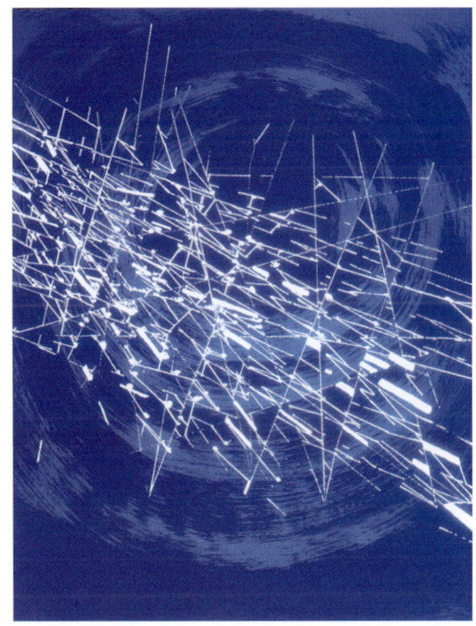

Cat.92

Vision in Time V (editioned posthumously, 2006)

Screenprint, four colours

76.0 x 58.0 (image and paper size)

Arches Velin Blanc 400gsm

Edition of 25. Carol Robertson, Graal Press

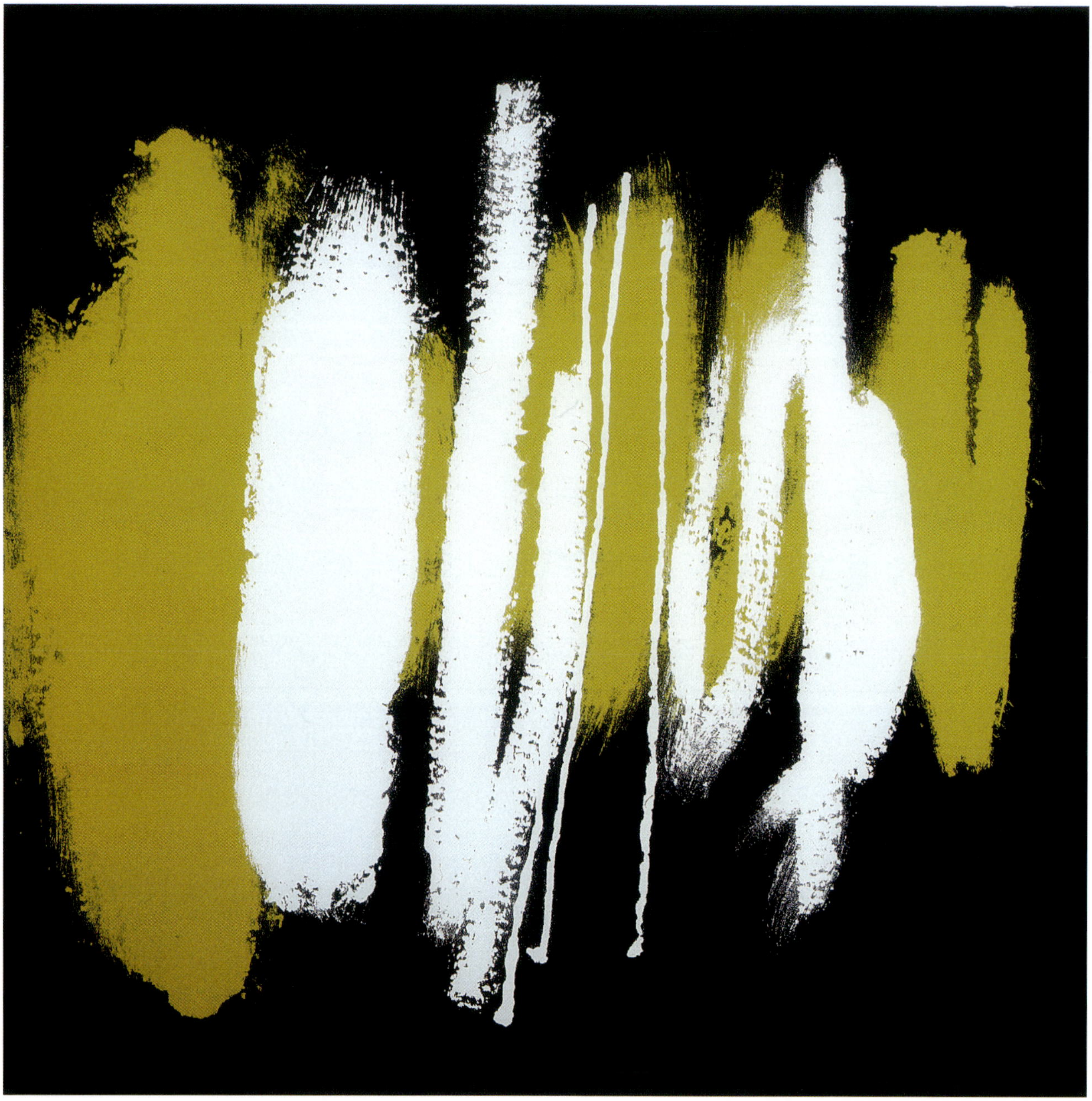

(x) Water Dance (Porthmeor) Series

Cat.93

Water Dance (Porthmeor) No. I, 2004

Screenprint, four colours

56.0 x 56.0 (image and paper size)

Arches Velin Blanc 400gsm

Edition of 70. Carol Robertson, Graal Press

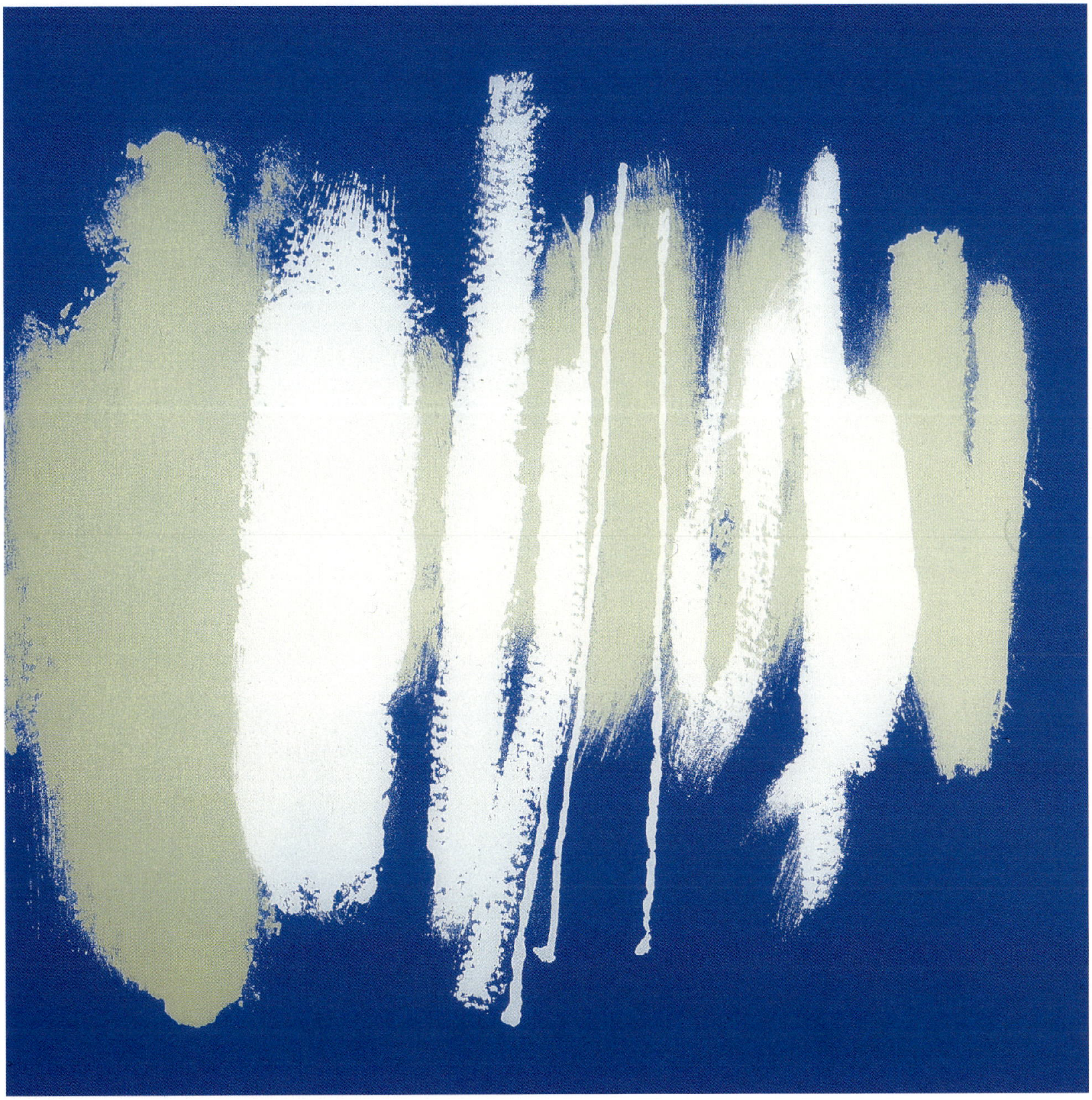

Cat.94

Water Dance (Porthmeor) No. II, 2004

Screenprint, three colours

56.0 x 56.0 (image and paper size)

Arches Velin Blanc 400gsm

Edition of 70. Carol Robertson, Graal Press

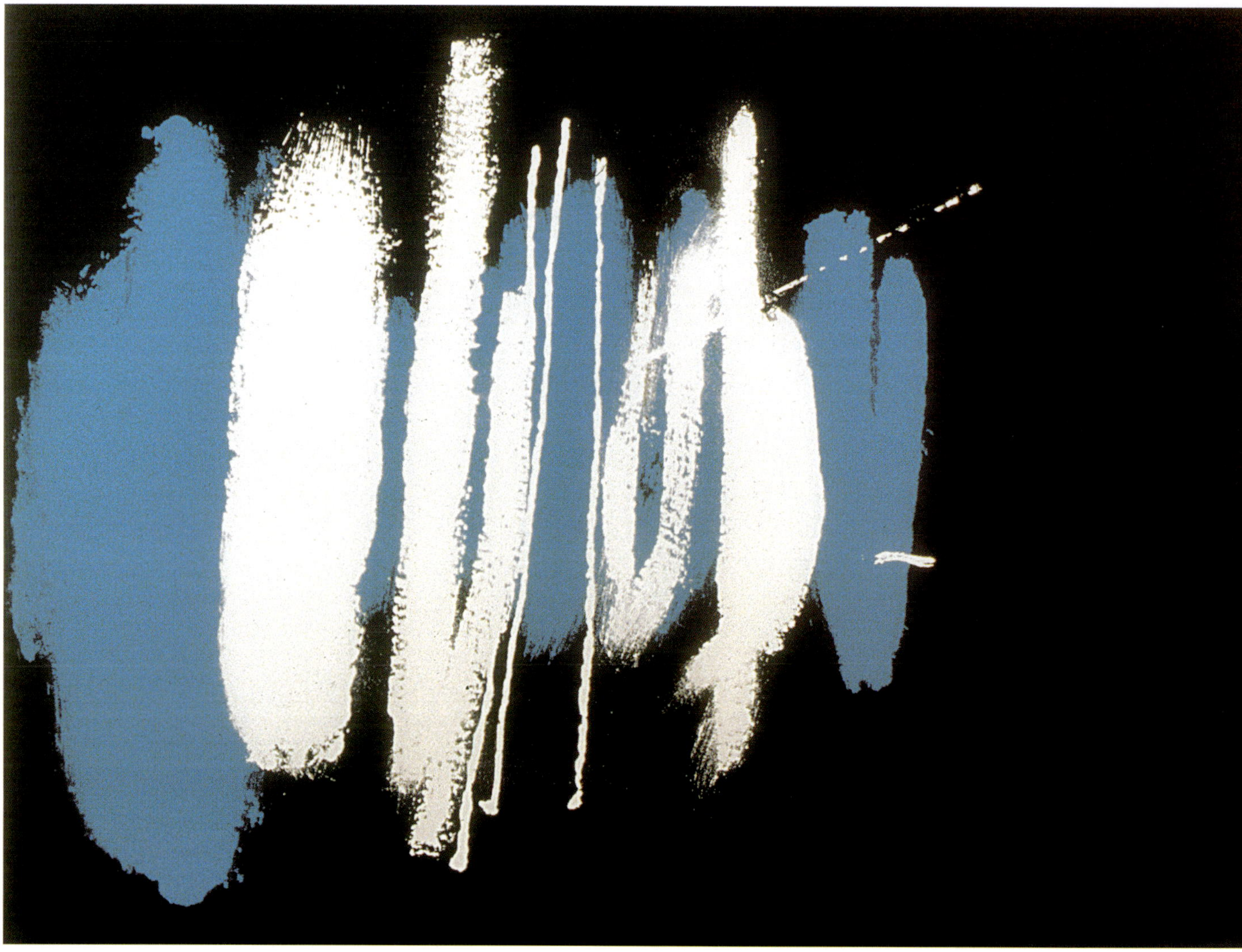

Cat.95

Water Dance (Porthmeor) No. III,
2004

Screenprint, three colours

56.0 x 76.0 (image and paper size)

Arches Velin Blanc 400gsm

Edition of 70. Carol Robertson, Graal Press

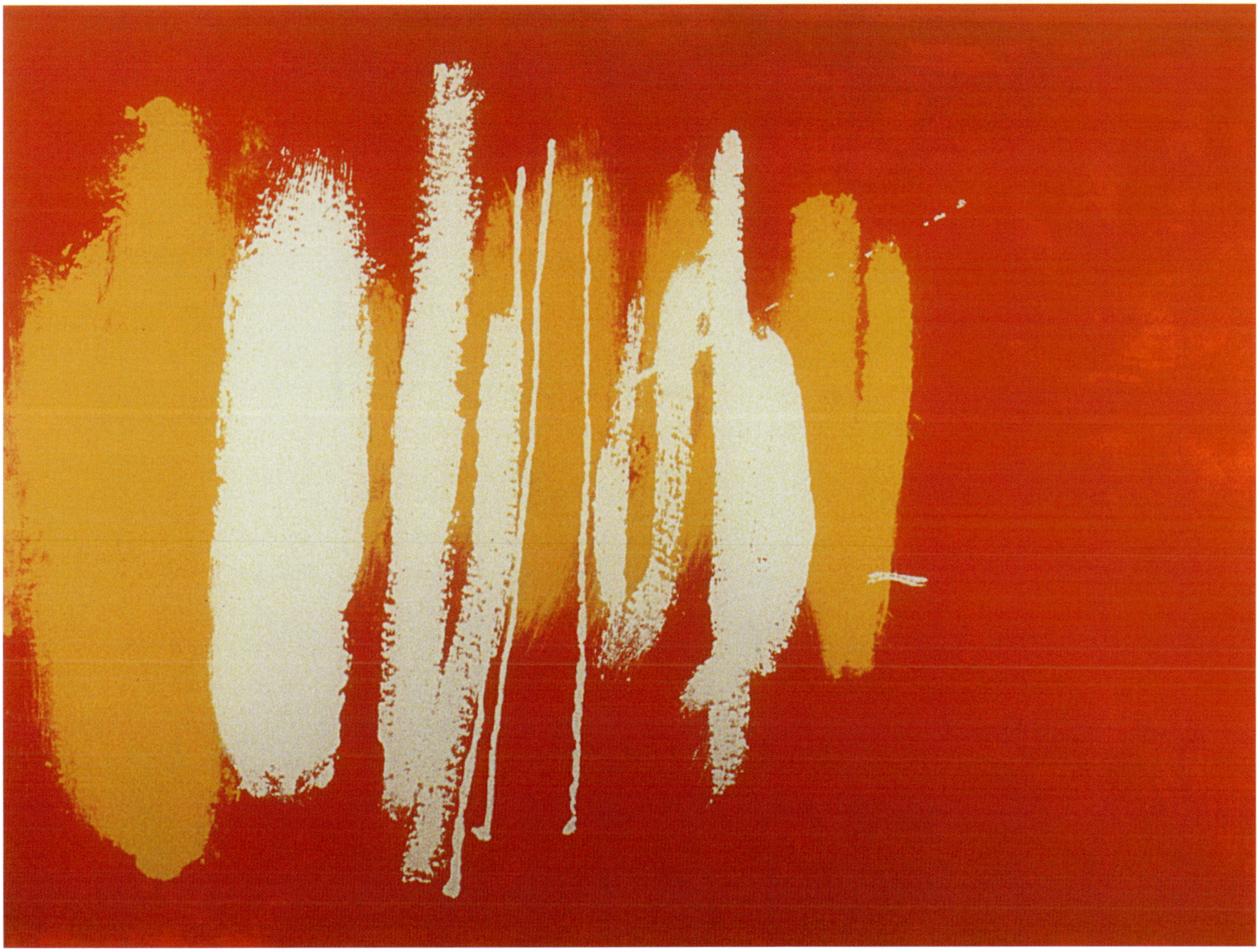

Cat.96

Water Dance (Porthmeor) No. IV, 2004

Screenprint, five colours

56.0 x 76.0 (image and paper size)

Arches Velin Blanc 400gsm

Edition of 70. Carol Robertson, Graal Press

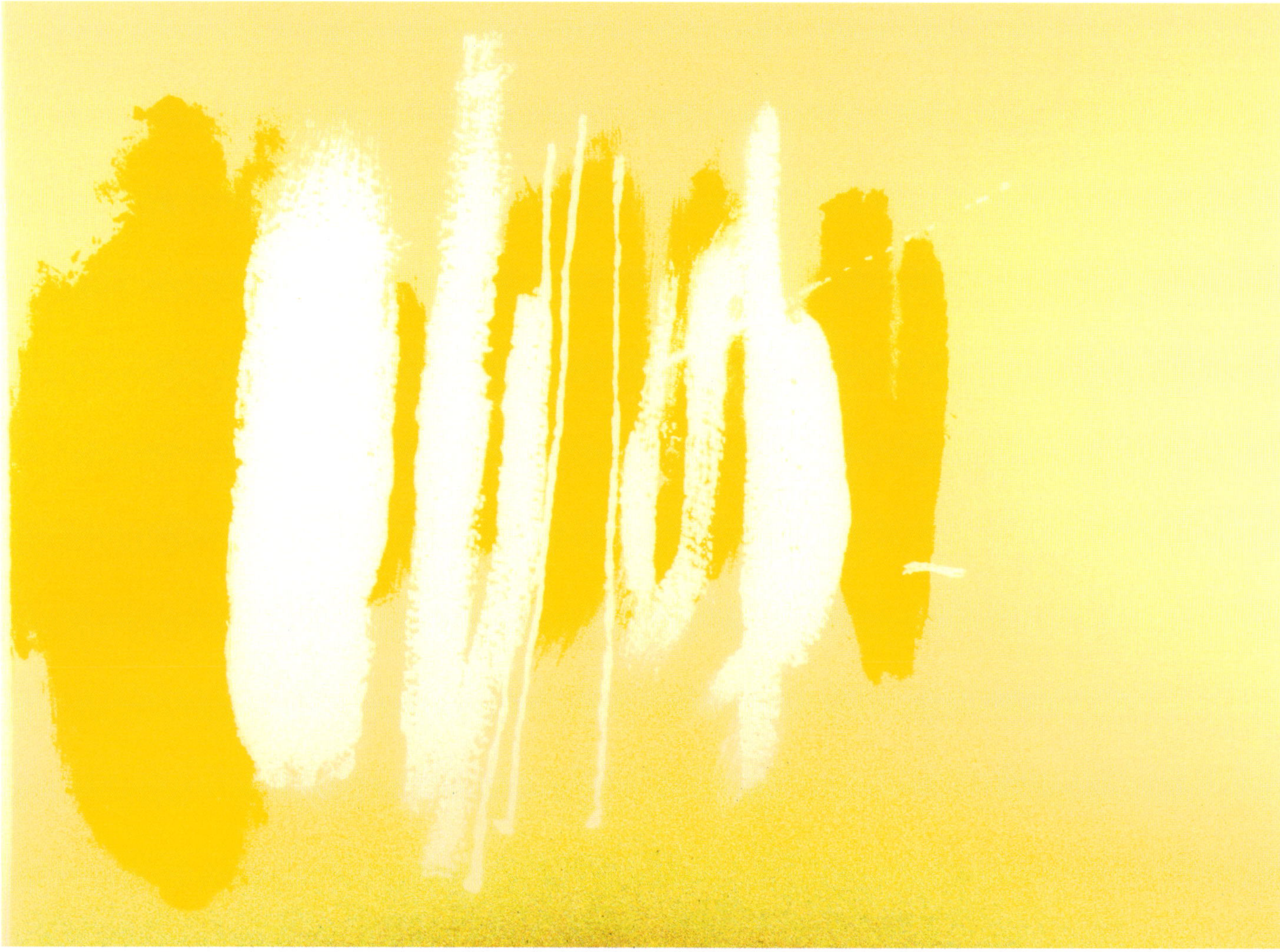

Cat.97

Water Dance (Porthmeor) No. V, 2004

Screenprint, four colours

56.0 x 76.0 (image and paper size)

Arches Velin Blanc 400gsm

Edition of 70. Carol Robertson, Graal Press

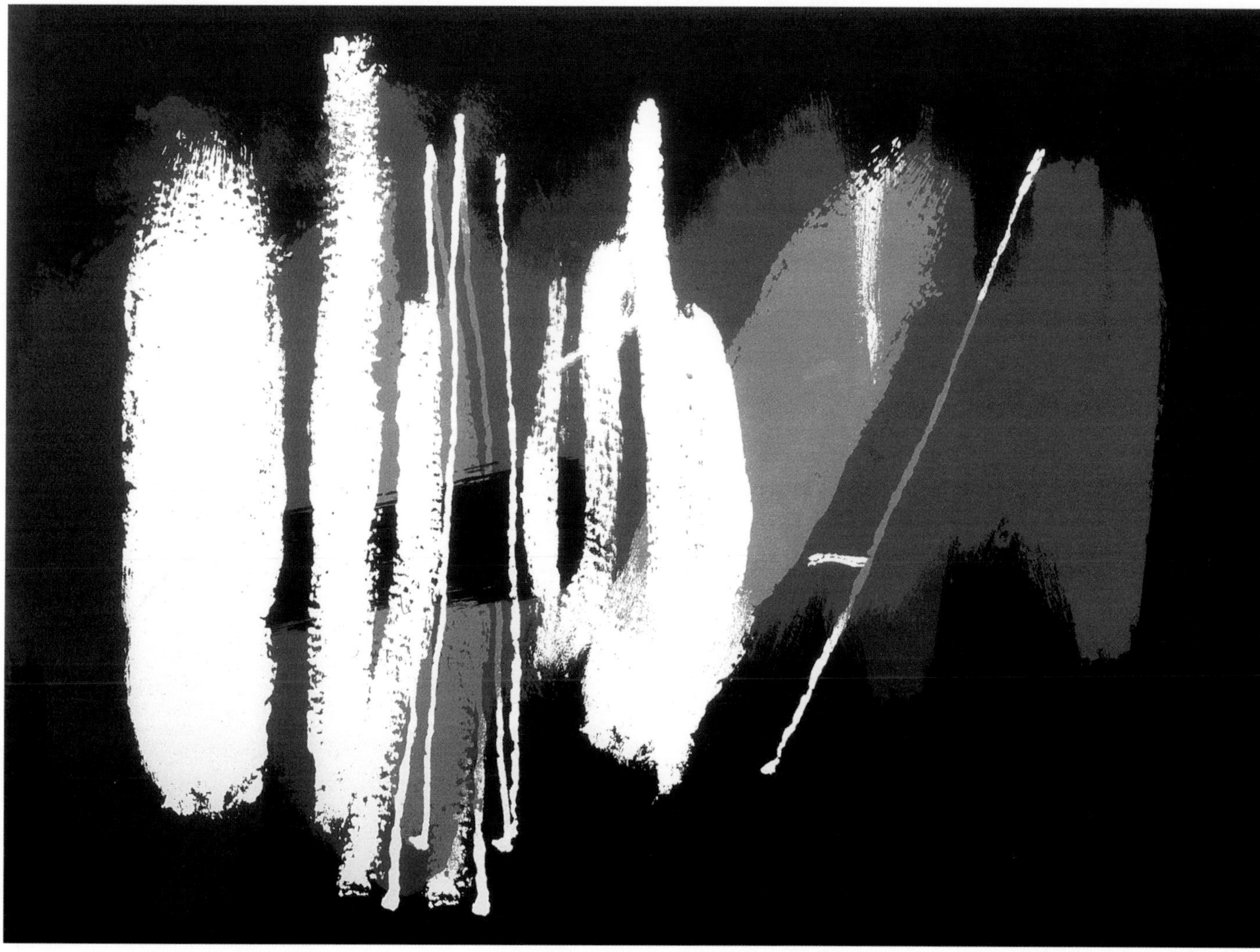

CAT. 98

Water Dance (Porthmeor) No. VI
(editioned posthumously, 2006)

Screenprint, eleven colours

56.0 x 76.0 (image and paper size)

Arches Velin Blanc 400gsm

Edition of 25. Carol Robertson, Graal Press

(xi) White Circle Series

Cat.99

White Circle Series I, 2003

Screenprint, six colours

56.0 x 56.0 (image and paper size)

Arches Velin Blanc 400gsm

Edition of 70. Carol Robertson, Graal Press

Signed and dated, lower right: *W Barns Graham 2003*; numbered, lower left

Note: In addition to painting on separation sheets, Barns-Graham cut out and positioned small paper shapes on clear sheets.

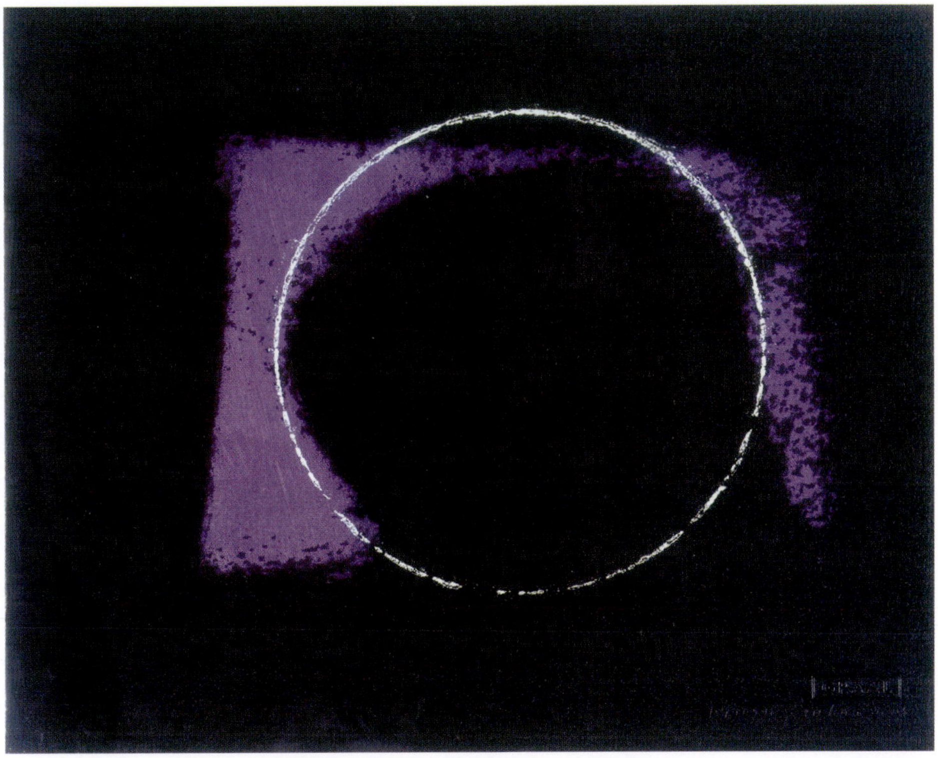

Cat.100

***White Circle Series II*, 2003**

Screenprint, six colours

34.0 x 41.0 (image and paper size)

Arches Velin Blanc 400gsm

Edition of 70. Carol Robertson, Graal Press

Signed and dated, lower right: *W Barns Graham 2003*; numbered, lower left

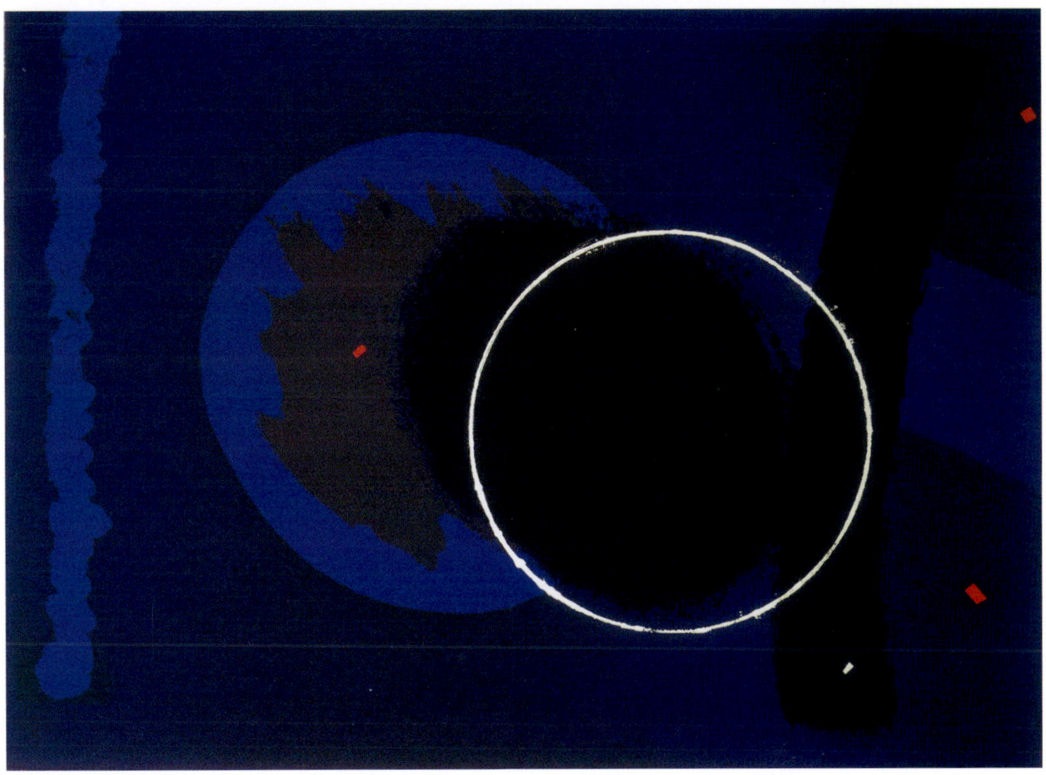

Cat.101

White Circle Series III (editioned posthumously, 2006)

Screenprint, fifteen colours

56.0 x 76.0 (image and paper size)

Arches Velin Blanc 400gsm

Edition of 25. Carol Robertson, Graal Press

Note: In addition to painting on separation sheets, Barns-Graham cut out and positioned small paper shapes on clear sheets.

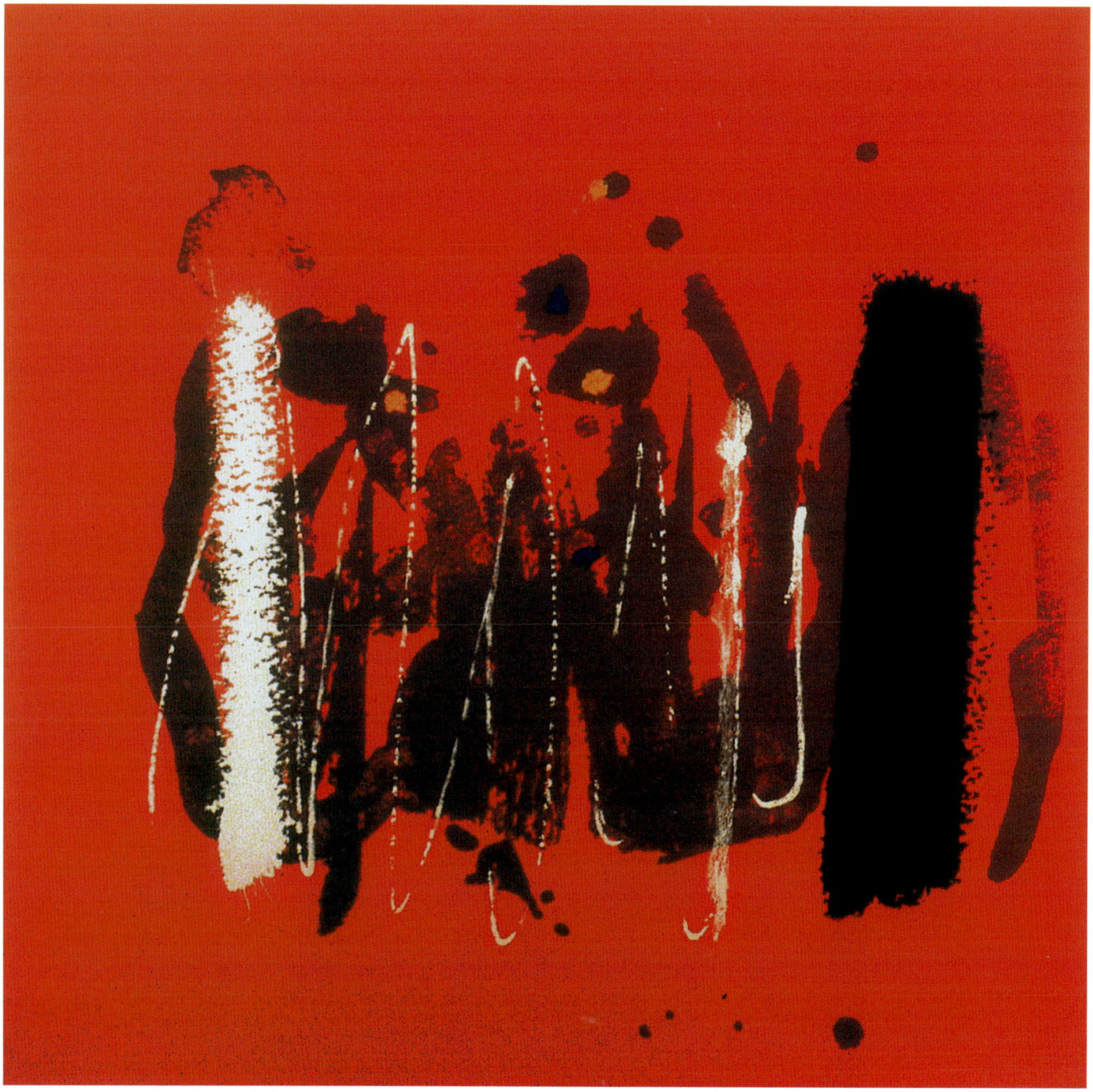

(xii) Wind Dance Series

Cat.102

Wind Dance Series No. I, 2004

Screenprint, nine colours

56.0 x 56.0 (image and paper size)

Arches Velin Blanc 400gsm

Edition of 70. Carol Robertson, Graal Press

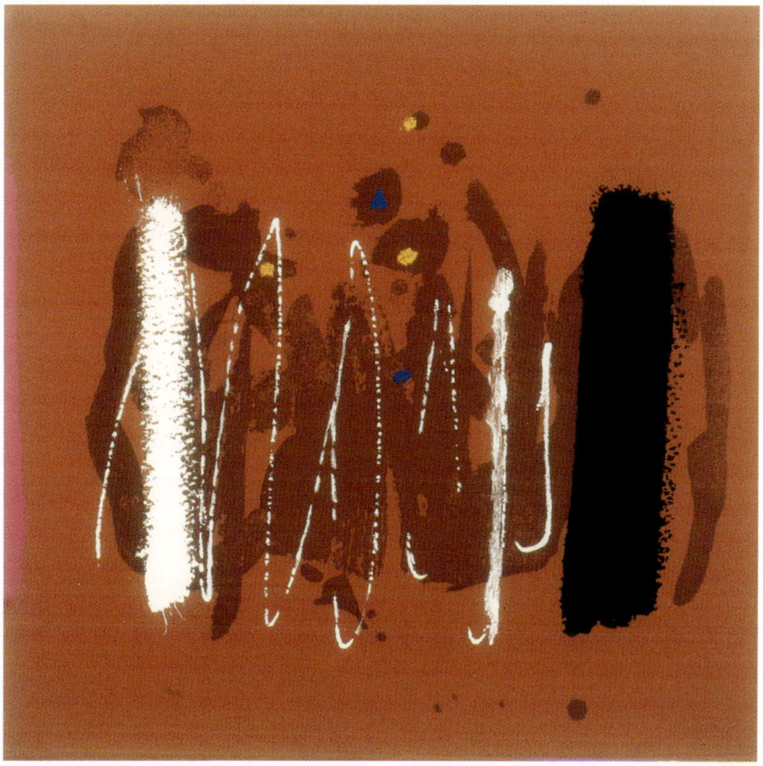

Cat.103

***Wind Dance Series No. II*, 2003**

Screenprint, ten colours

56.0 x 56.0 (image and paper size)

Arches Velin Blanc 400gsm

Edition of 70. Carol Robertson, Graal Press

Signed and dated, lower right: *W Barns Graham 2003*; not numbered

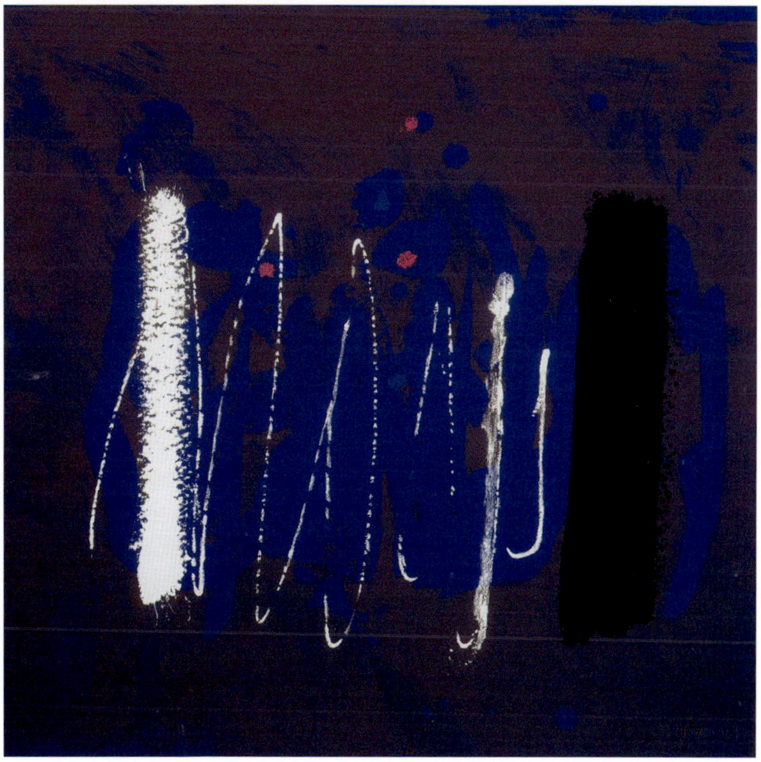

Cat.104

***Wind Dance Series No. III*, 2004**

Screenprint, eight colours

57.4 x 57.0 (image and paper size)

Arches Velin Blanc 400gsm

Edition of 70. Carol Robertson, Graal Press

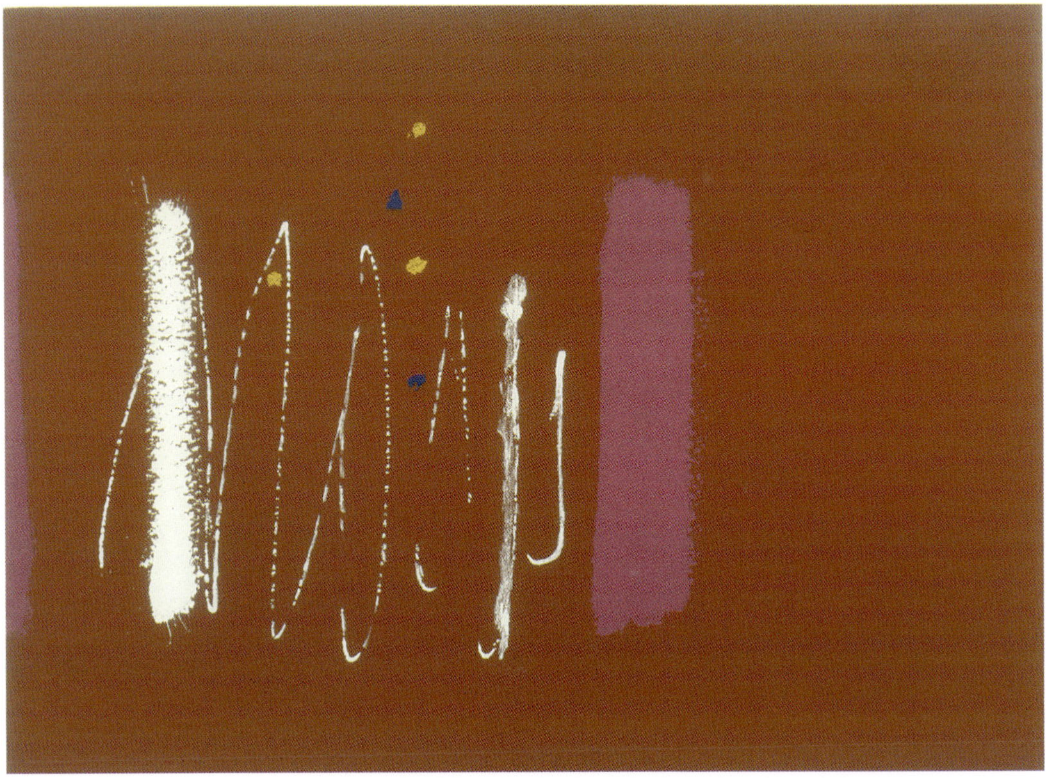

Cat.105
Wind Dance Series No. IV, 2003
Screenprint, seven colours
56.0 x 76.0 (image and paper size)
Arches Velin Blanc 400gsm
Edition of 70. Carol Robertson, Graal Press
Numbered, lower left, but not signed or dated

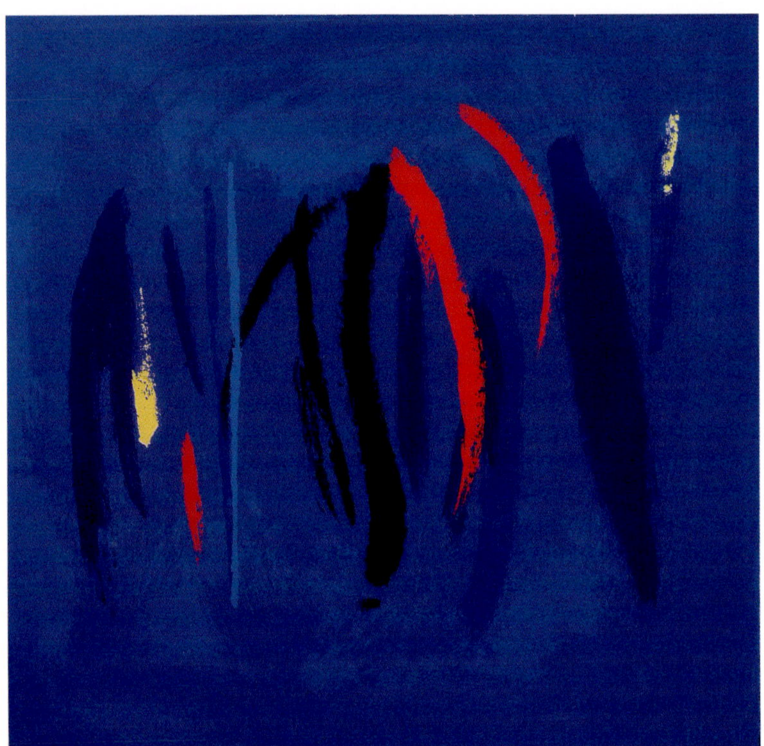

Cat.106
Wind Dance Series No. V
(editioned posthumously, 2006)
Screenprint, twelve colours
56.0 x 56.0 (image and paper size)
Arches Velin Blanc 400gsm
Edition of 25. Carol Robertson, Graal Press

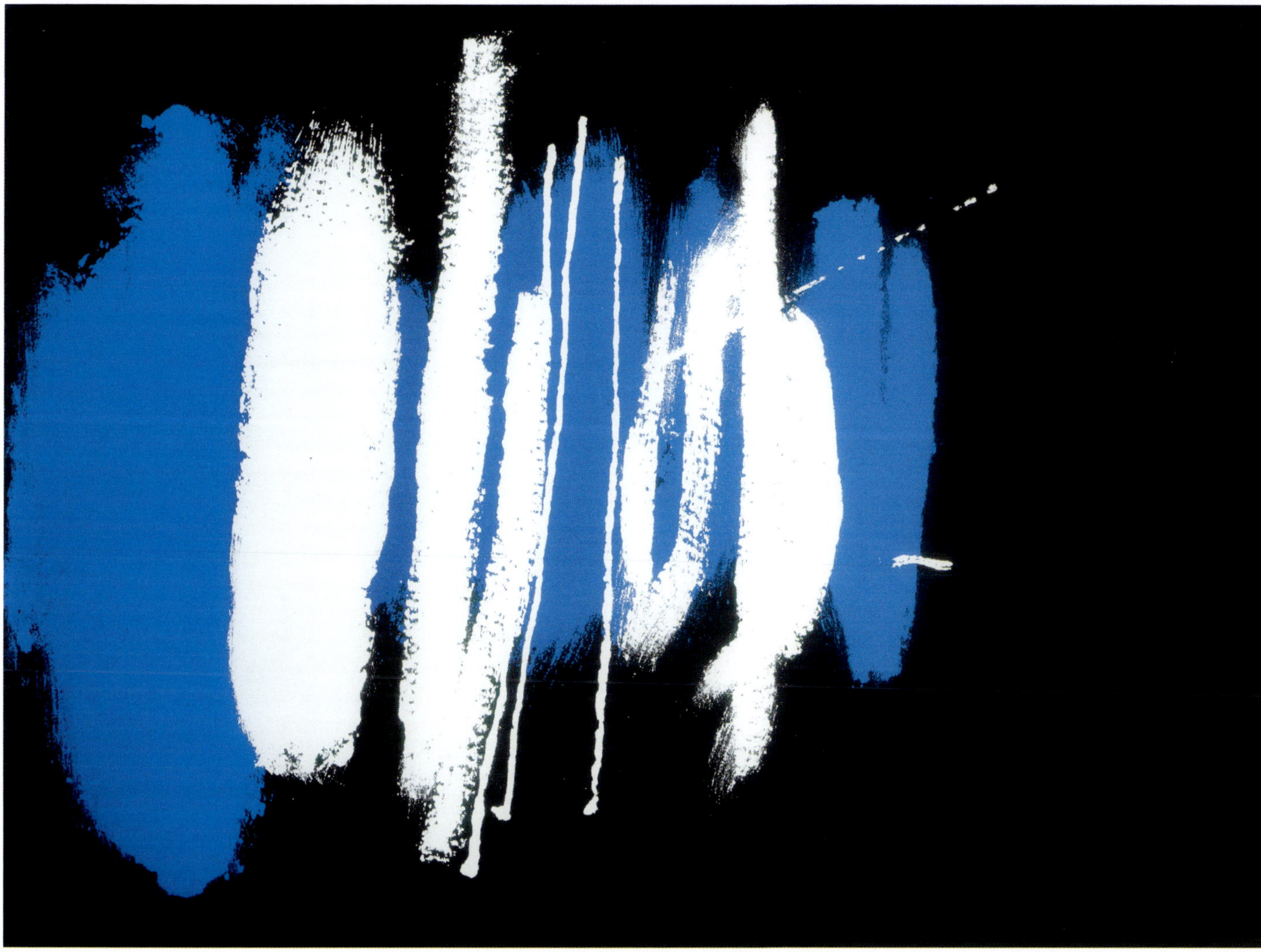

Cat.107

Water Dance (Porthmeor) No. VII
(editioned posthumously, 2007)

Screenprint, eight colours

22.0 x 18.5 (image and paper size)

Arches Velin Blanc 400gsm

Edition of 100. Carol Robertson, Graal Press

Note: A reduced version of *Water Dance No. III*, produced to accompany a limited edition of this publication.

Titles of print series made with Graal Press

Cobalt Playing Games Series
Earth Series
Millennium Series
Orange and Lemon Playing Games Series
Red Playing Games Series
Sunghrie Series
Time Series
Two Brushstrokes Series
Vision in Time Series
Water Dance (Porthmeor) Series
White Circle Series
Wind Dance Series

Concordance of posthumous prints

The following prints were published after the death of Wilhelmina Barn:

Cats 7, 8, 9, 45, 47, 49, 50, 51, 52, 53, 54, 55, 72, 74, 79, 81, 83, 84, 86, 87, 90, 91, 92, 98, 101, 106, 107.

GLOSSARY

Aquatint is a tonal *etching* method, the tone being made of powdered rosin heated and melted onto the etching plate. The acid bites into the spaces around the rosin, leaving a typically grainy texture. The image is made by successive immersions in acid, covering areas with acid-resistant stopping-out varnish, giving a deeper tone with each biting.

Blind stamp (or **printer's chop mark**): an impressed mark made on a print to identify the print studio that made the prints. It is not inked.

Carborundum print: in this method carborundum grit is mixed with a transparent medium which is painted onto a printing plate. When this is dry, the plate can be inked and the ink adheres to the gritty surface. When the result is printed the grit gives a textured or embossed surface to the print.

Colour etching: while etchings are usually monochrome, colour etchings can be made with a number of plates printed successively. As the paper, dampened for printing, may shrink as it dries, accurate registration of each plate can be difficult. Alternatively, several colours can be carefully applied to one or two plates 'à la poupée', with a little dolly-shaped rag.

Drypoint is an *engraving* technique using a sharp needle which throws up a burr on either side of the incised line. The way this burr holds the printing ink gives drypoint its characteristic rich, blurred effect. The burr is fragile and drypoints can only be printed in small editions.

Edition number: the number of prints made of one image. It is usually written on each print and expressed as, for example, 1/75. Some editions are limited because the printing plate will only last for a small number of prints, as in *drypoint*, for example. In other methods there is technically nothing to limit the number of prints taken so the edition is artificially limited. The edition number has traditionally been limited to 75, originally because above this number the print was presumed to be mass-produced and therefore liable to Purchase Tax. This practice was retained after Purchase Tax was replaced by Value Added Tax (VAT) in 1973.

Engraving is a method where the image is made by lines cut into a metal plate with a metal tool called a burin.

Etching is a method where a copper plate is first covered with an acid-resistant ground and the image is drawn through this, exposing the metal. The plate is immersed in acid, which bites the lines into the plate.

Frottage: rubbing.

Intaglio printing: here ink is carried in lines, grooves or pits which have been made in the surface of a plate, usually of copper or zinc. Ink is forced into the lines, and surplus ink is wiped off the surface of the plate. Dampened paper is placed on top, then a felt blanket, and these are passed through a roller press, the pressure of which forces the paper into the inked grooves. This produces the strong plate mark characteristic of intaglio printing. *Engraving*, *drypoint*, *etching* and *aquatint* are all intaglio methods (see separate entries).

Linocut: a method of *relief printing* using linoleum as a printing block.

Lithography is based on the principle that water and grease repel each other. The image is drawn on a stone or plate with a greasy pencil or special ink. The surface is dampened with water; a roller coated with greasy ink is then passed over the stone, but the ink only sticks to the drawing, being repelled by the water. The lithograph can reproduce a wide variety of tones, textures and effects, such as those of a pen-and-ink drawing, a delicate watercolour wash or a chalk drawing.

Monotype: a unique printed image which can be produced by making the image with paint or ink on a smooth glass plate and pulling one impression. Another kind of monotype is the *offset drawing*, where the image is made by inking the back of a sheet of paper and drawing on the front, making an image on a second sheet of paper underneath.

Non-toxic printmaking: many printmaking techniques have historically involved potentially hazardous chemicals: acids, oils and solvents for making plates, printing inks and cleaning materials. This meant that print studios contained toxic, flammable and volatile substances which have often had a serious effect on the health of printmakers. Fume cupboards, extractor systems and proper ventilation are expensive and take up space. In recent decades many printmakers have worked to develop systems for printmaking that eliminate these dangerous materials.

Off-set drawing: a method of *monotype*; also sometimes called **transfer drawing**.

Painting aids: different media that can be added to paint, such as pastes, gels, gloss or matte finishes, thickeners, emulsions and varnishes, and that affect the handling and appearance of the paint.

Positive: a transparent plastic sheet on which the artist makes autographic marks which can be transferred to a light-sensitive screen, stone or plate. (See also *separation*.)

Proof: a working or trial version of a print, or a print retained for archive and reference purposes, such as A/P = Artist's Proof; P/P = Printer's Proof; H/C = Hors Commerce (not for sale).

Relief printing: in this method ink is carried on the raised part of the printing surface. For example, a woodcut is made from a block of wood. The artist draws on the block and then wood is cut away from the lines of design leaving the drawing in relief. The ink is applied to the raised lines to make the print. *Linocut* is a method of relief printing.

Screenprinting: basically a stencil technique. A fine mesh (originally of silk, hence the terms *silkscreen* and *serigraphy*, but now more commonly a synthetic material) is stretched over a rectangular frame. Ink is forced through the mesh with a squeegee onto paper. Each colour in a print requires a separate screen. A complex image can be made up from more than twenty screens.

A stencil is applied to the screen to form the image. Simple screenprints can be made with cut-out stencils or by painting the screen with a stopping-out material, so that the ink only prints where the mesh is open. A development from this uses a light-sensitive emulsion for stopping-out. The screens are coated with the light-sensitive emulsion, which hardens when it is exposed to light. Where the light is blocked, the emulsion remains soft and can be washed away, leaving the mesh open.

The image is made by blocking the light with either a photographic negative or with marks made by the artist on a sheet of clear plastic. The screen and marked plastic sheet are held in contact and exposed to ultraviolet light. When the soft emulsion is washed away, it leaves the image as open mesh on the screen. When ink is passed through the open mesh of the screen it leaves a positive mark on the paper beneath the screen.

Separation: a transparent sheet used to make one layer or one colour of a printed image, particularly with reference to the photographic or digital deconstruction of images into their component colours for transferring to a printing matrix. Also used in the same meaning as *positive* (see above).

Serigraphy: a term sometimes used for *screenprinting*, based on the Latin word for silk, *sericum*.

Silkscreen: see *screenprinting*.

Soft-ground etching: this can be used to replicate the texture of a drawing. The acid-resistant ground is soft, and the image is made by drawing on a sheet of paper laid over the ground.

Stop-out: acid- or water-resistant substances used to block parts of an *etching* plate to prevent further biting in acid, or on a screen to prevent ink passing through the screen mesh in *screenprinting*.

Sugar-lift etching: a method where the marks are made on the plate with a water-soluble sugar solution. The brush marks are covered in *stop-out*, the plate is immersed into a bath of boiling water and the sugared areas dissolve and lift off to expose the brush marks, which can then be etched. A resin *aquatint* ground can be laid on the marks to add tonality.

Tusche: originally the German word for drawing ink, the word came to be used for the greasy crayons and liquid used in *lithography*. It now also refers to a variety of materials used to make images on plastic *separation* sheets for *screenprinting*.

CHRONOLOGY

1912	Born 8 June in St Andrews, Fife, Scotland.
1932–7	Edinburgh College of Art.
1940	Went to live in St Ives, Cornwall.
1942	Became a member of St Ives Society of Artists and Newlyn Society of Artists.
*c.*1943	Began printmaking, making monotypes and offset drawings.
1946	First meeting of Crypt Group, in her studio.
1949	Founder member of Penwith Society of Artists Resigned from St Ives Society of Artists.
	Visited Switzerland with the Brotherton family, climbing and drawing glaciers.
	Exhibition in George Downing's bookshop, St Ives, which included offset drawings and monotypes.
	Married David Lewis (marriage annulled 1963).
1950	Visited Italy, including Barbara Hepworth's Venice Biennale exhibition.
	Visited Scilly Isles.
1952	Took etching classes with John Wells and Peter Lanyon at Penzance School of Art, taught by Edward Bouverie Hoyton and John Tunnard.
	Exhibition at Redfern Gallery, London – *Recent Paintings and Glacier Constructions* – which included offset drawings and monotypes.
1953	Visited Paris.
1954	Visited Italy, including Ben Nicholson's Venice Biennale exhibition and Chiusure in Tuscany.
1955	Screenprinted table mat, made with Denis Mitchell, at Heal's Picture Gallery.
	Visited Italy and Sicily on Italian government International Scholarship for Professional Painting.
1956–7	On staff at Leeds School of Art.
1958	Lithography with Stanley Jones in St Ives.
	Visited Spain and Balearic Islands.
1960	Inherited Balmungo near St Andrews.
1961–3	Studio in London.
1962	Bought No. 1 Barnaloft, a studio residence overlooking Porthmeor Beach, St Ives.
	Visited United States with Contemporary Art Society.
1966	Visited Holland.
1971–2	Making linocut prints.
	Etching classes, St Ives.
1972	Screenprinting with Jim Whitlock, St Ives.
1973	Met Rowan James, who became friend and assistant.
1976	Took etching classes with Roy Walker, St Ives.
1977	Screenprinting with Ivan Polley, Edinburgh Printmakers.
1982	Took etching classes with Andrew Hambleton and Keith Fraser, Dundee Printmakers Workshop.
1984–5	Visited Orkney.
1988	Screenprinting with Fergus McLachlan, Dundee Printmakers Workshop, commissioned by Scottish Arts Council.
1989–92	Visited Lanzarote, Canary Isles.
1991	Visited Barcelona.
	Six-day visit to Curwen Chilford Studio, working with Stanley Jones and Kip Gresham, to make experimental screenprints. Also worked with them on two screenprints and one lithograph based on existing work.
1992	Honorary Doctorate from University of St Andrews.
1995	Screenprint with Kip Gresham: *Venetian Red.*
1996–7	Etchings with Rachael Kantaris, St Ives: *Scorpio I*, *Scorpio II* and *Eight Lines.*
1998	Screenprints with Alasdair Currie, Dundee Printmakers Workshop: *Spring* and *Summer.*
	Colour etching with Hugh Stoneman, Madron, Cornwall: *Eclipse.*
	Started working with Carol Robertson, Graal Press, Scotland.
1999	Honorary Member of Royal Scottish Academy (RSA) and Royal Scottish Society of Painters in Watercolours (RSW).
	Screenprint with Kip Gresham for King's College Portfolio: *Blue Light, Summer.*
	Exhibition in Brussels featuring thirteen prints, McGeary Gallery.
1999–2004	Worked with Carol Robertson and Robert Adam, of Graal Press, Scotland, mostly screenprints, but also etchings. Made 44 editioned prints in five years, plus 24 others proofed but not editioned at the time of her death.
2000	Honorary Doctorate from University of Plymouth.
2001	Awarded CBE for services to art.
	Honorary Doctorate from University of Exeter.
	W. Barns-Graham: A Studio Life, by Lynne Green, published.
2003	Awarded Honorary Doctorate, Heriot Watt University, Edinburgh.
2004	Died 26 January, St Andrews.

EXHIBITIONS

This list supplements and brings up to date the exhibition list in Lynne Green's 2001 publication *W. Barns-Graham: A Studio Life.* Apart from these most recent additions, it includes only exhibitions known to have contained prints. Once she had started making prints, Barns-Graham regularly sent them to the annual exhibitions of the Newlyn Society of Artists and the Penwith Society of Artists, with whom she exhibited continually from 1942 to 2002 and from 1949 to 2001, respectively.

1949 *Recent Drawings, Monotypes and Paintings, Glacier Drawings*, George Downing's Bookshop, St Ives, July 1949.

1952 *Recent Paintings and Glacier Construction*, Redfern Gallery, London.

1993 *Curwen Chilford: the First Four Years 1989–1993*, The New Academy & Curwen Galleries, London.

1994 *Painters' Prints*, Curwen Gallery, London.

1998 *Curwen Print Makers*, Curwen Gallery, London.

1999 *The Wilhelmina Barns-Graham Exhibition*, McGeary Gallery, Brussels.

2001 *W. Barns-Graham Prints*, Exeter University.
Art First in Print, Art First, London.
St Ives Past and Present, New Academy Gallery & Business Art Gallery, London.

2002 *W. Barns-Graham: A Celebration at 90*, The Scottish Gallery, Edinburgh.
W. Barns-Graham at 90: A Tribute from Art First, Art First, London.

2002–2004 *Wilhelmina Barns-Graham – Painting as Celebration*, Crawford Arts Centre, St Andrews and tour.

2004 *Wilhelmina Barns-Graham 1912–2004. A Tribute: Recent Paintings and New Prints*, Art First, London.

2005 *Wilhelmina Barns-Graham: Movement and Light Imag(in)ing Time*, Tate St Ives.

2006 *Wilhelmina Barns-Graham: Important Works from her Career,* Art First, London.
Wilhelmina Barns-Graham: Late Prints and Small Paintings, Dorseframe Pictures, South Petherton, Somerset.

BIBLIOGRAPHY

Adam, Robert, and Carol Robertson: *Screenprinting: The Complete Water-based System*, London, 2003

Allan, Christopher: *Elizabeth Blackadder Prints*, Lund Humphries, 2003

Archer, David: 'Terry Frost: printmaker', in Elizabeth Knowles (ed.), *Terry Frost*, Lund Humphries, 1994

Carey, Frances, and Anthony Griffiths: *Avant-garde British Printmaking, 1914–1960*, London, 1990

Castleman, Riva: *Prints of the Twentieth Century: A History*, London, 1976

Chamberlain, Walter: *Etching and Engraving*, London, 1981

Contemporary British Printmakers, exh. cat., St George's Gallery, 1 July – 30 August 1958 (available in the Tate Gallery Archive, Hyman Kreitman Research Centre, Tate Britain, London)

Cross, Tom: *Painting the Warmth of the Sun: St Ives Artists 1939–1975*, Penzance and Guildford, 1984

Cross, Tom: *Catching the Wave: Art And Artists In Contemporary Cornwall*, Tiverton, 2002

Davies, Peter: *St Ives Revisited – Innovators and Followers*, Abertillery, 1994

Gascoigne, Bamber: *How to Identify Prints*, London, 1986

Gilmour, Pat: Introduction to *Lithographs from the Curwen Studio: A Retrospective of Fifteen Years of Printmaking*, exh. cat., Camden Arts Centre, December 1973

Gilmour, Pat: *Artists at Curwen: A Celebration of the Gift of Artists' Prints from the Curwen Studio*, exh.cat., Tate Gallery, London, 1977

Gilmour, Pat: *The Mechanised Image: An Historical Perspective on 20th Century Prints*, London, 1978

Gilmour, Pat: 'Introduction', *Kelpra Studio: The Rose and Chris Prater Gift, Artists Prints 1961–1980*, exh.cat., Tate Gallery, London, 1980

Godfrey, Richard T.: *Printmaking in Britain*, Oxford, 1978

Gooding, Mel: 'Wilhelmina Barns-Graham: a study in three movements', in *Wilhelmina Barns-Graham, Movement and Light Imag(in)ing Time*, exh.cat., Tate St Ives, St Ives, 2005

Green, Lynne: *W. Barns-Graham: A Studio Life*, Lund Humphries, 2001

Griffiths, Antony: *Prints and Printmaking: An Introduction to the History and Techniques*, London, 1980

Griffiths, Antony: 'Monotypes', *Print Quarterly*, vol. 5, no. 1 (1988)

Hayter, S.W.: *About Prints*, London, 1962

Hodin, J.P.: 'W. Barns-Graham', *Art News & Review*, vol. 4, no. 2 (1952)

Kirker, Anne: *Collaborative Ventures, British Artists' Prints 1960s and 1970s*, Queensland Art Gallery exh. cat., Brisbane, 1989

Lewis, David: *St Ives 1939–64: Twenty-five Years of Painting, Sculpture and Pottery*, exh.cat., Tate Gallery [1985], revised edition, London, 1996

Oliner, Sheila: 'It's a beginning', *Printmaking Today*, vol. 3, no. 4 (Winter 1994)

Samuel, Gordon: 'The monotype 1900–1955', in Robin Garton (ed.), *British Printmakers 1855–1955*, Devizes, 1992

Samuel, Gordon and Nicola Penny: *The Cutting Edge of Modernity: Lino Cuts of the Grosvenor School*, Lund Humphries, 2002

Sidey, Tessa: *Editions Alecto: Original Graphics, Multiple Originals 1960–1981*, Lund Humphries, 2003

Spencer, Charles (ed.): *A Decade of Printmaking*, London, 1973

Stevens, Chris: *Bryan Wynter*, London, 1999

Tallman, Susan: *The Contemporary Print from Pre-Pop to Postmodern*, London, 1996

Val Baker, Denys: *Britain's Art Colony by the Sea*, 2nd edition, Bristol, 2000

Waverly, Peter: *Penzance School of Art 1853–2003*, Penzance, 2003

Wilhelmina Barns-Graham Exhibition Catalogues

Wilhelmina Barns-Graham: Paintings and Drawings, Crawford Arts Centre, St Andrews, 1982

Wilhelmina Barns-Graham Retrospective 1940–1989, City of Edinburgh Museums and Art Galleries, 1989

Wilhelmina Barns-Graham at 80: A New View, William Jackson Gallery, London, 1992

Wilhelmina Barns-Graham: New Paintings, Art First, London, 1995

Wilhelmina Barns-Graham: New Paintings, Art First, London, 1997

Wilhelmina Barns-Graham: An Enduring Image, Tate St Ives, 2000

Wilhelmina Barns-Graham Paintings, Art First, London, 2001

Wilhelmina Barns-Graham: A Celebration at 90, The Scottish Gallery, Edinburgh, 2002

Wilhelmina Barns-Graham at 90: A Tribute from Art First, Art First, London, 2002

Wilhelmina Barns-Graham 1912–2004. A Tribute: Recent Paintings and New Prints, Art First, London, 2004

Wilhelmina Barns-Graham: Movement and Light Imag(in)ing Time, Tate St Ives, 2005

Wilhelmina Barns-Graham: Important Works from her Career, Art First, London, 2006

Interviews

Author's taped interviews with:
Stanley Jones, 9 November 2005
Kip Gresham, 9 November 2005
Carol Robertson and Robert Adam, 29 May 2006.

Sheila Oliner, taped interview with Wilhelmina Barns-Graham, 16 September 1993.

The British Library Sound Archive, National Life Story Collection (NLSC): 'Artists' Lives':
Wilhelmina Barns-Graham: Tape Numbers F4747–4751, interviewer Tamsyn Woollcombe, recorded June 1994.
John Wells: Tape Numbers F4045–F4046, interviewer Tamsyn Woollcombe, recorded June 1994.

Archival material

Barns-Graham Archive (at the time of writing the ultimate destination of this archive has not yet been established; see www.barns-grahamtrust.org.uk):
Diaries 1940–2003
Artist's notebooks
Letters.

Tate Gallery Archive, Hyman Kreitman Research Centre, Tate Britain, London:
8717.1.2.292: Ben Nicholson Papers.
8613: Television South West: unedited typed transcript of interviews made between 2 August and 23 September. 1983, in connection with a television programme entitled 'Painting the Warmth of the Sun', broadcast April/May 1985.

Victoria and Albert Museum, Archive of Art and Design: Heal's Craftsman's Market scrapbook, AAD/1994/16/2693.

INDEX

NOTE: Page numbers in *italics* refer to illustrations; captions may also contain information.

Titles within series are indexed only where there is textual discussion of the individual work.